Swiftly Shifting Paradigms of English Language Teaching (ELT) in India

Swiftly Shifting Paradigms of English Language Teaching (ELT) in India

Dr. Ashok Kumar

AUTHORSPRESS
Publishers of Scholarly Books

Worldwide Circulation through Authorspress Global Network
First Published 2010
by
Authorspress
E-35/103, Jawahar Park
Laxmi Nagar, Delhi-110 092
e-mail: authorspress@yahoo.com

Swiftly Shifting Paradigms of English Language Teaching (ELT) in India
ISBN 978-81-7273-550-0

Printed in India at Tarun Offset, Delhi.

Foreword

The English Language Teaching (ELT) is no more restrained to books; the foremost task is given to the media and the Internet. A lot of newspapers are available in e-editions. There is a deluge of informative and interactive coverage, which is both formal and informal in form. ELT has survived in different setups and has the most profuse canvass to display the creative use of language, whether it is an everyday situation or moments of exceptional exchange, wherein a person is set to face a panel of interviewers. Subsequently, we see besides the shift to being formal, that the communicative need is more focused to deal with competition and the competitive spirit.

We see an insurgency in the field of media, and we see that the communication at all levels is reflecting the giant strides that the social networking has taken. Before we know it, the social networking has spread its tentacles far and wide. The ELT teacher has to assume the role of the social change facilitator too. Some of the agencies are grooming students for higher skills in language to increase their levels of employability. The Indians might lose their eminent standing of being versed in the English Language better than the neighbouring Asian countries.

A major thrust of the shifting of the focal point from English to native touch is due to the straightforward openness of the media convergence through the Internet and the radio transmission. English language teaching has shifted its spotlight to the existing modes and mediums. Therefore, we see that English Language Teaching is done more in the commercial premises of language-teaching sectors with the labelling of

American School of Language or *The British School of Language*, which try to cater to the market and the employability factors. We can come across a number of such institutions that promise of churn out the English speaking hordes to fit the career-demand markets. There are business schools that also cater to this corporate demand. The onus is to create an awareness that exists in the corporate sector, and English Language Teaching has to widen its curriculum, base and manner in which it has to be imparted. So there are the testimonies to the Swiftly Shifting Paradigms of English Language Teaching.

The present anthology is the best endeavour in this direction. Dr. Ashok Kumar has been able to put together in a distinct volume well argued innovative ideas of quite a number of academics from in and outside of India. The contributors have dealt with a variety of issues and aspects interrelated to the theme in depth. This anthology is thus rich in terms of multiplicity, variety as well as coverage. I am sure, those interested in English Language Teaching, as a field of study, or as an activity for advancement in career, and for enrichment in ELT, would find this volume gratifying, rewarding and thought-provoking.

Dr. Santosh Kumar Sheel
Joint Director,
State Council of Educational Research & Training,
Uttarakhand.

Preface

The dream of bringing out a volume about *Swiftly Shifting Paradigms of English Language Teaching (ELT)* in India would have not been translated into reality without the cooperation and guidance of my teachers, friends, and well wishers. I place on record my regards to Prof. Pashupati Jha (IIT, Roorkee), M.R. Verma Prof. & Head, Deptt. of English, Gurukul Kangari University, Haridwar. Prof. Binod Mishra (IIT, Roorkee), Prof. Saryug Yadav (RIE, Ajmer), Dr. G.S. Jha (Arunachal Pradesh), Shri Ramesh Chandra Shukla (Joint Director, SCERT Uttarakhand), Shri R.P. Singh (Deputy Director, SCERT Uttarakhand), Dr. Dharam Singh Saini, Minister of Education, (Govt. of Uttar Pradesh, India) for their academic guidance, sane suggestions and applauding my efforts from time to time. I also attest my love and cordiality to all my friends, family members and kinsmen who have encouraged me in my adventurous project.

I register my heartfelt gratitude to all the contributors for their scholarly contributions. Besides contributing their articles, they have been quite instrumental in reminding me of bringing the anthology well in time. I appreciate their continuous reminders, which have spurred me in my venture. Finally, I express my deep sense of gratitude to Sudarshan Kcherry, M.D., Authorspress, New Delhi, and his team for publishing this anthology both promptly and elegantly. I do hope that the book will successfully address the issues raised in the anthology and suggests remedies for the ELT challenges being faced in India today. The responses of the readers will act as the feedback in enduring the relevance of the anthology.

Every effort has been made to trace or contact all copy right holders. The publisher/editor will be pleased to make good any omissions or rectify any mistakes brought to their attention at the earliest opportunity.

—*Dr. Ashok Kumar*

Introduction

India is one of the largest hubs of non-native English speaking peoples of the world and, being one of the fastest emerging economies, certainly it will be as an intellectual hub of the world one day. Not only in urban but in rural parts of India too, it is frequently and extremely observed that young people are code-mixing and code-switching connecting English and other Indian languages to each other. Hindi, as used by half of the population of India, plays a role of the foremost sponsorer in code switching with English. With the introduction of new communicational devices like mobile and Internet, people use Hindlish—a language with established and deliberate code-switching between Hindi and English without bothering about the rules of grammar of any of the two languages where conveying meaning is the sole intention of the user, and they find it more comfortable than using any single language. So the use of both Hindi and English as literal languages are significantly affected by millions of SMS and e-mails everyday

Apart from messages and e-mails, shifting paradigms in ELT in India and other factors encouraging such use of languages are advertisement on mass media like TV and cable networks. In order to make their advertisements more motivating, alluring and fascinating, they use phrases like "Test Ka Tadka' or "Ye Dil Mange More". Some of the movies presenting themes of corporate world or domestic life of highly educated couples use a lot of Hindi and English all together which sometimes make difficult for anyone to find out where code switching takes place. The language, used by radio-jockeys on different F.M Radios, also provides a lot of use of Hindlish.

The anthology begins with an introductory research paper by **Dr. Ashok Kumar.** This paper provides a considerable estimation of the Communicative Approach (CA) and task-based approach with specific reference to the teaching and learning experiences of a group of English Language Teaching (ELT) practitioners and students in India. It is explored to facilitate even if the elemental doctrine of the approach has served the profession well, it is now time to contemplate over an emerging and diverse paradigm in the form of a context-based and task-based approach.

Alka Singh sharing her different experiences of legal English says that legal English, is based on accuracy. Even a small lapse of punctuation mark can mar the drafting and purpose of the document. It has a strong base on propriety of the academic discipline. In such a scenario and unwritten commandments, we may find that the use of Hinglish in written documents and oral communication is injurious and nasty sign not only for the Legal profession but almost for any field of ESP because ESP normally caters to the professional communication, and the professional setting is more articulated and disciplined than the literary or general framework of human and linguistic affairs.

Dr. Amrendra Sharma has concluded that no sober and efficient endeavour seems to have been done to distinguish the regional imbalances in India in terms of the excellence of educational accomplishment. Only if a standardised test could be administered to representative samples of students in different states in India, a comprehensive study of scores might provide information useful for educational planners and policy makers in the country, particularly to those involved in the field of education.

Dr. Anju Bala Agrawal in her comprehensive paper examines the need to hear language, write language, speak language and read language. She believes that computers can play an integral part in providing ELL students with valuable language experiences as they learn a new language. Verbal interaction and the use of a variety of language functions by English language learners can be facilitated by the use of the computer.

Dr. Anshu Surve in her innovative article considers that from *Officialese* in the colonial period, from *Globalese* in the postcolonial period, English is fast gaining the status of *Glocalese* (a combination of global and local English) during the years of decolonisation.

Dr. Arun Kumar Mukhopadhyay explores in a word, by dint of perfect resilience and adaptability, English today has shaken off its past colonial identity and merged in our national existence and voices the spirit of globalisation, so to speak, the call of the time which recommends the fusion of the local with the global.

Dr. Arvind Kumar in his psychoanalysis suggests that teacher needs to put off his age-old mantle of preacher at the altar; he has rather to create a learner-friendly environment in the classroom. Further exploring our aim as a teacher of English should not be to teach English for its own sake, but to motivate our students to speak and write language more effectively and proficiently.

Dr. Manju Ojha concludes that in India, English has long been the language of the government and the educated elite, and anyone who mixed Hindi and English was jeered at. "Hinglish" has become the hip voice of urban India, and thanks to the spread of cable TV and the popularity of Bollywood films its influence is reaching far beyond the cities. In a country with 16 national languages and more than 1,000 dialects, Hinglish is turning into a common tongue.

Dr. T. R. Muralikrishnan in his insightful article discovers that the language in the public domain can get transformed with the active interference of such code switching among the young users of Hindi. He further attempts to see the ways in which code switching can be a motivator to mitigate resistance among the people for using the market product consequently the language can be seen as a vehicle for promoting commercialisation.

Dr. Ram Sharma reveals that mother tongue should be used upto the highest level of instruction, but English should be taught both as a subject and as a library language at higher levels. After Hindi, English is the most commonly spoken or used language in India particularly in legal, financial, educational business and communicative systems The Secondary Education Commission recommended introduction of English along with Hindi at the end of junior basic stage, subject to the principle that no two languages should be introduced the same year. UGC also stressed the promotion of learning of the English language as a positive instrument of knowledge.

Dr. Sarika Dubey asserts that several theories relating to second language acquisition have their own importance in the field of research. In fact, they reflect a variety of perspective with regard to second language acquisition. Second language acquisitions follow a route in syntactical development. She further writes that conversational strategy influences the pace, the route of second language acquisition in number of a way. Conversation, articulate conversation is at the very centre of second language acquisition.

Shubho Ray in his insightful article reveals that language has an extremely critical role to play in unity in diversity since time immemorial. Vividness of mother tongues is noticed as we move from one state to another and find that the speakers of a particular dialect or language claiming their exclusiveness take a lot of pride. This creates fissure within the polity. The solution to these socio-linguistic problems is adoption of a pluralist approach towards language that will find some widely acceptable solutions.

Dr. Sunil K. Rai argues that the continuation of the study of English is both desirable and necessary. Knowledge of English has become essential for intellectual, cultural, economical and political relations with the rest of the world. Its study is indispensable for higher legal, technical and scientific education and technological evolutions.

Dr. Vikas Raval in his article scrutinises that India is a country of a billion people, and two official languages. Hindi and English are designated as the country's national languages. This situation has lead to the spontaneous creation of "Hinglish," a hybrid language combining elements of Hindi and English. He further aims to present the use of Hinglish in India through focusing on special features of Hinglish and how it differs from Standard English. He further explores certain common means of communication in hinglish, e.g., advertisement, announcement, instructions, newspapers, etc.

Dr. T.R. Muralikrishnan in this article attempts to make a study of prescribed English textbooks prepared by the SCERT for the schools in Kerala. He proposes that though the texts have enough knowledge based content for increasing the linguistic standards, in a gender perspective analysis, especially from the point of view of women, the content still continues to support the prevailing patriarchal values. The paper attempts to see the representation of women as stereotypes, in the role of domestic help and casting them in typical social models.

Dr. Nasrah M. Ismail aims at discovering the effectiveness of a proposed programme for developing phonological awareness skills for dyslexic students. The data showed that there are statistically significant differences between the experimental group and the control group on the post-test diagnostic reading test as well as the phonological awareness tasks, showing a significant increase in reading skills in the experimental group. It also reveals that there are statistically significant differences between the pre-test and post-test results for the experimental group on the phonological awareness test and diagnostic reading test. This shows that the experimental group had an increase in skills after having participated in the programme as seen on the post-test.

Aju Mukhopadhyay says that introduction of English and its teaching among the younger generation in India was talked about for some time but it became effective only when such personalities as Raja Rammohan Ray, T.V. Macaulay, David Hare and Hyde East came forward with great interest to induce the Government to take necessary steps to introduce it. Where we stand exactly is difficult to say at the moment but true it is that English language and Indian English Literature have occupied an enviable position throughout the world.

Dr. Sarika Dubey observes that Holistic Learning is considered to be the processes of learning Appropriated for promoting sustainable development. This paper aims to identify the three main components of holistic learning; the concept of deep learning, learning by doing (in real sector) and the interconnecting communication-based learning of which encourage learners, both from formal and non-formal education system, to share and learn with their learning partners. In building the real education for sustainable development, the cluster of learning practice is presented to be an example of opened learning process. The result from this practice will be the emerging change agents as well as the learning reform.

Dr. Sharda Iyer in her scholarly article views, there is no more justification for the century old accusation that we Indian are a nation of mimics, victims of English education which has conditioned the faculties of our perception so much so that we have failed to respond to the immediate situation.

Radha Kanta Mishra advocates the organisation of refresher courses and orientation programmes in the teaching of spoken English for generation of a host of well-trained and competent teachers, who will be capable of producing good students of remarkable communicability in English.

Ramesh Chandra Shukla in his highly brilliant article observes that the current status of English seems from its overwhelming presence on the world-stage and the reflection of this in the national arena. It is predicted that by 2010 a surge in English language learning will include a third of the world's people. The Indian economy in the 1990s has coincided with an explosion in the demand for English in our schools because English is perceived to open up world-class opportunities. The rigor of the secondary and higher secondary stage enables Indian students to compete successfully for education and for jobs globally. As a result, it is absolutely indispensable to reinforce this phase by providing greater triumph and also by improving quality and elements of education in a significant approach.

Dr. Archana Bahadur Zutshi in his excellent article very clearly mentions that before we know it, the social networking has spread its tentacles far and wide. There are 'Twitter', Facebook, Orkut, MSN and many such networks that are multiplying the available information into recipients' hands. The English Language Teaching is no more confined to books the major role is given to the media and the Internet. Newspapers are all available in e-paper editions. There is a deluge of informative and interactive coverage, which is both formal and informal in form. Hence the very format of teaching is undergoing a swift paradigmatic shift. The links are informative we have to filter the information, with the help of awareness among the teaching community. They have to be guiding light to the Internet crazed generation. They can guide the reading tastes of the young minds by taking the Twitter sessions both seriously and functionally as mediums of expression and creativity.

Dr. Ravindra Pratap Singh in his scholarly article observes that Hinglish or Inglish is smoothly gaining strong foothold in our speech communities. Hesitations in accepting it, is shattered in the postcolonial milieu. Willingly or unwillingly people are getting attracted to it. With such gestures, Hinglish merrily moves on, and this democratic trend and all-inclusive nature of English have spanned English as a universal language.

List of Contributors

Dr. Amrendra Sharma, Asst. Prof. of Linguistics, Dhofar University, Salalah, Sultanate of Oman.

Dr. Anju Bala Agrawal, Reader, Department of English, R.C.A.Girls' P.G. College, Mathura.

Dr. Anshu Surve, Dept. of English, The M.S. University of Baroda, Gujarat.

Dr. Archana Bahadur Zutshi, Sr. Lecturer, Deptt. of Humanities & Applied Sciences, S.M.S. Institute of Technology, Lucknow, U.P.

Dr. Arun Kumar Mukhopadhyay, K.M. Institution, P.O. Kenduadihi. Distt. Bankura, W.B. 722102.

Dr. Arvind Kumar, Dept. of English, S.K.K. Jain (P.G.) College, Khatauli, Muzaffarnagar, U.P.-251201.

Dr. Ashok Kumar, Deptt. of English, Urdu & Other Languages, State Council of Educational Research & Training Uttarakhand, Narendranagar, T. Garhwal, PIN-249175.

Dr. Manju Ojha, Lecturer of English, Law Department M. L. B. College, Gwalior, M.P.

Dr. Muralikrishnan T.R., Lecturer, Selection Grade, M.E.S College Marampally Aluva, Ernakulam District, 683107.

Dr. Ram Sharma, Sr. Lecturer, Department of English, Janta Vedic P.G. College Baraut, Baghpat, U.P.

Dr. Radha Kanta Mishra, Reader in English, D.A.V. College, Titilagarh, Orissa.

Dr. Ravindra Pratap Singh, Faculty Member English, Deptt. of English and Modern European Languages, University of Lucknow, Lucknow - 226007, U.P.

Dr. Sarika Dubey, Associate Professor, Vidya College of Engineering, Meerut, UP.

Dr. Sharda Iyer, Head Deptt. of English, Vasanta College for Women, Rajghat Fort, Varanasi, U.P. – 221001.

Dr. Sunil K. Rai, Deptt. of English, Mayo College Ajmer, Rajasthan.

Dr. Vikas Raval, Assistant professor in English, Nirma Institute of Technology, Ahmedabad (Gujarat).

Ms. Alka Singh, Lecturer in English, Deptt. of English, Dr. Ram Manohar Lohiya National Law University, Lucknow, LDA Scheme, Kanpur Road, Lucknow, UP, India Pin-226012.

Ramesh Chandra Shukla, Joint Director, State Council of Educational Research & Training, Uttarakhand, Narendranagar, Tehri Garhwal-249175.

Shubho Ray, Department of English, A. C. College, Jalpaiguri, West Bengal-735101.

Contents

1

Swiftly Shifting Paradigms of English Language Teaching (ELT) in India: A Study of Some Innovative Approaches

—Dr. Ashok Kumar

The worldwide spread of English has recently received much interest. Issues relating to the multifaceted roles of English around the world have been highlighted and purist positions about English challenged. In particular:

a) The assumption that British English is the only valid standard of English; and

b) The notion that the 'native speaker' is the only model that all learners should aspire to have been put to question.

Based on the premise that these positions are incompatible with the complex reality of English worldwide, the necessity of a paradigm shift in English language teaching (ELT) has been advocated, whereby such purist tenets would have to change. However, the impact of academic debate on language teaching practice has been marginal. I argue that this state of affairs is attributable not only to the predilection for a monochrome form of English in the ELT industry and pedagogical practice, but also to shortcomings within academic discourse.

The present study is a considerable estimation of the communicative approach (CA) and task-based approach with specific reference to the teaching and learning experiences of a group of English Language Teaching (ELT) practitioners and students in India. It is explored to facilitate even if the elemental doctrine of the approach has served the profession well, it is now time to contemplate over an emerging and diverse paradigm in the form of a context-based approach and task-based approach. The communicative approach has dominated English language teaching, it has resolutely established itself on a worldwide basis and there are good historical rationales for this. That the rationale of language is communicative competence and proficiency, and that communicative function and notions set in circumstances are a vital aspect of the equation, even though once radical, seems patently obvious to contemporary practitioners. Hymes's (1971) redefinition of Chomsky's (1965) observation of language aptitude, and the work of Wilkins (1976), Van E.k. and Alexander (1975) have provided a starting point for defining and subsequently developing the CA. Language is no longer seen as intangible grammatical set of rules, however of having applications in social contexts and as such it is not just about 'grammar' but moreover concerning functions and notions.

These days, it is intricate to envisage any practitioner, anywhere, disagreeing about this. A large number of us put CA into practice in our daily practice, and in parts of the world where this does not nevertheless transpire there are demands to shift in this approach. For many it is thus no longer an alternative to, but to a certain extent it is a substitution of, its audio-lingual or grammar translation predecessors. On the other hand, whether, subsequent to a quarter of a century of dominance, the CA, which comes from and was initially based in a Western milieu, still offers the most compelling paradigm. Through paradigm, we imply to a blueprint which is used to make sense or meaning from our experiences as language teaching practitioners and/or researchers. By approach we will take Lewis' (1993:2) definition of "an integrated set of theoretical and practical beliefs, embodying both syllabus and method...." The terms CA and communicative language teaching (CLT) are both used in this paper but by the CA we will be referring to the further theoretical, and by CLT to the further practical beliefs; simultaneously these attitude and practices comprise a paradigm which lead the dexterity.

Over the years, the CA has been significantly and comprehensively talked about. In the mid-1980's Swan's prominent and well-known critiques (1985a and 1985b) were approximately certainly the first to question several of the hypothesis of what was then still a recently up-and-coming approach. On the other hand, his conclusions that the approach is "likely to be seen as little more than an interesting ripple on the surface of twentieth-century language teaching" (1985b: 87) was precipitate, it has had a considerable impact, it is still largely with us and it has, to date, go forward but not been reinstated. Thompson endows with a prevailing justification of the CA by arguing that its critics have misconceived the role of grammar teaching, the primacy of speaking, the ways in which pair work and role-plays are used and the demands made on the teacher. Appreciably, on the other hand, Thomson (1996:14) concedes that the approach is not the final answer, "the next revolution in language teaching is already underway," but adds that an alternative will need to build upon the CA, "whatever innovations emerge, they will do so against a background of changes brought about by CLT, and will need to accommodate or explicitly reject those changes. Certain of them are too important to lose...." Our estimated inclination, as will turn out to be perceptible, recognises these considerable transforms and seeks to fabricate from them.

To a great extent, debates have focused on concern of educational aptness for Indian learners and a number of concerns have immediately been raised in the miscellaneous studies. A lot of works have acknowledged tribulations of executing the approach within unambiguous contexts, although all ultimately support an adapted version which takes into account local conditions. Several authors absolutely or unequivocally trail Holiday's peculiarity between a narrow interpretation which comes from, and is best suited to, a western European base, and a broader version which, "has within it the potential to adapt to all types of classroom context, provided it is informed by local knowledge" (Holiday, 1994:3) — a valuable feature, however one which nevertheless views context as secondary to the dominant paradigm, rather than the defining characteristic of an replacement. Further Kumaravadivelu's work (2001) endeavours a transfer in point of view by classifying limitations allied by way of CLT methodology and arguing for a meeting point on distinctive-ness, practicality and possibility within a post method paradigm. Conversely, the anticipated post-method situation, in spite of its momentous involvement to the study of methodology, has also been seen as adapting but ultimately maintaining the dominant paradigm. Bell (2003:326), for example, has characterised postmethod as a "... more holistic, redefined communicative language teaching...."

The intent behind investigating practitioner and student approach towards CLT and to consider whether the CA paradigm is still the most respectable. The method is based on a case study of 40 English language teachers and eight hundred students. Seventy two percent of the teachers informed not being exposed to CLT as students, but 57 per cent had received some training in it. All the teachers are with teaching experience varying from less than 1 year (20%) to more than 10 years (15%). The investigation of students' learning styles, their attitude to the teacher and teaching, including the use of materials, is acknowledged. Students came from a range of academic subject backgrounds including engineering, hotel and tourism, accounting and business and management. The English students were grouped according to their level.

There is no endeavour to determine what people say with what in point of fact transpires and further more qualitative advance would suggest extra insights. Even though all the questionnaires were anonymous, it may be that some of the replies are probably to imitate what the teachers and students think the researcher wants to read rather than their genuine way of thinking. It is recognised that a few of the questions have a propensity to be loaded and/or disingenuous. Such restrictions are entirely accepted and reveal the reality. On the other hand, in spite of the restrictions, it is considered that the data does suggest a number of valid insights and raises several genuine problems, which go further than the specificity of this study.

Reacting to the first question, regarding definition of CLT, the enormous majority (81%) of respondents enclosed language resembling communication. These definitions more or less match the philosophy discussed in the beginning. In feedback to question 2, each particular teacher described that they utilise CLT in their instructions. These two queries validate that the CA is the prevailing paradigm. Question 3 explores a number of perceptions and misunderstandings concerning CLT in apply. A great deal of data is created from Likert attitude scales of this type, and space does not authorise us to penetrate a detailed dialogue of all; yet, quite a lot of problems are demanded to emphasize.

Statement 1 (S1) specifies that whilst several would put fluency over accuracy, this contentious idea (arguably misconception) is by no means unanimously acknowledged. The huge mass (90%) of practitioners perceives students as being the centre of knowledge transmission and an apparent mass (69%) believes in an inductive approach through "struggling to communicate" which is most probably observed as being achieved through use of role play games etc. (62%). The idea that CLT places speaking above other skills (S5) are by no means collectively acknowledged and observations on error rectification are assorted (S6). The responsibility of bona fide material is extensively recognised (64%) even if the "all the time" allegation is obviously a controversial position. Seventy one per cent reported that CLT is effective for their students. Component 1 by and large points towards an understanding of what CLT is and an approval of many of CLT's vital system of belief.

Component 2 investigates problems nearby its accomplishment. In response to question four 100 per cent reported finding problems when executing CLT in their classroom. The problems, as the table below indicates, are varied but mainly relate to the level of students, to their responsibility and to their learning styles. Class size, the time period of lessons and, to a lesser extent, the demands of the examination system are also significant. When asked to elaborate on problems or offer other limitations the vast majority focused on their students and reported that their level or their learning style (shyness) made CLT difficult to implement. A number of teachers identified the deferential nature of Indian society as an encumbrance. This statistics recommends that it is not so much that teachers do not appreciate CLT, or do not have access to resources and equipments but that context restrains accomplishment.

The majority problematic concern indicated in the two parts of the questionnaire is, on the one hand, a clear understanding and widespread endorsement of CLT and its effectiveness and, on the other hand, a universal recognition of problems with implementation. Such problems have been reported elsewhere (Karavas-Doukas, 1996) and are apparently marked yet in the present days. At the same time as with the data generated from the teacher's questionnaire, space does not permit a detailed discussion of all the data; however a number of significant issues are worth highlighting. In contrast to the teachers who reported mixed views, the vast majority of students (74%) expressed a preference for accuracy over fluency. Many students (50% +) reported a learning style where loss of face, shyness and a reluctance to question the teacher are important factors and there is an overwhelming preference for a deductive teacher-centered learning style. Such views clearly raise questions about the relevance of some of CLT's essential belief.

A large number of specific findings are worth noting. Questions 8 and 9 show that a majority do not recognise the notion of the teacher as a "facilitator" and the student as "generator of knowledge," nor do they accept an emphasis on a student-based struggle to communicate (though this question with its explicit exclusion of grammar and lexis is admittedly ambiguous). These responses support the views of many teachers who identified lack of student comfort with aspects CLT. Other answers in this section seem to contradict some of those reported in Part 1. For example, 66 per cent approve of role-play, games, etc., and yet many have indicated desire for work on accuracy and a shyness to speak. With authenticity, it is interesting to note that one of the most problematic tenets of CLT that "the native speaker is best" has been endorsed by 84 per cent of the learners.

In spite of teachers' obligation to CLT and their great effort to put it into practice, the response to question 15 shows that 69 per cent of students did not recognise any of the items in Part 2 number 3, 8-14 as actually taking place in their classrooms. Of the minority, 31 per cent of students who recognise items 8-14 as occurring, the largest number of responses (19%) indicated item 10; language tasks through role-plays instead of teaching grammar and vocabulary as taking place mainly. The negligible number (3%) identified number 13 as taking place and we have previously remarked on the native speaker concern.

Reacting to question 17, a total of 82 per cent depicted having learnt English "well" on their course, and in response to question 18, 71 per cent reported differences between their university experience and their school experience of learning English. If, for the majority, CLT is perceived as not, or at best partially, being achieved, what might account for this response? The limitations of question 19 give no meaningful answer to this but we might speculate that perhaps it is the use of more communicative textbooks as compared to secondary schools. The final question (20), despite being open-ended, provided an overwhelming uniformity in responses. Ninety per cent commented that they felt too shy to speak and express opinions.

The collective reactions from teachers and learners heave issues which question the authority and the practicality of a number of the essential doctrine of CLT. All teachers appreciate and state to utilise the approach and nevertheless all have problems with its implementation. Furthermore, countless students have pointed out a fondness for a certain learning style, which is fundamentally incompatible with CLT. Earlier reactions to problems of this type have been to adjust CLT to restricted environment in order to make it extra applicable. Conceivably this is because it is seen as the lesser evil to the historical alternatives of audio-lingualism or grammar translation. However such a reaction attempts to reconcile the contradictions within CLT but fails to question the value of the paradigm itself. It is perhaps a fear of going backwards has hindered substitutes that might take us further.

"When a paradigm shift takes place, we see things from a different perspective as we focus on different aspects of the phenomena," says Jacobs and Farrell (2001). The paradigm shift proposed here, as Bax (2003: 280-281) has argued, is to see that aspects CLT are now having a negative effect due to misplaced priorities on what the teacher should do, which draws attention away from the context of teaching and learning. The alternative does not negate the view that language is about communication, but it does question the universal validity of the CA. With the C-b-A comes a view of methodology as being only one of several factors in language learning and teaching and that other methods and approaches which are often dismissed as "traditional" and "old-fashioned" may be equally valid. The educational structure for a C-b-A is that language learners learn best in teaching and learning environments that are harmonious with their learning styles and expectations—this is greatly influenced by civilisation, ethnicity and society. National educational goals need to reflect this and not uncritically adopt approaches which raise as many questions as they seek to answer. This case study suggests that teachers recognise problems with CLT implementation particularly in relation to learner expectations. The challenge is surely for practitioners to work with these expectations and styles rather than try to fit them into an inappropriate model; a C-b-A, it is suggested might offer a more realistic framework.

In general, a conventional ELT curriculum lists learning items in terms of structures, functions, notions and vocabulary that are then set in conditions and which usually incorporate a variety of expertise (reading, writing, listening and speaking). This prevailing approach has been characterised as product-orientated because it centres on what is to be learnt or on products (White, 1988). The problem with this approach, as Nunan (1988) has pointed out, is that input cannot be equated with output and that teaching cannot be equated with learning. In short, what the teacher teaches is not what the learner learns. It is a problem which is compounded within our proposed EIL framework. Nunn (2005:61-62) has argued that linguistic, communicative and other kinds of competences have not been adequately addressed in relation to EIL and goes on to argue that "... international communication seems to require the ability to adjust to almost infinitely diverse intercultural communication situations." An alternative approach can be characterised as process-orientated because it focuses not on items to be taught and learned, but on what the learner does with the language. A task-based approach is very much process-orientated because it focuses on "learning through doing," i.e., on tasks. Tasks mean different things to different people and the work of Ellis (2003) has been particularly helpful in documenting and discussing these issues. With authentic tasks students are asked to complete activities which are likely to be carried out in real life once the student has left the classroom.

The most significant vagueness to task-based approaches is that they are measured unfeasible and removed from every-day teaching and learning contexts. It is an argument which we have never really acknowledged because the approach can be implemented at various levels—it is really about encouraging learners to do useful, interesting and meaningful activities with language and this can be applied in a range of contexts. This work goes a considerable way to addressing these objections. However, once computers are introduced into the ELT curriculum, and our discussion to date touches upon the case for doing so, then task-based approaches become arguably the only way to effectively take into account the changes in language that we have identified. We have already noted rapidly changing, subject to trend and fashion and vary in different contexts. It is very easy to devise simple, achievable tasks which encourage students to use email to communicate with each other, their tutors and the wider world; likewise it is not difficult to find useful meaningful ways in which student access and even post information on the web.

The needs of the learners and the contexts in which they work will ultimately determine the most appropriate tasks. For example, Jarvis presents far-reaching statements of how such thoughts can be realised with English for Academic Purposes students. Related thoughts can be utilised with general English students, they might for example be asked to prepare a travel itinerary for a visitor to their country, province or city. This could involve accessing websites to note and decide upon the best places to visit, using the web and email to arrange flight bookings to and from the city, negotiating amongst themselves (via email) on the best options etcetera. There must be literally hundreds of task-based activities of this type across the globe which involves students using computers to access information and to communicate with others. The task is specified and students generate appropriate language, with help as required. Achievement is calculated by the extent to which the task is lucratively accomplished and the language is viewed as the tool to achieve the ends; it is not prescribed. The learners are viewed as working with tools which belong to them as much as to anyone else.

Computers are, on the one hand, impacting on the way in which we define our subject matter and, on the other hand, are also impacting upon the English language, upon the subject matter itself. This new age would seem to go hand in hand with task-based approaches and represents challenges for everyone involved in ELT. For practitioners, applied linguists and educators there is a changed dynamic in which computers have now become much more than a tool or a tutor for developing language skills. This traditional distinction (Levy, 1997) would no longer seem adequate. Warschauer and Healey (1998) have observed that it is now less a question of the role of computers in the language classroom and more a question of the role of the language classroom in an information technology society.

Language teaching instruction is evidently inflowing an innovative and fundamentally uncultivated segment and we would seem to be at a junction. Warchauer and Kern (2000) have identified this as a "sociocognitive phase" where, unlike in preceding phases, students intermingle with each other and the world via the computer. A great deal of work has focused on the value of computers in learning or second language acquisition on the implications of the content of teaching itself, i.e., the syllabus. Yet less contemplation appears to have been given to how we see, define or classify our learners.

We have discovered that a task-based curriculum recommends a way advance and practitioners will need to replicate upon what is practicable within their own contexts. In addressing these confronts we will evidently require to widen a sense in which English belongs to the students and their beneficiary countrymen and women just as much as anyone else and to do this we will need to avoid classifying the vast majority of users as "foreign" or "second" language learners. ELT would seem to be at a crossroads and it is enriching to see that much of the impetus for transformation is coming from, and driven by, practitioners and students.

The CA has been a functional and practical paradigm, which is why a C-b-A substitute needs to build on it and from it. On the other hand, it is historically set in the last quarter of the last century. An era, which viewed English as a foreign or second language will perhaps inevitably tend to export so-called "enlightened" approaches for teaching, collectively with hypothesis in relation to learning. The move to no longer view English as a foreign or second language although as a global language provides further support for a C-b-A. If language belongs to the mainstream of non-native speakers immediately as much as it does to the marginal native speakers, then their familiarity, in their precise contexts, should significantly manipulate its delivery. The export of at times unsuitable, unworkable and culturally loaded teaching approaches is consequently swapped with the predominance of context. An up-and-coming debate which began with Bax's article and has been supplementary developed here—whether we ultimately see things from a diverse outlook and an innovative C-b-A paradigm materialises, only time will enlighten. Further investigation, dialogue and dissemination are evidently considered necessary, and the inquiry of realistic accomplishment of a C-b-A is conceivably the subsequently foremost challenge for the ELT vocation.

Works Cited

Bax, S. (2003). "The End of CLT: A Context Approach to Language Teaching." *English Language Teaching Journal*, 57(3), 278-287.

Bell, D. (2003). "Method and Post Method: Are They Really so Incompatible?" *TESOL Quarterly*, 37(1), 325-336.

Biber, D., Johansson, S., Leech, G., Conrad, S. and Finegan, E. (1999). *Longman Grammar of Spoken and Written English*. Harlow: Longman.

Breen, M. and Littlejohn, A. (Eds.). (2000). *Classroom Decision-Making Negotiation and Process Syllabus in Practice*. Cambridge: Cambridge University Press.

Burns, A. and Coffin, C. (Eds.). (2001). *Analysing English in a Global Context*. London and New York: Routledge.

Cameron, K. (Ed.). (1999). *CALL Media Design and Applications*. Lisse: Swets and Zeitlinger.

Chambers, A. and Davies, G. (Eds.). (2001). *ICT and Language Learning*. Lisse: Swets and Zeitlinger.

Chapelle, C. (2000). *Computers Applications in Second Language Acquisition*. Cambridge: Cambridge University Press.

Chomsky, N. (1965). *Aspects of the Theory of Syntax*. Cambridge: MA. MIT Press.

Crystal, D. (2003). *English as a Global Language* (2nd Edition). Cambridge: Cambridge University Press.

__________ (2001). *Language and the Internet*. Cambridge: Cambridge University Press.

Dudeney, G. (2000). *The Internet and the Language Classroom*. Cambridge: Cambridge University Press.

Egbert, J. and Hanson-Smith, E. (Eds.). (1999). *CALL Environments: Research, Practice, and Critical Issues*. Alexandria, Virginia: TESOL Inc.

Ellis, R. (2003). *Task-based Language Learning and Teaching*. Oxford: Oxford University Press.

Ellis, G. (1996). "How culturally appropriate is the communicative approach?" *English Language Teaching Journal*, 50(3), 213-218.

Graddol, D. (2000). *The Future of English?: A Guide to Forecasting the Popularity of the English Language in the 21st Century* (2nd Edition). The British Council.

Holiday, A. (1994). "The House of TESP and the Communicative Approach." *English Language Teaching Journal*, 48(1), 3-11.

http://www.asian-efl-journal.com

Hymes, D. (1971). "Competence and Performance in Linguistic Theory" in R. Huxley & E. Ingram (Eds.) *Language Acquisition: Models and Methods*. (pp.2-28). NY: Academic Press.

Jacobs, G. and Farrell, T. (2001). "Paradigm Shift: Understanding and Implementing Change in Second Language Education." *TESL-EJ* 5/1. http://www-writing.berkeley.edu/TESL-EJ

Jarvis, H. (2004). "Investigating the Classroom Applications of Computers on EFL Courses at Higher Education Institutions." *Journal of English for Academic Purposes*, 3(2), 111-137.

______________ (2003). "Integrating Information and Communication Technology into English for Academic Purposes by Utilising the Skills of Practitioners and Students." *The English Teacher*, 6(3), 291-297.

______________ (2001). "Internet Usage of English for Academic Purposes Courses." *Re Call*. *13*(2),

______________ (in press). "Issues of Computer Mediated Communication (CMC) for English Language Teaching." *British Journal of Education Technology*.

______________ and Atsilarat, S. (2004). "Shifting Paradigms: From a Communicative to a context-based approach." *Asian EFL Journal*, 6 (4).

Karavas-Doukas, E. (1996). "Using Attitude Scales to Investigate Teachers' Attitudes to the Communicative Approach." *English Language Teaching Journal*, 50 (3), 187-198.

Kumaravadivelu, B. (2001). "Towards Post Method Pedagogy." *TESOL Quarterly*, 35(4), 537-559.

Levy, M. (1997). *Computer-assisted Language Learning*. New York: Oxford University Press.

Lewis, M. (1993). *The Lexical Approach.* London: LTP.

Li, D. (1998). "It's Always More Difficult Than You Plan and Imagine: Teachers' Perceived Difficulties in Introducing the Communicative Approach in South Korea." *TESOL Quarterly,* 32 (2), 677-703.

Maurer, J. and Schoenberg, I. (1998). *True Colors: An EFL Course for Real Communication.* New York: Longman.

McCarthy, M. and O'Dell, F. (1994). *English Vocabulary in Use.* Cambridge: Cambridge University Press.

McKay, S. (2002). *Teaching English as an International Language.* Oxford: Oxford University Press.

Nunan D. (1988). *The Learner-Centered Curriculum.* Cambridge: Cambridge University Press.

Nunn, R. (2005). "Competence and Teaching English as an International Language." *Asian EFL Journal, 7*(4), 61-74.

Phan Le Ha. (2005). "Towards a Critical Notion of Appropriation of English as an International Language." *Asian EFL Journal, 7*(4), 34-46.

Phillipson, R. (1992). *Linguistic Imperialism.* Oxford: Oxford University Press.

Rao, Z. (2002). *Chinese Students' Perceptions of Communicative and Non-communicative Activities in EFL Classroom. System,* 30(1), 85-105.

Sano, M., Takahashi, M., Yoneyama, A. (1984). "Communicative Language Teaching and Local Needs." *English Language Teaching Journal,* 38(3), 170-176.

Sinclair, J. (Ed.). (1987). *Looking up: An Account of the Co-build Project in Lexical Computing.* London & Glasgow: Collins ELT.

Soars, J and Soars, L. (1996). *New Headway English Course Intermediate.* Oxford: Oxford University Press.

Sperling, D. (1998). *Internet Guide* (2nd Edition). New Jersey: Prentice Hall Regents.

Swan, M. (1985a). A Critical Look at the Communicative Approach (1). *English Language Teaching Journal,* 39 (1), 1-12.

____________ (1985b). "A Critical Look at the Communicative Approach (2)." *English Language Teaching Journal,* 39 (2), 76-87.

Teeler, D. with Gray, P. (2000). *How to Use the Internet in ELT.* Harlow: Longman.

Thompson, G. (1996). "Some Misconceptions about Communicative Language Teaching." *English Language Teaching Journal,* 50(1), 9-15.

Van Ek, J. and Alexander, L. (1975). *Threshold Level English*. Oxford: Oxford University Press.

Warschauer, M. (2002). "Languages.com: The Internet and Linguistic Pluralism." In Snyder (Ed.), Silicon literacies: *Communication, Innovation and Education in the Electronic Age,* (pp. 62-74). London: Routledge.

______________ and H :aley, D. (1998). "Computers and Language Learning: An Overview." *Language Teaching, 31,* 57-71.

______________ and Kern, R. (Eds.). (2000). *Network-based Language Teaching: Concepts and Practice.* New York: Cambridge University Press.

White, R. (1988). *The ELT Curriculum: Design, Innovation & Management.* Oxford: Blackwell.

Wilkins, D. (1976). *Notional Syllabuses,* Oxford: Oxford University Press.

Yu, L. (2001). "Communicative Language Teaching in China: Progress and Resistance." *TESOL Quarterly,* 35(1), 194-198

Zhao, Y. (2003). "Recent Developments in Technology and Language Learning: A Literature Review and Meta-analysis." *CALICO Journal,* 21(1), 7-27.

2

Effects of Regional Variations on Language Learning: Some Pedagogical Implications

—*Dr. Amrendra Sharma*

Introduction and Background Information

It is a well-known fact that regional variations (imbalances) in India in terms of economic growth, industrial expansion, employment opportunities, rate of literacy, per capita income, rural per capita expenditure on education and educational standards are becoming more and more pronounced. According to All India ASER Report (*Assessment Survey Evaluation Research*, 2008), 0.6 per cent children between six and 14 years in Tamil Nadu do not attend school, in Kerala this percentage comes down to 0.2% and in Bihar the number of such children is as high as 5.7 per cent. In Maharashtra, the children in this age group constitute 1.5 per cent of the total number of children. Based on a situation analysis presented by the *UNICEF* (1991) states like Maharashtra, Tamil Nadu, Karnataka, Gujarat and Kerala have been labelled as some of the forward states in the field of education, whereas Bihar has been described as one of the educationally backward states.

'Backwardness,'as defined by the UNICEF or UNESCO, in this context, is based on the percentage of young boys and girls attending school. According to this situation analysis, about 57 per cent of the total number of rural children between six and 14 years in Tamil Nadu attend school, In Kerala this percentage goes up to 88.16 per cent, and in Bihar the number of such rural children is as low as 32.57 per cent. In urban areas the school-going children in this age group constitute 79.30 per cent of the total number of urban children in Maharashtra. In Kerala, such children constitute 91.71% of the total number of children in urban areas. In Bihar, school-going children in this age group constitute only 64.36 per cent of the children living in urban areas. If we take into account the National Family Health Survey -3 (NFHS-3, released on 11 October 2007), the literacy rates of Kerala, Mizoram and Bihar are 100 per cent, 89.9 per cent and 54.1 per cent respectively. This speaks volume about the wide disparity with regard to literacy among various states. The same disparity is reflected in the annual expenditure of per student pursuing education in rural India in 1995-96 in the report of National Sample Survey Organisation (1998). To illustrate, the annual expenditure per students in rural India in Dadra & Nagar Haveli, Nagaland and Bihar is Rs. 1863, 1210, and 230 respectively. Thus we witness disparities on different levels across different states. In a micro level, the same variations are likely to be found among different districts of a state too.

No serious and systematic attempt seems to have been done to perceive the regional imbalances in India in terms of the quality of educational attainment. Only if a standardised test could be administered to representative samples of students in different states in India, a comprehensive study of scores might provide information useful for educational planners and policy makers in the country, particularly to those involved in the field of education. For want of time no such ambitious plan was undertaken for the purpose of this research and attention was confined to a micro study inside the State itself in the field of English teaching at the Intermediate stage. The main objective of this research, therefore, is to ascertain whether the scores obtained by Intermediate students in different parts of Bihar are more or less identical or whether they indicate a severe imbalance.

Research Methodology

A standardised grammar test, consisting of 100 items and based on 10 grammatical points was administered to 2,900 Intermediate students of Bihar at the entry point and also terminal point of their programme. (Henceforward 'students' will refer to the Intermediate students of Bihar, a state of the North India). An intermediate programme is considered to be a pre-university programme and it follows the school final, i.e. class X. This standardised test was naturally based on Intermediate syllabus, and it was also found that the school final syllabus (i.e., secondary school syllabus) had almost the same grammatical components. Therefore, it was assumed that students should be familiar with each and every grammatical point of the test.

Findings and Discussions

Tables 1-2 listed below are intended to provide information regarding the average score in English obtained by Intermediate students in different parts of Bihar at the end of the two years Intermediate course.

Table 1
Mean Scores of Science Students (District-wise) at the Terminal Level

District	*Mean*
1. Patna	66. 45
2. Deoghar	48. 78
3. Bhagalpur	48. 40
4. Munger	47. 77
5. Dumka	45. 86
6. Sahibganj	40. 67
7. Darbhanga	38. 95
8. Muzaffarpur	37. 70

Table 1 shows that from the point of view of attainment in English there are severe imbalances in different parts of the state. This is obvious from the fact that the average score obtained by Intermediate students of science in Muzaffarpur is only 37.70 per cent whereas the average score obtained by Intermediate students of science in Patna is 66.45 per cent.

Table 2 shows that among the students of arts this disparity is slightly lower than the disparity in the students of science. But it is present in a big way, nevertheless. As is evident from

Table 2
Mean Scores of Arts Students (District-wise) at the Terminal Stage

District	*Mean*
1. Patna	49. 81
2. Munger	43. 02
3. Deoghar	41. 46
4. Muzaffarpur	40. 98
5. Bhagalpur	40. 69
6. Sahibganj	37. 64
7. Dumka	37. 15
8. Darbhanga	33. 11

Table 2, the students of arts in Darbhanga obtained an average score of 33.11 per cent only whereas students of arts in Patna obtained an average of 49.81 per cent in English. In other words, the average score of the Intermediate students in Patna is approximately 50.43 per cent higher than the average score obtained by the students of Darbhanga. The information given in Table 2 does not tally with the information given in Table 1 in matters of details. For example, Bhagalpur occupies the 3rd position in Table 1 but it occupies the 5th position in Table 2. Dumka occupies the 5th place in Table 1 but it occupies the 7th position in Table 2. In spite of these variations what emerges in the form of indisputable findings on the basis of these two Tables (1-2) is the fact that students of both science and arts in Patna attained a significantly higher score in English than the students in other parts of the state. It is the same syllabus and the same course.

Teachers teaching Intermediate courses are, by and large, transferable from one part of the state to another. Teachers in Intermediate colleges get the same salary and nearly the same facilities, and from the point of view of the quality of input on the teaching side there is no substantial difference between institutions of Intermediate teaching in Patna and in other parts of the state. However, Patna, the capital of the state, has a definite edge over other parts of the state in matters of students' attainments of English. In spite of all that a government can do and in spite of the best planning, a certain amount of regional imbalance is bound to be there even in the most highly developed countries of the world. There are certain types of disparities in matters of opportunity which people have to learn to live with. The capital will be capital and the state will be state, and in spite of the government's best efforts to provide equal opportunities to people in different parts of the state, a certain amount of imbalance will perhaps be there. The findings listed in Tables 1 & 2 show, however, that the disparity in Bihar is not of a marginal or peripheral nature and that something serious needs to be done about them at the level of planning.

Conclusion and Implications

The test administered at the end of the two years Intermediate course shows a serious imbalance in students' attainments. Students of science in Muzaffarpur, for example, got an average score of 37.70, the students of science of Darbhanga had an average score of 40.67, but the students of science in Patna had an average score of 66.45. This regional imbalance in students' attainments manifests itself not only in the case of science students but in the case of students in other faculties as well. Students of arts in Darbhanga, for example, had an average score of 33.11, and students of arts in Dumka, for example, got an average score of 37. 15 but the students of arts in Patna earned an average score of 49. 81. All over the world students in the capital have certain advantages which students in the interior parts may not have. A certain amount of regional imbalance is likely to be there in spite of the best planning even in the most developed countries of the world but in the state of Bihar the regional imbalance in students' attainments seems to be too large to be ignored.

This project, therefore, may be taken as an eye-opener for educational planners and course designers. They may think of conducting a diagnostic test and providing extra-teaching hours to students according to their needs or they may provide remedial classes to the disadvantaged groups of students so that the variations in language proficiency of students across the different areas of a state can be minimised. Besides, what is true about microcosm is true about macrocosm as well. The issue of regional variations is not specific to Bihar only. In fact, Bihar represents the whole of Northern India. In a broader sense, it presents a microscopic view of the whole country where the efforts and efficiency of different organisations need to be reassessed in view of these regional imbalances and some positive measures can be taken to minimise these imbalances.

Works Cited

All India ASER (Assessment Survey Evaluation Research) *Report*. (2008). *School Enrolment and Out of school (Age 6-14)*. Retrieved 15 March 2010 from http://www.asercentre.org/asersurvey/aser08/data/in/in-enr-o8.php.

National Family Health Survey -3 (NFHS-3). (2007). *Indian States Ranking by Literacy Rate. Wikipedia.* Retrieved 10 March 2010 from http://e.wikipedia.org/wiki/Indian states ranking by literary rate.

National Sample Survey Organisation (NSSO). (1998). *Rural per Capita Expenditure on Education in India.* Retrieved 01 March 2010 from http:///www.karamyog.org/rural development/rural development 7007.htm.

Sharma, A.K. (*2001*). *Teaching and Testing English Grammar*. New Delhi: Bahri Publications.

United Nations Children's Fund. (1990). *India, Situation Analysis 1990: Some highlights*. New Delhi: UNICEF. pp 54-55.

3

A Programme for Developing Phonological Awareness and Its Effect on Reducing English Reading Disabilities (dyslexia) for Intermediate Stage Students in Shifting Paradigms

—*Dr. Nasrah M. Ismail*

Introduction

Kirk & Chalfant (1984) confirmed that "the problem of reading and language is the essence of learning disabilities, and these disabilities fall under the classification of academic learning disabilities faced by students in different class levels" (p. 17).

After more than 20 years of researching the acquisition of reading skills, it seems the greatest difficulty that children face in learning to read fluently is the development of basic reading skills. The number of children with limited English proficiency in US public schools has risen dramatically in the past 20 years and continues to grow (Gunn, Smolkowski, Biglan, Black, and Blair, 2005). If native speakers of English are having difficulty learning to read, it stands to reason that the EFL students around the world, especially in Arabic-speaking countries, will be expected to have similar or even increased difficulties.

Numerous studies of students learning English suggest that phoneme awareness, coupled with letter knowledge enables students to grasp the alphabetical principle that underpins the development of word recognition and spelling (Share, 1995,

Caravoles, Hulme, & Snowling, 2001; Muter, Hulme, Snowling, & Stevenson, 2004). Allocating time to phonemic awareness and alphabetic instruction can improve reading (Foorman, Schatschneider, Eakin, Fletcher, Moats and Francis, 2006). The central role of phoneme awareness in the development of reading in English is clearly established (e.g., Torgeson, 2002). Persistent deficiency in phoneme awareness is present in English-speaking individuals with dyslexia (e.g., Bruck, 1992; Vellutino, Fletcher, Snowling, & Scanlon, 2004).

Phonological Awareness Definitions

Broadly defined, phonological awareness refers to the ability to perceive and manipulate the sounds of spoken words or phonemes along with sensitivity to the sound structure and the ability to consciously access and manipulate phonemes of a language. This is generally agreed upon by various researchers (Goswami & Bryant, 1990; Petryshen, Kaplan, Liu, and Field, 2000; Vloedgraven and Verhoeven, 2009). Not only had this but Naples, Chang, Katz, & Grigorenko (2009) considered that phonological awareness is a reading-related process. Phonological awareness is an oral language that is strongly related to reading skill and the basis for phonological decoding (Lundberg, Frost, & Peterson, 1988; Rohl & Pratt, 1995; Share, 1995; Castles & Coltheart, 2004). Hoover and Gough (2008) defined it by the ability to identify and manipulate onset, rhyme and syllable.

Phonological awareness is necessary to understand and absorb the principle of the letters on which the writing system of the language is based; if we want to have students with good reading, they must be sensitive to the internal construction of words. If students understand that words can be divided into individual sounds and these sounds can be collected into words, they will be able to use their knowledge of the relationship between the letter and sound to read and to form words (e.g., Geudeus, Sandra, & Broeck, 2004; Caravolas, Volý'n, & Hulme, 2005; Seki, Kassai, Uchiyama, Koeda 2008; Roman, Kirby, Parrila, Wade- Woolley, & Deacon 2008; Hoover and Gough, 2008; Roch & Jarrold, 2008).

Phonological awareness is to understand the different ways in which: (1) the division of oral or verbal language to the smallest elements can be used. Any oral language can be divided in various ways, including the division of the sentences to words, words into syllables and prefix, onset and rhyme end and to the sounds or single individual phonemes; (2) the sounds can be used, including the deletion or addition or replacement of clips or sounds such as in minimal pairs where the sound /k/ can be replaced by /m/ in the word "can" (Share, 1995; Chard & Dickson, 1999).

Phonological awareness is a comprehensive concept that includes activities such as deleting phonemes, blending and segmenting of words into onset and rhyme. Phonological awareness is important for reading in English (McBride-Chang, Cho, Liu, Wagner, Shu, Zhou, Cheuk, and Muse, 2005).

According to Chen, Li, Wu and Shu (2004), phonological awareness consists of two parts: (1) Phonemic Awareness is the most important level in the levels of phonological awareness, by which is meant that the student understands that words consist of individual sounds or phonemes. And it is the ability to use these sounds, either by dividing, blending or changing them for the composition of new words. (2) Onset and rhyme awareness.

The Relationship between Phonological Awareness and Dyslexia

According to the World Federation of Neurology (1968) developmental dyslexia is frequently defined as a deficit in learning to read despite adequate intelligence, motivation, and conventional instruction or a disorder in children who, despite conventional classroom experience, fail to attain the language skills of reading (cited in: Gaddes, 1985, p. 274). Similarly, Snowling (2000) concludes that children with developmental dyslexia suffer from severe reading problems despite normal intelligence and teaching, and in the absence of any obvious sensory deficit.

In contrast to acquired dyslexia, which results from a neural insult to a fully developed system, developmental dyslexia is a disorder that prevents the developing reading system from becoming efficient and automatised. Westbury and Buchanan (2006) conclude that deep dyslexics should show an increased error rate for abstract words that have more phonological neighbours than few, as compared with matched concrete words.

A number of researchers have identified two reading related processes found to be principally deficient in individuals with specified reading disability: phonemic awareness and rapid naming (e.g., Ackerman, Holloway, Youngdahl, Dykman 2001; Pennington Cardoso-Martins, Green and Lefly, 2001).

According to a common current opinion, developmental dyslexia, a specific difficulty in learning to read, is frequently related to phonological problems (e.g., Awaida & Beech, 1995; Caravolas, et al., 2005; Beech & Beauvois, 2006). In other words, a deficit in phonological processing occurs so frequently in dyslexia that it is often considered to be the 'core' deficit (Mody, Studdert-Kennedy, and Brady, 1997; Landerl, Fussenegger, Moll & Willburger, 2009).

Many researchers have clearly shown that there is a deficit in phonetic awareness in children and adults with dyslexia. Phonological awareness is strongly related to reading ability (Callua, Giannopulua, Escolanoa, Cusinb, Jacquier-Rouxb & Dellatolas, 2005; Seki, et al., 2008; Roman, et al., 2008; Ziegler, Castel, Pech-Georgel, George, Alario, & Perry, 2008; Liu, Shu & Yang 2009; Vaessen, Gerretsen & Blomert, 2009). Moreover, the deficiencies in the awareness of sound play an important role in the deficit of reading impairment (MacDonald & Cornwall, 1995; Caravolas, et al., 2005; Plaza & Cohen, 2005). The impairments in phonology can adversely affect development in reading, so it can be concluded that phonology and reading performance are interrelated (Beech & Beauvois, 2006). Bonte & Blomert (2004) indicating that the failure to adequately develop these phonological skills may underlie difficulties in reading and/or spelling such as experienced in developmental dyslexia.

About the difficulty of dyslexics in applying phonological awareness, Desroches, Joanisse & Robertson (2006) conclude that it is possible that students' problems in judging the initial sounds of words are due to difficulty explicitly applying phonological knowledge. Goswami (1999) also emphasizes that students with reading disabilities make less use of rhyme analogy cues in reading, compared to normal readers.

Phonological Awareness Training

"Remedial teaching is highly individualised teaching based on diagnostic study of the child`s unique problems and needs. It is highly individualised also in skills that are selected for emphasis, in the materials used, and in the varied approaches that help different students to achieve the general basic skills" (Harris & Sipay, 1975, p. 313).

Bradley and Bryant (1983) affirmed that reading skills are not inherent aptitude but they are acquired skills that can be taught and developed through educational and training organised programmes, as well as confirmed silent reading skills were developed through phonological awareness programs.

Castles and Colthear (2004) conclude that phonological awareness should have been trained. While clearly there are strong theoretical and practical reasons for teaching phonological awareness along with other reading-related skills (e.g. letter–sound correspondences), such designs compromise the ability to infer a direct causal link between phonological awareness as an independent variable and reading as a dependent variable.

Many recent reviews assured that training students to read right from childhood, it saves a lot of time, effort and money that is spent on teaching students how to read, and therefore must follow a successful reading programme to teach students how to read. Rivers (1981) stated that "the expert teacher has to recognise that he needed a clear and compelling necessity to adopt a program of reading to help him to cope with reading difficulties, and this contributes to the achievement of the kind of education that the community wants" (p.12).

Critical levels of phonological awareness can be developed through carefully planned instruction and this development has a significant influence on children's reading and spelling achievement (Ball & Blachman, 1988). Kjeldsen, Niemi and Olofsson (2003) suggested that training must be strictly systematic in order to be effective. They added this if phonological awareness is one of the causes of good reading development, then training in this skill would be highly desirable.

Through their studies Laing and Espeland (2005), and Saunders and Defulio (2007) confirmed that early intervention through phonological activities can facilitate early reading process and spelling. That's because the students through these activities can detect rhyme, know the sounds of letters and how to segment the word into smaller parts.

Moreover, several studies focusing on the early training of phonological awareness were able to show that children trained during the last year of kindergarten outperformed untrained control children in reading and spelling at school such that training phonological awareness in kindergarten was also successful for children at risk for dyslexia (e.g., Lundberg, et al., 1988; Schneider, Küspert, Roth, Visé, & Marx, 1997; Schneider, Roth, & Ennemoser, 2000).

Performance on phonological awareness tasks distinguishes clearly between those who have acquired the ability to associate letters with speech sounds and those who have not (Treiman, 2000). Moreover, there is increasing evidence that many children encounter difficulty developing phonological awareness without direct instruction in the phonemic segmentation of spoken language, and how letters represent those segments (Byrne, Fielding-Barnsley & Ashley, 1996). Milhim (2002) also has argued that "the failure of students in the acquisition of reading skills is mainly due to the lack of training students through the learning processes by their teachers" (p.297).

Several empirical studies of the field, for example, Kennedy and Backman (1993), Caravolas, et al., (2005), confirmed that children are developing in reading when phonological awareness training has a meaningful way and is integrated with the process of education. They found that phonological awareness training helps the children to understand that there is a relationship between the systemic patterns of spelling words and their pronunciation as well as the correlation between the perception of written words and audio elements in the early stages. Leppanen, et al., (2007) found that phonological awareness training contributes to the development of early reading performance in children, especially when the language is a second language such as English, French and German.

Similar to the above results, through their study Bradely and Bryan, 1983) regarding the effectiveness of the training on phonological categorisation and on the classification of concepts, found that children of (five-seven) years old have weakness in the phonological preparation and confirmed that their reading skills developed as well as their phonological classification.

Many studies that used phonological awareness programmes for developing reading skills affirmed that the experimental group performance is better than the control group in knowing letters, reading words and word identification, for example, Khalil (2003) asserted that the programme led to development of the children's language skills (listening, speaking and the readiness for the reading and the writing). Lenz and Hughes (1990), Kennedy and Backman (1993) found that the training on analysing the structure of the word and word recognition led to develop the understanding of the students with reading disabilities and a decrease of word recognition mistakes during the reading.

Ball and Blachman (1988) examined the effects of seven weeks of phoneme segmentation training on groups of kindergarten children. All of the children received the same instruction in language activities and in letter names and sounds, but only part of the children received phoneme segmentation training. The results showed that phoneme segmentation training has positive impact on reading skill. Similarly, Baker, Torgesen and Wagner (1992) studied 87 third- graders concerning the independent role of the orthographic skills in several different types of reading tasks. The authors found that orthographic processing skill makes a significant independent contribution to each type of reading skill and suggest that fluent access to visual word representations may play a special role in the facilitation of reading connected text.

The Problem of the Study

Although the process of learning to read has received unprecedented attention, it is still a big problem for students with learning disabilities. A lot of studies mentioned that (Rankhorn, England, Collins, Lockavich & Algozzine, 1998) 80 per cent of the students with learning disabilities find various reading skills difficult. In addition, Harris and Sipay (1985, p.15) confirmed that 25 per cent of regular school students need special remediation.

This researcher suggests that a phonological awareness program provides assistance for students with reading disabilities. If the intervention is provided early for students, then they will not have as many reading problems in their early school years; for example, Vloedgraven and Verhoeventhe (2009) have some significant implications for the early identification of children with reading problems and dyslexia through phonological awareness. Also if they were to provide help for students with reading disabilities in the early stages, the potential for later success in reading would be greater. For these reasons, recent trends in special education began to design tools for the diagnosis and treatment programmes for children at the age of four.

The phonological awareness theory offers a well established explanation of the mechanisms of reading difficulties in terms of phonological abilities (Vellutino, et al., 2004). Different phonological deficits have been shown to accompany characteristics of dyslexia and there is a documented relationship between performance on phonological tasks and reading skills. The more knowledge students have about the constituent sounds of words, the better they tend to be at reading. However, most research in support of this hypothesis has been carried out with English readers, whereas phonology could play a role in the difficulties of dyslexic readers in all alphabetic systems (Bednarek, Saldaña, Garcia, 2009).

Although the subject of phonological awareness has received much attention, there are many issues that need to be addressed. Researchers are still looking for ways to determine how and what kind of education is necessary or required for those who are dyslexic. According to Boets, Wouters, Wieringen, Ghesquière, (2006) there are between 5 and 15 per cent of the school students cannot deal with the symbols of language (i.e. the acquisition of reading skills), although they have good mental capacity, educational efforts are being made in the classroom and the economic situation appropriately.

Because Saudi students have had access to English language education from the seventh grade (intermediate school), this researcher chose this particular level for the survey of the phonological awareness programme to help those students in English reading with the hope of decreasing the number of students with English reading disabilities in the future. In doing phonological awareness training, teachers will more closely and directly satisfy their students' immediate needs for these skills, while helping them to increase their self-confidence in English language learning. Another reason for doing this research is because there are only a limited number of studies that address the issue of phonological awareness in native Arabic speakers of English as a second language, especially in Saudi Arabia.

This study addresses the following hypotheses:

- There are significant differences between the experimental group scores and the control group on the post-test of diagnostic reading test, namely, the experimental group students scored higher than the control group.
- There are significant differences between the mean scores of the experimental group and the control group on the post-test of phonological awareness test.
- There are significant differences between the mean scores of pre-test and post-test of the diagnostic reading test as well as the phonological awareness test. The experimental group scores are higher than in the post-test.
- There are no significant differences in the mean scores of the post-test and the follow up of the diagnostic reading test and phonological awareness test for the experimental group.

Method

Participants

Two schools (Al Arba'ain School and Al Mutawista Al Oula) were randomly chosen from the schools of Taif. The participants were (511) females at the first grade level of intermediate school. According to their achievement scores in the mid-term exam and their participation with the teachers in the class, this researcher asked the teachers to identify the students who had disability in reading English, so the sample was (87) girls. After testing the students with the Mental Abilities Test (Abd–El-Fatah, 1984) and the diagnostic reading test, four students were excluded because of their low IQ scores and six because of their normal achievement. The final sample was 77 students that were divided into two groups; experimental (40 females) and control (37 females). The average age of the students (M = 13.4 years, SD = 0.577). T-test shows that there are no differences between the experimental group and control group on the diagnostic reading pre-test, the phonological awareness pre-test, age and IQ scores.

To diagnose the students with reading disabilities this researcher followed four steps:

I. English teacher's referral for the students who have reading disabilities from the teacher's opinion,

II. IQ student's score on the Mental Abilities Test is 90 and over,

III. Diagnostic reading student's score below the general average of their peers by one standard deviation at least in two subtests from the four subtests.

Table 1

Cut Scores that are Used in Identifying the Sample

Tests	*Mean*	*SD*	*Cut scores*
Reading Aloud	24.211	6.306	17
One Minute Reading	23.305	5.465	17
Word Recognition	5.427	1.287	4
Silent Reading	27.821	6.800	21

Measures

Phonological awareness tasks

1. Rhyme detection

In this task this researcher shows a page for the student that has a picture or a word at the top and three pictures/words at its bottom. The student was as' ed to determine; for example: which picture/word starts with the same sound as..... There were three practice items with corrective feedback and ten (10) test items without feedback; each item consists of three words.

2. Phoneme deletion

After the presentation of the word response, the target word was pronounced along with a phoneme to be deleted. After the identification of the initial sound of the word, the student had to delete the first sound and say the remaining part of the word. For example, after repeating the word 'seat' the student was asked what word would be left if said without the /s/. The total number of items was 10 test items without feedback that the researcher selected them from the students' book and three practices with corrective feedback. The phoneme deletion process addressed all possible positions in the word.

3. Phoneme substitution

After the presentation of the word response alternative, the target word was pronounced along with a phoneme to be changed. The student was asked to say (e.g., /cat/) and then change the first sound to (/h/). There were three practices with corrective feedback and 10 test items without feedback. The phoneme substitution process addressed all possible positions in the word (initial, middle and end sound).

4. Rhyme application task

After the presentation of the two words response alternatives, then the target words were pronounced. The task required the student to give a word that rhymed with the words presented orally by the experimenter (e. g., /hen/pen) and then the student says (e.g. ten). After three practice trials with corrective feedback, 10 test items were presented without feedback.

5. Verbal fluency

Students needed to name as many words as s/he could within 1 min. starting with a particular letter. The researcher chose B, S, F.

6. Syllable segmentation

In contrast to the other tasks, the phoneme segmentation task required an oral response. The target word was presented both visually and auditorily. The student was asked to divide simple words into parts of phoneme-size and pronounce each of the phonemes in the word in the proper order. Three examples of an item were presented with corrective feedback. The target words contained two to five phonemes. Twelve test items were used without feedback.

Procedure

The six tasks were administered individually in a quiet room in the school by the researcher and they were administered in the same order to all participants. Each task took approximately five minutes to complete. Every task started with three practice items in which the experimenter provided immediate feedback to facilitate understanding of the task and each task contained 10 test items except the syllable segmentation task has twelve test items. But verbal fluency subscale does not have a limited number of words.

Item validity and internal consistency for phonological awareness tasks in the current study:

The corrected item-total correlation ranged from 0.350 to 0.527 ($p < 0.01$), suggesting adequate item validity. While for the corrected item, Subscale 1(rhyme detection) the correlation ranged from 0.417 to 0.607 ($p < 0.01$), for the Subscale 2 (phoneme deletion) the correlation ranged from 0.393 to 0.696 ($p < 0.01$), but for the Subscale 3 (phoneme substitution) the correlation ranged from 0.492 to 0.689 ($p < 0.01$); for the Subscale 4 (rhyme application) the correlation ranged from 0.42 to 0.78 ($p < 0.01$) for the Subscale 6 (syllable segmentation) the correlation ranged from 0.46 to 0.65 ($p < 0.01$), suggesting adequate item validity.

The internal consistency was high for the total scale (spilt half reliability = 0.910), as well as for Subscale 1 (spilt half reliability = 0.745) Subscale 2 (spilt half reliability = 0.843), Subscale 3 (spilt half reliability = 0.689), Subscale 4 (spilt half reliability = 0.728), Subscale 5 (spilt half reliability = 0.861), and Subscale 6 (verbal (test retest = 0.725). The mean total score was 29.228 (SD = 9.315).

The mean for Subscale 1 was 7.14 (SD = 1.75), for Subscale 2 was 5.36 (SD = 2.18), for Subscale 3 was 3.68 (SD = 1.89), for Subscale 4 was 3.22 (SD = 1.89), for Subscale 5 was 3.36 (SD = 1.091), and the mean for Subscale 6 was 3.94 (SD = 1.99). While the correlation between factors ranged from 0.34 to 0.68 and between factors and total score ranged from 0.30 to 0.71. ($p < 0.05$ to $p < 0.01$), the validity for subscale 5 (verbal fluency) was from the correlation between its scores and rapid naming test (0.751).

Diagnostic Reading Test

It contains four subtests; a reading aloud passage, a one minute reading list of words, a word recognition test and a silent reading passage. It was applied individually in a suitable and quiet room in the school. It took 10 minutes to complete.

1. Reading aloud passage

This test was designed to measure the students' ability to read correctly as well as to understand. This researcher selected the passage from the students' book. The researcher put five questions on the passage to check the understanding of the student. The maximum score for the test is 75: 65 for the passage and 10 scores for the questions.

2. One minute reading list

This test was designed to measure the students' ability to read the words. The words were chosen from the students' book. The maximum score was 42 according to the number of the 42 words in list. Students with no sign of reading ability obtained 0 points. Each word was worth one point when read correctly.

3. Word recognition

This test was designed to measure the students' ability to listen carefully to recognise the word that she heard among four alternatives. This test consists of 10 items. Each sentence contains four words. The researcher says the word and then the student points to the word after hearing it; 10 points for the whole test, 1 mark for each correct recognition.

4. Silent reading passage

This researcher selected the passage from the students' book and put five questions related to the passage to measure the students' understanding; 50 scores for the all questions and 10 points for each correct answer.

Validity and Reliability for Diagnostic Reading Test in the Current Study

The predictive validity for the diagnostic reading test was concluded by correlations coefficients between the scores of the diagnostic reading test and the students' mid-term scores, for total scale ($r = 0.87$; $p < 0.01$); for subscale 1 (Reading aloud passage) ($r = 0.83$; $p < 0.01$), for subscale 2 (One Minute reading) ($r = 0.79$; $p < 0.01$), for subscale 3 (Word recognition) ($r = 0.85$; $p < 0.01$), for subscale 4 (Silent reading passage) ($r = 0.77$; $p < 0.01$). The reliability for total scale was (spilt half reliability = 0.89), but for subscale 1 (spilt half reliability = 0.89), for subscale 2 (spilt half reliability = 0.85), for subscale 3 (spilt half reliability = 0.91), and for subscale 4 (spilt half reliability = 0.87). The mean for Subscale 1 was 24.211 (SD = 6.306), the mean for Subscale 2 was 23.305 (SD = 5.465), the mean for Subscale 3 was 5.427 (SD = 1.287), the mean for Subscale 4 was 27.821 (SD = 6.800).

Training Programme

The highly structured phonological awareness training programme included 50 experimental students implemented in three weekly sessions. The training period started in the beginning of February 2008 and was continued until May 2008. The programme consisted of 48 sessions; four sessions per week and it continued for three months. Tools and aids that were used in the programme are cards, pictures, word cards, toys, letter cards and songs that have rhymed words. The programme was evaluated through the pre-tests and post-tests, through the comparison between the experimental and control groups scores and also through the follow up in developing reading skills after one month from stopping the programme.

Table 2: The Differences between the Experimental Group and the Control Group on the Diagnostic Reading Post-test

Variables	*Experimental group*			*Control group*						
	N	*Mean*	*SD*	*N*	*Mean*	*SD*	*T-test*	*d.f.*	*Sig.*	*Effect size*
Reading aloud	40	21.180	4.984	37	14.106	2.631	7.598	75	0.001	1.732
One minute reading	40	21.520	6.329	37	15.440	5.245	4.510	75	0.001	1.028
Word recognition	40	5.820	1.101	37	4.830	1.070	3.944	75	0.001	0.899
Silent reading	40	24.080	6.951	37	15.043	3.471	7.038	75	0.001	1.605

Effect size is small = 0.2, moderate = 0.505, high = 0.84, 1 or over it means strong effect (Morad, 2000, p.248).

Results

The results generally conformed to my tentative expectations that significant differences would be found between the means of the experimental group and the control group on the diagnostic reading post-test which confirmed the correction of the first hypothesis; the mean of experimental group was higher than the control group. This researcher explains that the positive results of the experimental group are due to the effects of the program which includes a lot of reading activities that the students share with each other.

This result agrees with the results of many studies (e.g., Geudens, et al., 2004) confirmed that the awareness of reading skills cannot grow spontaneously but through a training programme. Boets, Ghesquière, Wieringen, and Wouters also (2007) asserted that the significant relationship between phonological awareness and reading has a positive impact on achievement.

In addition, Al Batina, Al Rashedan, Al Sabila and Al Khatita (2005) mentioned that there are some reasons that make the student unable to read the word if he has no specified strategy to follow, and he does not know how to connect between phonemes and there meanings. Furthermore, it is difficult for them to read the word through its phonemes or its segments. This means that reading programmes are a necessity for students with reading disabilities to develop their reading skills (p.145).

Table 3 indicates that there are differences between the two groups in the phonological awareness post-test and its factors; for the experimental group (M = 38.08, SD = 4.810), for the control group (M = 24.957, SD = 4.787). This result agrees with the result of Leppanen, Aunola, Niemi, Nurmi (2007) who that stated phonological awareness is an important factor in teaching reading correctly and it facilitates the reading process and its accurateness. It also has a major effect on understanding and fluency.

In addition to, this hypothesis agrees with results of many studies (e.g. Seki, et al., 2008; Geudeus, et al., 2004; Durand, Hulme, Larkin & Snowling, 2005; Boada & Pennington, 2006; Coch, Hart & Mitra, 2008) which affirmed that phonological awareness helps the students to gain reading skills. Additionally,

Table 3: The Differences between the Experimental Group and the Control Group on the Phonological Awareness Post-test.

Variables	*Experimental group*			*Control group*						
	N	*Mean*	*SD*	N	*Mean*	*SD*	*d.f.*	*T*	*Sig.*	*Effect Size*
Rhyme dictation	40	7.620	1.323	37	5.064	0.987	75	9.432	0.001	2.150
Phoneme deletion	40	6.380	1.850	37	5.319	1.944	75	2.422	0.05	0.552
Sound substitution	40	5.280	1.539	37	3.787	1.944	75	4.194	0.001	0.956
Rhyme application	40	5.620	1.159	37	3.553	1.348	75	7.128	0.001	1.625
Verbal fluency	40	5.660	1.493	37	3.319	1.002	75	7.936	0.001	1.809
Word segmentation	40	6.520	1.344	37	3.745	1.113	75	9.703	0.001	2.212
Total	40	38.080	4.810	37	24.957	4.787	95	11.833	0.001	2.698

Effect size is small = 0.2, moderate = 0.505, high = 0.84, 1 or over it means strong effect (Morad, 2000, p.248).

they prove that students with reading difficulties have less phonological awareness than normal students since they lack in their perception of phonological awareness process.

Table 4

The Differences between the Pre-test and the Post-test on the Phonological Awareness Tasks for the Experimental Group

The Variables	*Mean Differences*	*Std. Error*	*T. Test*	*d.f.*	*Sig.*	*Effect Size*
Rhyme detection	2.860	0.234	12.222	39	0.001	1.728
Phoneme deletion	1.640	0.153	10.719	39	0.001	1.312
Phoneme substitution	1.540	0.236	6.525	39	0.001	0.946
Rhyme application	2.320	0.272	8.529	39	0.001	1.183
Verbal fluency	2.340	0.263	8.897	39	0.001	1.258
Syllable segmentation	2.640	0.292	9.041	39	0.001	1.213
Total	14.290	0.878	16.276	39	0.001	1.926

Effect size is: small=0.2, moderate =0.505 , high =0.84 , 1 or over it means strong effect (Morad, 2000, p. 248).

We can explain these differences in the light of the importance of phonological awareness and the importance of its training, as well as showing the teaching style that the researcher follows during the programme. The table also shows that the effects are indeed powerful (e.g. Lenz & Hughes, 1990; Torgeson, et al., 1992; Kennedy & Backman, 1993; Lovett & Steinbach, 1997).

The current results are also quite similar to the findings of Kennedy and Backman (1993) who mentioned that training students in phonological awareness led to developing the dyslexic students' understanding of word recognition mistakes during reading. Lastly, training has a positive effect on reading achievement.

Many studies asserted that students make good progress in reading when they have good phonological training; when this training becomes an essential part of the instructional process (e.g.

Roch & Jarrold, 2008; Roman, et al., 2008; Seki, et al., 2008). This table also suggests that students in the experimental group who performed poorly prior to training improved their performance.

Table 5

The Differences between the Pre-test and the Post-test on the Diagnostic Reading Test for the Experimental Group

The Variables	*Mean Differences*	*Std. Error*	*T. Test*	*d.f.*	*Sig.*	*Effect Size*
Reading aloud	6.500	0.495	13.131	39	0.001	1.857
One minute reading	6.680	0.734	9.101	39	0.001	1.115
Word recognition	1.360	0.206	6.602	39	0.001	1.043
Silent reading	8.920	0.589	15.144	39	0.001	2.272

Effect size is: small=0.2, moderate =0.505, high =0.84, 1 or over it means strong effect (Morad, 2000, 248).

However, the study reveals that there are no statistically significant differences between the first post-test and the second (follow up) post-test which was administered a month after the first post-test on the phonological awareness test and diagnostic reading test

Moore, Rosenberg and Coleman (2005) indicate that enhanced performance in the trained children was maintained in a delayed test five–six weeks following training. They further suggest that relatively long-lasting improvements are possible with more restricted training.

Discussions

The findings of the current study supported earlier research of Lundberg, et al., (1988) which showed training in phonological awareness strongly facilitates reading acquisition. It also agrees with the results of Kjeldsen et al. (2003) that proved to be a treatment effect on both the early literacy variables, which are letter-knowledge and reading.

In short, phonological awareness training is important and of great interest to readers, at any level, with learning difficulties, and that awareness can be developed by the reading process. This facilitates the process of acquiring reading skill. The current findings support previous literature that has suggested that individuals with reading disability have poorer phonological awareness (e.g., Boada & Pennington, 2006).

Conclusion

Through phonological awareness children with dyslexia can be identified early and the teacher can follow the system offered by this program follows. Reference points from the programme can be left with the teachers to follow with the students. This researcher wants the teacher to also think of words phonologically through the planning and teaching of the lessons, especially with those dyslexic students, to direct their attention to the segmenting of words or blending. Students with reading problems could be given homework or class work which concentrates on the phonological aspect of reading. The teacher can take notes on the individual dyslexic students that can be used by others on what methods of teaching were useful and beneficial to the students. The teacher can also note what the common problems existed between the dyslexic students, which might be of benefit to such a program of concentrating on the phonological aspects of learning to read.

Following this structure, each teacher could select among the tasks to compose a session. The teacher could also introduce a new concept or a new procedure.

Works Cited

Abd-El-Fatah, F. (1984). *Mental Abilities Test*. Cairo: El-Nahda EL-Masriya.

Ackerman, P.T., Holloway, C.A., Youngdahl, P.L., Dykman, R.A. (2001). The double- deficit theory of reading disability does not fit all. *Learning Disabilities Research & Practice, 16,* 152–160.

Awaida, M. & Beech, J.R. (1995). Children's Lexical and Sublexical Development while Learning to Read. *Journal of Experimental Education, 63,* 97-113.

Baker, T.A., Torgesen, J.K., & Wagner, R. K. (1992). The role of orthographic processing skills on five different reading tasks. *Reading Research Quarterly, 27,* 334 -345.

Ball, E.W., & Blachman, B.A. (1988). Phoneme segmentation training: Effect on reading readiness. *Annals of Dyslexia, 38,* 208-225.

Bednarek, D., Saldaña, D., Garcia, I. (2009). Visual versus phonological abilities in Spanish dyslexic boys and girls. *Brain and Cognition 70,* 273–278.

Beech, J.R. & Beauvois, M.W (2006). Early experience of sex hormones as a predictor of reading, phonology and auditory perception. *Brain and Language, 96,* 49-58.

Boada, R. & Pennington, B.F. (2006). Deficient implicit phonological representations in children with dyslexia. *Journal of Experimental Child Psychology 95,*153–193.

Boets, B. Ghesquière, P. Wieringen, A.V and Wouters .J. (2007). Speech perception in preschoolers at family risk for dyslexia: Relations with low-level auditory processing and phonological ability. *Brain and Language 101,* 19–30.

Wouters, J, Wieringen, A.V. Ghesquière, P. (2006). Auditory temporal information processing in preschool children at family risk for dyslexia: Relations with phonological abilities and developing literacy skills. *Brain and Language, 97,* 64–79.

Bonte, M. L. & Blomert, L. (2004). Developmental dyslexia: ERP correlates of anomalous phonological processing during spoken word recognition. *Cognitive Brain Research 21,* 360–376.

Bruck, M. (1992). Persistence of dyslexics' phonological awareness deficits. *Developmental Psychology, 28,* 874-886.

Byrne, B., Fielding-Barnsley, R., & Ashley, L. (1996). What does the child bring to the task of learning to read. A summary of the New England reading acquisition projects. *Australian Journal of Psychology, 48,* 119–123.

Callua, D. Giannopulua, I. Escolanoa, S. Cusin,F. Jacquier-Rouxb, M. & Dellatolas, G. (2005). Smooth pursuit eye movements are associated with phonological awareness in preschool children. *Brain and Cognition 58,* 217–225.

Caravolas, M.; Volý'n, J. & Hulme, C. (2005). Phoneme awareness is a key component of alphabetic literacy skills in consistent and inconsistent orthographies: Evidence from Czech and English children. *Journal of Experimental Child Psychological, 92,* 107-139.

Castles, A. & Colthear, M. (2004). Is there a causal link from phonological awareness to success in learning to read? *Cognition, 91,* 77–111.

Chard, D.J & Dickson, S.V. (1999). Phonological awareness: Instructional and Assessment Guidelines. *Intervention in School and Clinic, 34,* 261-270.

Chen, R.C.A.; Li, W.; Wu. M.X. & Shu, H. (2004). Phonological awareness of bilingual and monolingual Chinese children. *Journal of Educational Psychology, 96* (1), 142-151.

Coch, D.; Hart,T.; & Mitra,P. (2008). Three Kinds of Rhymes: An ERP Study. *Brain and Language, 104,* 230-243.

Desroches, A. S. Joanisse, M. F. & Robertson, E. k. (2006). Specific phonological impairments in dyslexia revealed by eyetracking. *Cognition 100,* 32–42.

Durand, M.; Hulme, C.; Larkin, R. & Snowling, M; (2005). The cognitive foundations of reading and arithmetic skills in 7-10 years old. *Experimental Child Psychology, 91,* 113-136.

El Batina, O.M., El Rashedan, A.M., El Sabila, A. A. &e l Khatita, S.M. A. (2005). *Learning disabilities, Theory and practice,* 2nd Ed. Oman: Dar El- Maysara.

Foorman, B. R., Schatschneider, C., Eakin, M. N., Fletcher, J.M., Moats, L.C., and Francis, D.J. (2006).The impact of instructional practices in Grades 1 and 2 on reading and spelling achievement in high poverty schools. *Contemporary Educational Psychology, 31,* 1-29.

Gaddes, W.H. (1985). *Learning Disabilities and Brain Function, A Neuropsychological Approach, (2nd Ed).* New York, Berlin, Tokyo, Springer–Verlag New York Inc.

Geudeus, A.; Sandra, D. & Broeck, V. W. (2004). Segmenting two-phoneme syllables: developmental differences in relation with early reading skills. *Brain and Language, 90,* 338-352.

Goswami, U. (1999). Causal connections in beginning reading: The importance of rhyme. *Journal of Research in Reading, 22*(3), 217–240.

& Bryant, P. (1990). *Phonological skills and learning to read.* London: Erlbaum.

Gunn,B., Smolkowski, K., Biglan, A.,Black, C., and Blair, J (2005) Fostering the development of reading skill through supplemental instruction: results for Hispanic and non-Hispanic students. *The Journal of Special Education, 39* (2), 66-85.

Harris, A.J. & Sipay, E. R. (1975). *How to increase reading ability (2nd Ed).* United States of America. David McKAY Company.

Hoover, A. W. & Gough, B. P. (2008). The reading acquisition framework- an overview. http://www.sedl.org/reading/framework/overview.html 18/7/2008.

Kennedy, K. & Backman, J. (1993). Effectiveness of the lindamood auditory discrimination in depth program with students with learning disabilities. *Learning Disabilities Research and Practice,* 18, (4), 253-259.

Khalil, E.A. (2003). Effectiveness of program in expressive activities for developing some language skills for preschool child. Unpublished Ph. D. dissertation. The institution for childhood studies: Ain Shams University.

Kirk, S. A. & Chalfant, J. C. (1984). *Academic and Developmental Learning Disabilities, (2nd Ed)*. Denver, London: Love Publishing Company.

Kjeldsen, A.-C., Niemi, P. & Olofsson, A. (2003). Training phonological awareness in kindergarten level children: consistency is more important than quantity. *Learning and Instruction 13*, 349–365.

Laing, S. P. & Espeland, W. (2005). Low intensity phonological awareness training in a preschool classroom for children with communication impairments. *Journal of Communication Disorders 38*, 65–82.

Landerl, K., Fussenegger, B., Moll, K., & Willburger, E. (2009). Dyslexia and dyscalculia: Two learning disorders with different cognitive profiles. *Journal of Experimental Child Psychology, 103*,309–324.

Lenz, B.K. & Hughes, C.A. (1990) A word identification strategy adolescents with learning disabilities. *Journal of Learning Disabilities, 23* (3), 149- 158.

Leppanen, U., Aunola, K., Niemi, P., Nurmi, J-E. (2007). Letter knowledge predicts grade 4 reading fluency and reading comprehension. *Learning and Instruction,* 1-17.

Liu, W., Shu, H., & Yang,Y. (2009). Speech perception deficits by Chinese children with phonological dyslexia. *Journal of Experimental Child Psychology,* 103,338–354

Lovett, M. & Steinbach, K. K. (1997). The effectiveness of remedial programs for reading disabled children of different ages: Does the benefit decrease for older children? *Learning Disabilities Quarterly, l20,* (3), 189-210.

Lundberg, I., Frost, J., & Peterson, O. (1988). Effects of an extensive program for stimulating phonological awareness in preschool children. *Reading Research Quarterly,* 23, 263–284.

MacDonald, G. W & Cornwall, A. (1995). The relationship between phonological awareness and reading and spelling achievement eleven years later. *Journal of Learning Disabilities. 28* (8), 457-528.

McBride-Chang, C. Cho, J. Liu, H. Wagner, R. K. Shu, H. Zhou, A. et al. (2005). Changing models across cultures: Associations of phonological awareness and morphological structure awareness with vocabulary and word recognition in second graders from Beijing, Hong Kong, Korea, and the United States. *Journal of Experimental Child Psychology* 92,140–160

Milhim, S. M. (2002). *Learning Disabilities*. Jordan, Oman: Dar El-Maiysara.

Mody, M., Studdert-Kennedy M. and Brady S. (1997). Speech perception deficits in poor readers: auditory processing or phonological coding? *Journal of Experimental Child Psychology, 64*, 199–231.

Moore, D. R., Rosenberg, J. F., & Coleman, J. S. (2005). Discrimination training of phonemic contrasts enhances phonological processing in mainstream school children. *Brain and Language 94,* 72–85.

Morad, S. A. (2000). *Statistical Methods for the Social, Educational and Psychological Sciences.* Cairo: El-Anglo EL-Masriya.

Muter,V. Hulme,C., Snowling, M., & Stevenson, K.E. .(2004). Phoneme, rimes, vocabulary and grammatical skills as foundations of early reading development: Evidence from a longitudinal study. *Developmental Psychology, 40,* 665-681.

Naples, A. J., Chang, J. T., Katz, L. & Grigorenko, E. L. (2009). Same or different? Insights into the etiology of phonological awareness and rapid naming. *Biological Psychology, 80,* 226–239

Pennington, B.F., Cardoso-Martins, C., Green, P.A., Lefly, D.L. (2001). Comparing the phonological and double deficit hypotheses for developmental dyslexia. *Reading and Writing 14,* 707–755.

Petryshen, T. L., Kaplan, B. J., Liu, M. F. and Field, L.L. (2000). Absence of significant linkage between phonological coding dyslexia and chromosome 6p23-21.3, as determined by use of quantitative-trait methods: confirmation of qualitative analyses. *Am. J. Hum. Genet.* 66:708–714.

Plaza, M. & Cohen, H. (2005) Influence of auditory – verbal, visual – verbal, visual and visual- visual processing speed on reading and spelling at the end of grade 1. *Brain and Cognition, 57,* 189-1194.

Rivers, W.M., (1981). *Teaching Foreign- Language Skills (2nd Ed.).* The University of Chicago Press. Chicago and London.

Roch, M. & Jarrold, C. (2008). A Comparison between word and nonword reading in Down syndrome: The role phonological awareness. *Journal of Communication Disorders.41,*305-318.

Rohl, M., & Pratt, C. (1995). Phonological awareness, verbal working memory and the acquisition of literacy. *Reading and Writing, 7,* 327–360.

Roman, A. A.; Kirby,.J. R; Parrila ,.R. K; Wade- Woolley, L. & Deacon ,S. H. (2009).Toward a comprehensive view of the skills involved in word reading in grades 4 , 6 and 8. *Journal of Experimental Child Psychology, 102* (1), 96-113.

Saunders, J.K & Defulio, A. (2007). Phonological awareness and rapid naming predict word attack and word identification in adults with mild mental retardation. *American Journal on Mental Retardation, 112* (3), 155-166.

Schneider, W., Küspert, P., Roth, E., Visé, M., & Marx, H. (1997). Short- and long-term effects of training phonological awareness in kindergarten: Evidence from two German studies. *Journal of Experimental Child Psychology, 66,* 311–340.

Schneider, W., Roth, E., & Ennemoser, M. (2000). Training phonological skills and letter knowledge in children at risk for dyslexia: A comparison of three kindergarten training programs. *Journal of Educational Psychology, 92,* 284–295.

Seki, A.; Kassai, K.; Uchiyama, H.; Koeda, T. (2008). Reading Ability and Phonological Awareness in Japanese Children with Dyslexia. *Brain & Development, 30,* 179-188.

Share, D.L. (1995). phonological decoding and self-teaching: Since qua non of reading acquisition. *Cognition, 55,*151-218.

Snowling, M.J. (2000). *Dyslexia.* Oxford: Blackwell.

Torgesen, J.K.; Morgan, S.T. & Davis, C.(1992) Effects of two types of phonological awareness training on word learning in kindergarten children. *Journal of Educational Psychology, 8,* (3), 364-370.

(2002). The prevention of reading difficulties. *Journal of School Psychology, 40,* 7-26.

Treiman, R. (2000). The foundations of literacy. *Current Directions in psychological Science, 9* (3), 89-92.

Vaessen, A., Gerretsen P. & Blomert, L. (2009). Naming problems do not reflect a second independent core deficit in dyslexia: Double deficits explored. *Journal of Experimental Child Psychology 103,* 202–221.

Vellutino, F. R., Fletcher, J.M., Snowling, M.J., & Scanlon, D.M., (2004). Specific reading disability (dyslexia): What have we learned in the past four decades? *Journal of Child Psychology and Psychiatry.*

Vloedgraven, J. Verhoeven, L. (2009). The nature of phonological awareness throughout the elementary grades: An item response theory perspective. *Learning and Individual Differences 19,* 161–169

Westbury, C. & Buchanan, L. (2006). Toward a frontal lobe disconnection model of deep dyslexia: The role of semantic feedback in phonological false memories. *Journal of Neurolinguistics, 19,* 124–156.

Ziegler, J.C., Castel, C., Pech-Georgel, C., George, F., Alario, F. & Perry, C. (2008). Developmental dyslexia and the dual route model of reading: Simulating individual differences and subtypes. *Cognition, 107,* 151–178.

4

Shifting Paradigms and the Role of R.M.S.A in English Language Teaching in India: Fostering Creativity

—*Ramesh Chandra Shukla*

A Global Language in a Multilingual Country

Why English

English in India today is a symbol of people's aspiration for quality education, and a fuller participation in national and international life. Its colonial origins, now forgotten or irrelevant, its initial role in independent India was tailored to higher education (as a" library language," a "window on the "world"). Now it is felt to be insufficiently inclusive socially and linguistically. The current status of English seems to have its overwhelming presence on the world stage and the reflection of this is in the national arena. It is predicted that by 2010 a surge in English language learning will include a third of the world's people (Graddol, 1997). The opening up of the Indian economy in the 1990s has coincided with an explosion in the demand for English in our schools because English is perceived to open up opportunities (Das 2005).

The liberalisation of the Indian economy ushered in all kinds of reasons. To learn English language earlier in the century students who had specialised in English joined either teaching or the civil services, now a new spectrum of job opportunities has opened up. There are now countries that need trainers to equip their employees.

Meaning of Creativity

There are divergent views on the nature of creativity. Two major areas exist in which this term is used. On the one hand, it refers to a special type of thinking or mental functioning that is called divergent thinking ('jara hat ke'). On the other hand, it refers to the generation of products that are perceived to be creative such as works of arts, architechture or music. But in the case of school children, Cropley leans towards the first of these two opinions, and adopts the stance that creativity is 'the capacity to get the ideas, specially original, inventive and noble. Creativity may be mathematically expressed as follows:

Creativity = Logical thinking + Divergent thinking

This is based on intuition but has a conscious aim. When one is applying divergent thinking in a practical problem solving matter, divergent thinking produces many new ideas. Some of them seem to be useful for finding solutions, and a process of logical thinking will make a summary of these fruitful ideas. After reviewing various definitions of creativity Dettann and Havinghurst (1962) concluded, "Creativity is the quality which leads to the production of something new and desirable. The new product may be new to the society of merely new for the individual who creates it."

Fostering Creativity

Two phases—'convergence thinking' and 'divergent thinking' are—closely related to creativity. In convergence thinking, emphasis is laid on activities that are directed towards a correct answer while divergent thinking, on the contrary, emphasizes diversity of ideas. It opens up the multiplicity of ideas. Students using a divergent approach to the solutions of problems begin to look at problems in a new light and results in creativity. Hence, divergent thinking paves the way for producing something quite new. Learning experiences should be provided to students for using divergent thinking. Imagination is the beginning of creation. Hence, the teacher should help for the students train their imagination, imagination is more important than knowledge. For while knowledge defines all us currently know and understand imagination points to all we might yet discover and create. Creative imagination enables students to raise new questions, new possibilities and to regard old problems from a new angle. Imagination should not atrophy. It should not be stimulated. This can be done only in an encouraging atmosphere in English language class. Moreover, teachers must encourage originality and heterogeneity, if creativity is to be encouraged. While solving problems teachers should not demand one uniform answer but allow different opinion and expressions. Problem solving is a framework of pattern within which creativity takes place.

Rashtriya Madhyamik Siksha Abhiyan (R.M.S.A.)

Secondary education is a crucial stage in the educational hierarchy as it prepares the students for higher education and also for the world of work. Classes IX and X constitute the secondary stage. The normal age group of the children in secondary classes is 14-16 whereas it is 16-18 for higher secondary classes. The rigour of the secondary and higher secondary stage enables Indian students to compete successfully for education and for jobs globally. Therefore, it is absolutely essential to strengthen this stage by providing greater success and also by improving quality in a significant way.

The population of the age group 14-16 was 8.55 crore in 2001 as per the census data. The estimated population of this age group as on March 2005 was 9.48 crore which was likely to increase to 9.70 crore as on March 2007, i.e., at the beginning of the Eleventh Five, Year Plan. This is likely to stabilise at round 9.70 Crore in 2011. The gross enrolment ratio for classes IX to XII in 2005-06 was 40.49 per cent. The figure for classes IX and X was 52.26 per cent whereas that for classes XI to XII was 28.54 per cent.

With the liberalisation and globalisation of the Indian economy, the rapid changes witnessed in scientific and technological world and the general need to improve the quality of life and to reduce poverty, it is essential that school leavers acquire a higher level of knowledge and skills than what they are provided in the eight years of elementary education, particularly when the average earning of secondary school certificate holder is significantly higher than of a person who has studied up to class VIIII. It is also necessary that besides general education up to secondary level, opportunities for improvement of vocational knowledge and skill should be provided at the higher secondary level to enable some students to be employable. Consequently, for ICT it is important and the importance of English language has its unique place in modern macro life.

Main Objectives

i) To ensure that no child is deprived of secondary education of satisfactory quality due to gender, socio-economic, disability and other barriers.

ii) To ensure that all students pursuing secondary Education receives good quality of education.

iii) To improve the quality of secondary education resulting in enhanced intellectual, social and cultural learning.

iv) Achievement of the above objectives would also, inter-alia, signifies substantial progress in the direction of common school system.

Approach and Strategy for Secondary Stage

1. Access
2. Quality
3. Equity

English in our schools and the level of introduction of english

The visible impact of the presence of English is that everyone is today demanding it at the very initial stage of schooling. The English teaching profession has consistly recommended a relatively late (class IV, V and VI) introduction of English and this is reflected in spirit in policy documents. The dissatisfaction with this recommendation is evident in the mushrooming of private English-medium schools and the early introduction of English in state school systems. The popular response to systemic failure has been to extend downwards the very system that has failed to deliver. The level of introduction of English has now become a matter of political response to the people's aspirations, rendering almost irrelevant an academic debate on the merits of a very early introduction. There is a problem of systematic feasibility and preparedness, for example, finding the required number of competent teachers. But there is an expectation that the system should respond to popular needs rather than the other way round.

We perceive this question in various ways. First, we hope through multilingualism to counter some possible ill effects such as the loss of one's own language(s), or the burden of sheer incomprehension. Second, we describe what can realistically be achieved in given situation, supplemented with affirmation action interventions where necessary, the aim is to identify delivery system for comprehensible input to the child, whether in the classroom or outside it. For a fuller understanding of the issues around the early introduction of English, we have included an assessment of the "critical period" or "sensitive window" which entails a very early introduction of English.

Variety and Range of English Teaching in India

The teaching and earning of English today is characterised by, on the one hand, a diversity of schools and linguistic environments supportive of English acquisition and, on the other hand, by systematically pervasive classroom procedures of teaching a textbook for success in examination modulated by teacher beliefs influenced to varying degrees by inputs form the English-language teaching profession.

One way to broadly characterise English-teaching situations in India is in terms of (a) the teachers' English language proficiency (TP) and (b) the exposure of pupils to English outside schools, i.e., availability of English in the environment for language acquisition (EE). The reference parameters for school class classification is Nag-Arulmani (2000). Kurrien (2005) thus identifies the four types of schools below:

a) 11, TP, EE (e.g., English-medium private/government–aided schools), proficient teacher, varying degrees of English in the environment, including as a home or first language.

b) 1 TP, 1EE (e.g., new English-medium private schools many of which use both English and other Indian languages): teachers with limited proficiency children with little or no background in English; parents aspire to upward mobility through English.

c) 1TP, 1EE (e.g., government–aided regional–medium schools): schools with a tradition of English education along with regional languages established by educational societies, with children from a variety of backgrounds.

d) 11TP, 11EE (e.g. government regional–medium schools run by district and municipal education authorities): They enrol the largest number of elementary school children in rural India. They are also the only choice for the urban poor (who, however have some options of access to English in the environment). Their teachers may be the least proficient in English of these four types of schools. Nag-Arulmani (2005) has findings through their research that schools with class libraries read better than those in schools where reading is restricted to monotonous texts and frequent routine tests of spelling lists.

Goals for a Language Curriculum

A National curriculum can aim for: A cohesive curricular policy based on guiding principles for language teaching and acquisition, which allows for a variety of implementations suitable to local needs and resources and which provides illustrative models for use.

English cannot stand alone; it needs to find its place

– Along with other Indian languages.
– In relation to other subjects.

Language acquisition inside and outside the classroom

Second language pedagogy, more than the teaching of any other curricular subject, must meet the most stringent criterion of universal success, the spontaneous and appropriate use of language for at least everyday purposes.

A common cognitive academic linguistic proficiency

Language in education should ideally and ordinarily build on such naturally acquired language ability, enriching it through the development of literacy into an instrument for abstract thought and the acquisition of academic knowledge. We can then speak of a "cognitive academic linguistic proficiency" (cf. Cummins, 1979) as language and thinking skills that build on the basis of a child's spontaneous knowledge of language. This is the goal of language education and education through language. (This discussion has most often been in the context of language education in the mother tongue.)

- Such cognitive and academic skills, moreover, arguably transferable across language, to a second language, the transferability is one of the premises for recommending a relatively late introduction of English that language–in-education proficiency, developed in the child's language, would then naturally extend to a new language. The dissatisfaction with this recommendation is attributed to two factors.
- The unsatisfactory achievement level of academic linguistic proficiency in the first language(s) in, for example, reading and writing, thus the failure to provide an academic base for the second language. There are data to show (Nag-Arulmani 2005) that 40 per cent of children in small towns, 80 per cent of children in tribal areas and 18 per cent of children in urban schools cannot read in their own language at the primary stage; these disparities widen and translate into general academic failure at later stages.
- The failure to ensure the spontaneous working knowledge of English on which higher order skills (such as reading with inferential comprehension, and working with conceptual clarity) can be built.

Within the eight years of education guaranteed to every child, it should be possible in a span of about four years to ensure basic English language proficiency. This would include basic literacy skills of reading and writing. But for this the teaching of language in general must achieve a better success in our schools, or literacy skills are transferable. Alternatively, if English is insisted on as a medium at very early stages, its teaching should ensure better success in literacy in other languages, as documented by West (1941).

English at Secondary Level: High Order Skills Vocabulary, Reading and Literature

Lexical knowledge is now acknowledged to be central to communicative competence, and the acquisition and development of second language. Even in a first language "...Where the grammar of a language is largely in place by the time a child is 10 years old..., vocabulary continues to be learned throughout one's life time" (Schmitt 2004:4). The foundation for vocabulary development and writing at later level is through reading extensively with comprehension and interest.

The debate on "instructed" and" incidental" vocabulary acquisition suggests that the very large vocabulary required of a high school student for academic purpose is not acquired in all or-none," taught" manner, but built up gradually and incrementally through reading (cf. Crashen 1989, Schmitt 2000). When language is adequately taught in the early years, the learner can naturally build up these high order skills independently, with some guidance from the classroom. Research has also shown us that greater gains accrue when language instruction moves away from the traditional approach of learning definitions of words (the dictionary approach) to an enriched approach, which encourages associations with other words and contexts (the encyclopedia approach) (Fawcett and Nicholson 1991 et al. 1991).

Traditionally, language lear..ing materials beyond the initial stages have been sourced from literature, prose, fiction and poetry. While there is trend for inclusion of a wider range of more contemporary and authentic texts (due both to a functional orientation of the language curriculum and a broader definition of what constitutes literature), accessible and culturally appropriate pieces of literature continue to play a pivotal role. Most children think of the English class as a place in which to read stories. The use of language to develop the imagination is a major aim of later language study. Provision may in addition be made in the curriculum for the optional study of literatures in English, British, American and literatures in translation, Indian, Commonwealth, European and so on. Simultaneously, English for specific purpose (ESP) approach can be adopted where necessary and feasible. (Formulaic use of language, such as an in tourist' phrase books, do not presuppose any systematic or spontaneous knowledge of the language, and are excluded from our purview.) These approaches will serve as precursors of specialisations to follow in the study of language at the undergraduate level. Instead, the language learner is an active decision-maker in the language learning process and creative generator of newly acquired language.

In a language learning class, the contexts, experiences and language learning preferences of each and every language have an impact on the rate at which second language is learned. The learner's cultural background is perceived as a significant factor in the language learning process, as it has a direct impact on second language learning. Any mismatch between the ESL classroom culture and the learner's home culture can impede the second language learning process. Therefore, using and including the learner's culture for ESL learning is gaining ground.

As the learner has become an active participant in the language learning process, the role of the teacher has undergone a change from being a knowledge provider to that of a facilitator in the language learning process. The teacher provides the learner with opportunity to use and develop the target language. The ESL teacher has become a mediator by helping the learner in identifying, framing and using the second language in such a way that earning becomes permanent. The teacher is a more partner as he/she helps the learner in making language learning choices in keeping with their preferred learning styles, strategies and linguistic needs. These changes lead us to the following implications regarding ESL teaching: proficiency in a second language needs to emerge holistically and naturally through the use of functional language used for authentic purposes.

English as a Second Language (ESL)

Views regarding English as a second language (ESL) have changed significantly in the last 30 years or so. Several previously held hypotheses have changed leading to the emergence of new methods of developing proficiency in English as a second language. Traditional ESL methods and approaches, which focused on the form and structure of English, have been found contradicting the natural development of language. This made the language learning process more tedious and cumbersome for the learner. Methods of learning English with the help of pattern practice, details and repetitive grammar exercises have been found wanting in replicating the real language use by the learner. The ESL classrooms have become more learner- and activity-centred rather than remaining teacher-centred. Teachers and learners are perceived as being partners in the learning experience.

These changes in our approach to ESL are a result of current views about language, second language learning and about the role that teachers and learners play in the language learning process. Language is perceived as a complex, vital and constantly changing system of communication whose sum is larger than its parts. Language is no longer conceptualised on the basis of units that constitute it, such as the sounds, letters, syntactic rules or words, but the meaning inherent in and conveyed by the interaction of these units within a social or functional context is all important (Chaika 1982, Lindfors 1987). There has been a significant change in our perception of language learning too. It is now perceived as an active endeavour, in which the learner plays a significant role, generating the language he or she is learning. The learning process is individualised and affected by the learner's culture and content.

The role of the learner has changed from that of a passive recipient of knowledge about the language he or she is learning. No longer is it necessary for learners to apply rigid language rules. Instead, the language learner is an active decision maker in the learning process and a creative generator of a newly acquired language. In a language learning class, the contexts, experiences and language learning preferences of each and every language have an impact on the rate at which a second language is learned. The learner's cultural background is perceived as a significant factor in the language learning process, as it has a direct impact on second language learning. Any mismatch between the ESL classroom and the learner's home culture can impede the second learning process. Therefore, using and including the learners for ESL learning is gaining ground.

As the learner has become an active participant in the language learning process, the role of the teacher has undergone a change from being a knowledge provider to that of a facilitator in the language learning process. The teacher provides the learners with opportunity to use and develop the target language. The ESL teacher has become a mediator by helping the learner in identifying, focusing, framing and using the second language in such a way that learning becomes permanent. The teacher is more a partner as he/she helps the learner in making language-learning choices in keeping with their preferred styles, strategies and linguistic needs.

These changes lead us to the following implications regarding ESL teaching:

a) Proficiency in a second language needs to emerge holistically and naturally through the use of functional language used for authentic purposes.
b) Content of instruction is a significant component of language learning.
c) There is no one single method suitable for the needs of all ESL learners.

The second language learner would be benefited if the class tasks:

a) Focus on meaning making by the learner.
b) Are the functional and help them fulfil their social academic and vocational language needs.
c) Are culturally familiar.

Choices of Teaching Approach

The field of teaching ESL has been characterised by what Stern (1985) has called a "century-old obsession" with the search for the perfect method to get second language learners to become proficient in the target language. Over the years, a range of methods has been tried successfully or otherwise. Some of these methods are as follows.

1) The Grammar Translation Method

The reaching of grammar in the first half of the century was dominated by the grammar translation method. The emphasis, in this method, was on the organisation of language at the sentenced level, in terms of parts of speech, such as subject, verb, adjective and adverb. Its goals were based on the idea that the purpose of learning a second language was to read its literature and to benefit form the mental discipline and intellectual development in learning a foreign language. Translation was seen as a way of studying and analysing the rules of the language. Its focus was on rules, and the grammar came to be seen as the class of teaching the rules of grammar.

2) The Direct Method

The direct method, sometimes known as the natural method, was based on the belief that a language could best be taught by its active use in the classroom. The teacher began attempting to teach the target language in a way that was similar to first language acquisition. It incorporated techniques designed to address all the areas of Grammar Translation namely, oral communication, spontaneous use of language, and developing the ability to think in the target language. There was to be a direct connection between concepts and the language to be learned.

3) The Oral Approach and Situational Language Learning:

The oral approach was the accepted British approach to English language teaching by the 1950's. Language teaching, as part of Oral–Situational Approach, began with the spoken language. Lessons were taught orally. The target was the language of the classroom. New language points were introduced and practised situationally. Vocabulary selection procedures were followed to ensure that an essential general vocabulary was covered. Items of grammar were graded, following the principle that forms should be taught before complex ones; sufficient lexical grammatical basis was established. Therefore; language was viewed as a purposeful activity related to goals and situations in the real world. The learner developed from being a passive listener to an active participant while the teacher acted as a model, along with a cue-provider for the learners. The lessons were, usually, teacher–directed, with the teacher deciding the pace.

4) The Audio Lingual Method

The Audio-Lingual Method was based on a behaviourist approach to learning. The language was broken down into grammatical structure, which learners practised by process of mechanical habit formation such as memorising and drills. The focus was on the target language being presented in the spoken form before they were seen in the written form. Aural-oral training was provided as foundation for the development of other language skills. The learner had little control over the content pace or style of style of learning, while the teacher controlled the direction and pace of learning. This was followed by a major paradigm shift in language teaching. The quest for alternatives to grammar-based approaches and methods led to several directions. While, on one hand, such innovative methods as Total Physical Response Silent Way Suggestopedia were developed outside of mainstream language teaching, on the other hand, the communicative movement shifted the focus away from grammar to a different view of language learning.

Communicative Language Teaching

CLT referred to a diverse set of principles that reflected a communicative view of language learning. It could be used to support a wide variety of classroom procedures. Since its inception, CLT has passed through a number of different dimensions of the teaching learning process. In its first phase, the primary concern was the need to develop a syllabus that was compatible with the notion of communicative competence. This led to proposals from the organisation of syllabuses in terms of notions and functions, rather than grammatical structures (Wilkins 1976). In the second phase, CLT focused on procedures for identifying learner's need and this resulted in proposals to make needs analysis an essential component of communicative methodology (Munby, 1978). In the third phase, CLT focused on the kinds of classroom activities that could be used as the basis of communicative methodology, such as group work, task-work and the information–gap activities (Prabhu, 1987).

Johnson and Johnson (1998) identify five core characteristics that underlie current applications of communicative methodology:

I. Appropriateness of Language reflects the situations of its use and must be appropriate to the situation, depending on the purpose of the communication. Thus, learners may need to be able to use formal, as well as, casual styles of speaking.

II. Message Focus Learners need to be able to create and understand messages, i.e., real meanings. Hence, the focus on information sharing and information transfer in CLT activities.

III. Psycho-linguistic Processing CLT activities seek to engage learner in the use of cognitive and other processes that are important factors in second language acquisition.

IV. Risk–taking Learners are encouraged to make guesses and learn from their errors by going beyond what they have been taught; they are encouraged to employ a variety of communication strategies.

V. Free practice CLT encourages the use of holistic practice involving the simultaneous use of variety of sub-skill, rather than practising individual skills one piece at a time.

Then characteristics of communicative methodology, just cited, address very general aspects of language learning and teaching that are now largely accepted as self-evident and axiomatic throughout the profession. Today, CLT continues in its classic form (Richards and Rodgers 2KI), as is seen in a huge range of course books and other teaching resources based on the principles of CLT. In addition, it has influenced many other language teaching approaches and methods that subscribe to a similar philosophy of language teaching.

In the communicative view of language, language learning is characterised as a process of developing the ability to do things with language (as opposed to learning about language). In fact, there is not one, but a cluster of approaches which parade under the general label "communicative," all of which characterise language learning as the development of communication skills. Recent approaches recognise the limitations of language transfer and suggest that, at some stage, learners should be encouraged to engage in class in some of the behaviours they will require to use outside. While part–skills, practice might involve some non communicative activities, such as drills, learners will also be expected to engage in substantial whole-skill practice.

Some proponents of communicative methodologies see the prior specification of objectives as redundant believing that my classroom activities which engage the learner in any sort of communicative language use will provide the necessary and sufficient conditions for learning (Krashen and Terrell, 1983). But, what happens in a class should relate, in some principled way, to what was planned to happen, even though it is unlikely there will ever be a neat one–to-one relationship between intention n and reality.

Making the Final Choice

The complexity of the second language learner is indicated by the complexity of theories that attempt to explain the process. As Spolsky (1988) points out, a theory of second language learning must take into account the following:

- There is no single criterion according to which a second language learner can get to know the target language.
- Different combinations of conditions will lead to all possible language proficiency outcomes.
- Second language learning is a social act that takes place within a social context.

In India, from a variety of backgrounds, people seek to learn English as a second language. They form a heterogeneous group with varying abilities and sociolinguistic profiles. The social components interact with individual preferences, making the language learning process rather complex and personalised. Therefore, one cannot argue for a single method that can be identified and implemented successfully across a range of schools. Then, it is left to the teachers to identify and use appropriate methods based on the needs of the target learner group. To this end, a language laboratory can aid an impressive range of language learning activities and support learners while they work on individual pair or group assignments.

The Language Laboratory

Before installing a language laboratory one must know exactly what purposes the laboratory will fulfil and what benefits can be derived from its use. Once it is clear how the laboratory will serve the needs of learners and faculty, one must decide what teaching strategies will be used and what type of research will be carried out, and then determine what machines and materials are required to implement them. Involving learners and teachers in the planning and use of a new laboratory would generate interest and cooperation. Learners could be asked to suggest the workstations, timings of the laboratory and how best it could provide an environment conducive to study. It can enrich and enliven our course by better motivating learners, offer them additional guidance and practise, allow more creativity and give more time to perform and practice tasks. Teachers could be asked about preferred equipment, integrating the laboratory with their course and software. Teachers can engage in more person-to–person communication. It is a place where they can have access for literary linguistic and methodological research, and use their authorising programmes to supplement their courses with audiovisual experiences or computer-assisted tasks. However, they must know the basic purpose for each media and the proper techniques for using laboratory equipment before they can use the software properly.

Examples of Some Latest Laboratories

Digital Laboratory: This laboratory empowers teachers to work with their existing teaching materials such as transparencies, audio-cassettes/tapes, videotapes, DVDs and so with minimal advanced preparations.

Logo Laboratory: This laboratory employs a virtual language laboratory teaching model. Teachers create multimedia assignments in advance; use authentic language materials, learners individually access and work on the assignments at any time from any computer PC.

Smart Class Virtual Recorder: This software package by Robotel provides a basic language laboratory platform. It enables learners to review digital audio and multimedia, and content and record a separate audio response track, either on their local workstation's hard drive or on a central file server. It empowers learners to work at their pace, and provides simple lesson authoring tools for teachers who want to assemble their own digital lessons. Practice licences, which support unlimited play back and recorded capability, are provided without cost, to encourage learners to practise their language learning skills at home.

There has been a remarkable upsurge in interest in using electronic media to facilitate instruction and conduct research. In addition, the growth of the multimedia and telecommunication industries means that there is a constantly improving rapidly in ceasing variety of ready-made software available. While the laboratory is the best suited for self-paced instruction we can also use media devices in the classroom to help an entire group understand and practise key points. For instance, the teacher can show a scene from a play on the video, provide a brief computer track to ensure that learner comprehend the dialogue in the scene and enhance learners' interest through the added dimension provided by music or sound effects.

The language laboratory can increase productivity, assist the improving the quality of instruction and foster professional development. Today the laboratory has become almost indispensable and is heavily frequented by learners and faculty. Just like the telecommunications media, the language laboratory is here to stay. These laboratories can be established in DIETs and SCRT /RIE/SIET of every state and union territory. They can serve the same purpose to the learners. Nobody can deny that we have a considerable majority of slow learners (SL) in the classroom.

Instructional Considerations for Slow Learners

Slow learners exhibit academic problems and perform below their chronological age and grade level peers academically. Their poor academic performance is attributed to low intellectual ability. Additionally, there are other reasons that slow down the academic performance of some individuals.

Who are Slow Learners?

Slow learners are those who are not performing well in school, yet are not eligible for special education services. They do not qualify for special education services because their IQ scores are too high for consideration as a child with mental retardation and with a learning disability (Mercer, 1995). The myth is that only children with learning disabilities and mental retardation deserve special help and that low learners have learning challenges because they are too lazy and too unmotivated to learn. Hence slow learners tend to be ignored and they eventually drop out of school and add to the burden of being unemployed are unemployed. Even if they do not drop out of school, they fail at an alarming rate (Shaw, Grimes & Bukman, 2005). Hence, it is critical that we examine the variables that slow down the learning process of certain individuals. Once the variables are identified, teachers will be able to use appropriate teaching methodologies that would help slow learners succeed academically. 'Slow learners' is a phrase that seems to be used to refer low ability students who have problems understating, transferring and generalising information. Learning is a complex process and involves five stages of information processing such as input, perception attention, memory and output. When the ability level is low, the individual seems to have problems with taking in information, interpreting, information, storing information and retrieving and reproducing the information.

This ultimately slows down the learning pace of the student who falls more and more, behind as s/he moves one grade level to another. Not all slow learners have low intellectual abilities. Some individuals do not succeed academically and become classified as slow learners for reasons such as maturational lag, developmental delay, mismatch of learning and teaching styles, health and sensory impairments, lack of attention, poor motivation, ineffective teaching, lack of language development ,irrelevance of curriculum, etc. Bender (1957) popularised his theory of 'maturational lag' to explain the learning problems that some individuals experience. According to this theory, each person has a preset timetable for development that varies from individual to individual. When the various mental processes mature at different rates, some mental abilities develop slowly in some persons. According to Ames (1968) this theory explains that problems in learning are created because students are asked to perform tasks before they are ready.

Some slow learners may not be ready to learn because of the cognitive differences or may not have developed the appropriate problem-solving strategies to interpret complex tasks, a challenging quiz or the materials presented by the teachers. They may not have the prerequisite skills to understand certain tasks because they may be young for a particular grade level (birth-date effect). They may need more time, they may need the task to be explained again and again, they may need more practice activities to understand the task (Mercer, 1997).

The education of slow learners should be approached from a developmental perspective. According to Piaget, each individual goes through four stages of intellectual development: sensory motor stage (0-2 years), pre-operational stage (2-7 years) concrete operational stage (7-12 years) and formal operational stage (above 12 years). What educators forget is that some students tend to stay longer in one stage, and speeding up the developmental process may only slow down the learning process. The teacher may assume that the student is in the third stage of intellectual development based on the child's age when the student is still lingering in the second stage because of low ability. What happens is a mismatch between the student's ability and teacher expectations.

Teaching practices for each stage of the development sequence should be carefully selected and applied. Teachers must identify the cognitive capabilities and limits of the individuals at various points in development, so that age appropriate tasks are presented to the students. Learning takes place in five stages: acquisition stage, proficiency stage, maintenance stage generalisation stage and adaptation stage. The way the teachers teach and what they teach should match the stage of learning the students are in. Idol (1983) & Smith (1981) emphasize that the stages of student learning are fundamental to implementing effective instruction and successful learning. Matching teaching procedures and content with the student's stage of learning is very critical for learning to take place. When the teacher does not teach to the stage that the student is in., the student exhibits learning problems.

Ignoring the learning style of students is another variable that exacerbates learning problems. Learning problems frequently are not related to the difficulty of the subject matter but rather to the type and level of cognitive process required to learn the material (Keefe, 1988). Gregore and Ward (1977) claim that if educators are to successfully address the needs of the individual they have to understand what 'individual' means. They must relate teaching style to learning style. When the learning preference of the student clashes with the teaching preference of the instructor, not only is it frustrating to the student and the instructor but also the communicative process breaks down and the learning fails. Keefe (1991) describes learning style as an indicator of how a student learns and likes to learn. As an instructional strategy, it informs the cognition, context and content of learning.

Learning styles are the sensory channels through which individual give, receive and store information. Most students learn with all of their modalities but have certain strengths and weaknesses in a specific modality (Reiff), 1992). These avenues of preferred perception include kinesthetic/tactual auditory, and visual (Eiszler, 1983). Stronck (1980) describes the kinesthetic/ tactual learners as the ones who try things out, touch, feel and manipulate. Auditory learners respond well to lecture and discussion. Visual learners learn by seeing, and they have greater recall of concepts that are presented visually (Barbe and Swashing, 1979). A review of literature shows that student including slow learners score higher on tests when they are taught and tested in their preferred modalities (Dunn & Dunn, 1978). They may be slow learners who do not show cognitive weaknesses but perform poorly in the classroom because they are instructed through other modalities of learning and not through their preferred ones. Having discussed some of the variables that cause learning to slow down, here are some strategies that might be used to help learners succeed academically.

- Slow learners need to be academically challenged like everybody else.
- Each student's strengths and weaknesses need to be identified and specifically addressed.
- Slow learners need to be provided with an enriched environment through numerous experiences and opportunities for learning. Especially in the case of a maturational lag, development is stimulated through multiple opportunities for learning.
- Teachers may design creative activities that will improve memory, attention, problem-solving skills, comprehension language development, etc.
- Slow learners may be paired up with peer tutors who will provide study guides, lecture notes, copies of overheads, etc.
- If needed slow learners may be provided with extra time or assigned less work.

- Longer assignments may be broken down into shorter ones. A 30-minute long assignment may be broken down into six five-minute assignments.
- The slow learners may be allowed more time to understand and think through the instructional materials.
- Teachers may need to use simple concrete language when teaching and giving directions to slow learners. A series of directions need to be broken down and given one at a time.
- Teaching may focus on a single concept and gradually move to more abstract ideas. When the student experiences problems understanding the concept, the teacher may check if the student has prerequisite skills needed.
- In teaching new concepts to slow learners, teachers may use manipulative or demonstrations. They may use a variety of activities to teach and reinforce the concepts taught.
- Teachers should repeat information especially with those learners who experience maturational lags.
- Information should be presented in bite-sizes to slow learners. Too much of information at one time will confuse the slow learner.
- Teachers need to present information through visual and auditory channels and kinesthetically. Eiszler (1983) claims that varying teaching strategies to address all channels promote learning, no matter what students' preferences of cognitive styles are. Dunn (1979) showed that all learners tend to increase their academic success when varied multi-sensory methods were used as a form of instruction.
- Computers and other technology applications help the slow learner in all academic areas. Today's different kinds of software help with tutoring drill, simulation, and practice activities. Technology is very useful because it is self-pacing and individualised, and increases time on task. With its sound and colour effects it is very motivating to the slow learners (Smith, Polloway, Pattón and Dowdy, 2007)

These are just a handful of techniques that may help slow learners achieve academic success. What is important in the education of slow learners is that teachers evaluate and understand the individual needs of each student, and use appropriate teaching strategies that will maximise the educational outcomes of this population of students.

Which English?

In its primary spoken form, language is a continuum of social or geographical dialects that are mutually intelligible at adjacent locations, whereas locations separated geographically, socially or in time may become unintelligible. Most speakers command more than one spoken dialect or register of language (for example, formal and informal varieties). Western varieties of language after the invention of print have tended towards standard variety that serves as the norm particularly in education and academic life. This is necessary given the relative permanence of such communication.

Discussions on what model of English is appropriate for India centre mostly around the pronunciation (i.e. English), and secondarily on lexis or vocabulary. The criterion for an acceptable pronunciation has to be intelligibility. David Crystal's (2004) concept of a tri-dialectal model with speakers moving smoothly from a regional dialect (such as Punjabi English or Tamil English), to a national dialect (Indian English), or an international dialect where required, seems to be a feasible one. The success of young Indians at call centre jobs shows that 'accent training' is a matter of learning obvious regionalisms arriving at a neutral speech style. This is achieved in large part by learning to show down speech speaking to a rhythm, and articulating with clarity, factors that improve the sound of speech in any language.

As far the sounds themselves are concerned, spoken "Indian English" has been described as having some pan-Indian characteristics such as long vowels in stead of diphthongs, retroflex consonants instead of alveolar ones. Many more characteristics of 'Indian English' reflect the mother tongues of the speakers, given the fact that India is a nation but 'Indian' is not a language. The less obtrusive these mother-tongues characteristics are the more acceptable the pronunciation of the other tongue. It is also a common experience that a person may understand more than one speech, just as he understands many accents, other than his own.

Coming to lexis, linguistically the vocabulary of a language is an open class that enriches a language the more it borrows. It is well known that the strength of the English vocabulary lies in the richness of its sources. Standard dictionaries currently have supplements of words commonly occurring in English used in India. There surely cannot now be any reason to keep these words out of the classroom. We include in lexis the idiomatic use of prepositions: in a bus rather than on a bus, and the use of into in mathematics: the latter means the division of one number by another in British English, but multiplication of two numbers in India. Such usages need not be seen as non–standard grammar.

As for the rest, we expect a comprehensible input rich curriculum to trigger the formation of a linguistic system in the mind that approximates to standard varieties (cf. Prabhu 1987, for more discussion). It is obvious that we do not think that the Indian English is an inferior variety nor is the Indian teachers' English inferior, once proficiency–a basic grammatical competence in the language–is ensured. But a national curriculum must envisage compatibility of inputs for all kinds of learners. Popular opinion has already forced the revision of a stance whereby English was available to only a special class few at the onset of schooling and to others only later. We would not now want some learners to learn "English" while others rest content with "Indian English." We see the attainment of a standard, internalised English competence as both practicable and desirable.

The question of the model of English to teach should (in any case) not loom as large in the teachers' mind as to prevent the acquisition of any English at all. Nor should simple lack of competence in English masquerade as "Indian English," pending a more systematic documentation of this variety. In a wider context, there is a great demand for teachers (and teacher educators) from India in the global market. This should give us greater confidence about our linguistic abilities in English.

Suggestions

Teachers

- All teachers who teach should have basic proficiency in English.
- All teachers should have the skills to teach English in ways appropriate to their situation and levels based on knowledge of how languages are learnt.

These two suggestions have implications for the content of pre-service and in-service teacher education programmes.

Curriculum

- A variety of materials should be available to provide an input-rich curriculum, which focuses on meaning.
- Multilinguality should be the aim in English–medium as well as regional–medium schools. Similarly language across–curriculum perspectives should be adopted.
- This has implication for textbook design and choice of appropriate methods (class libraries and media support).

Evaluation

- Evaluation to be made an enabling factor for learning rather than impediment. Ongoing assignments should document a learner's progress through the portfolio mode. Language evolution need not be tied to an achievement with respect to syllabi but must be reoriented to the measurement of language proficiency.
- National benchmarks for language proficiency should be evolved as preliminary to the preparathion of a set of English language tests.

Works Cited

Framework for Implementation of Rashtriya Madhyamik Shiksha Abhiyan, pp 1-65, H.R.D.Min.

Spolsky, B. (1988). "Bridging the gap: A General Theory of second Language Learning." *TESOL Quarterly*. 22: 377-96.

www.robotel.com

www.edu/celop/mu/call/instal.html

www.connectededucation.com

Littlewood, (1981). "Communication Language Teaching An Introduction to Cambridge." Cambridge University Press.

McDonough and show. (1993). "Materials and Methods in ELT: A Teacher's Guide. Oxford: Blackwell.

Chomsky, Noam. (1975) "Reflections on Language." New York: Pantheon Books.

Crystal David, (2004). *The Language Revolution*. Cambridge, Malden MA: Polity Press.

Cummins J. (1979). Linguistic Interdependence and the Educational Development of Bilingual Children. *Review of Educational Research* 49: pp. 222-51

Krashen, Stephen D. (1989). We Acquire Vocabulary and Spelling by Reading: Additional Evidence for the Input Hypothesis. *Modern Language Journal*, 73:4, pp. 440-64.

_____________ D and Tracy D. Terrell (1983). *The National Approach: Language Acquisition in the Classroom*. Hayward CA: Almery Press.

Kurrien, John (2005). *Notes for the Meeting of the National Focus Group on Teaching of English Primary Stage*. Ms. NFG – English.

Nag-Arulmani S. (2005). *Language Attainments and Learning Opportunities: Printers for a New Curriculum Frame Work*. Ms, NFG-English.

Prabhu N.S. (1987). *Second Language Pedagogy*. Oxford. New York: Oxford University Press.

Tickoo, ML. (2004). *ELT in India*. New Delhi: Orient Longmen.

Dunn R., and Dunnk. (1978). *How to Create Hands–On Materials: Instructor*. pp. 134-141.

_____________ (1979). "Learning – A Matter of Style, Educational Leadership." 36 (6), 430-432.

Eislzer, CF, (1983). *Perceptual Preferences as an aspect of adolescent Learning styles, Education*. 103 (39, 23) 242.

Keefe. J.W. (1991). *Learning Style Cognitive and Thinking Skills*. Reston. VA National Association of Secondary School Principals.

Mercer C. (1995). Learning Disabilities and Criteria used by Stat Education Department. *Learning Disabilities Quarterly*. 19. 217-232

_____________ (1997). *Students with Learning Disabilities Upper Saddle River*. NJ: Prentice Hall.

Chaika E. (1982). *Language: The Social Mirror*. Rowley: Newbury House.

5

English in India Today: Re-situating the Perspective from a Multilingual to a Bilingual Context

—Dr. Arun Kumar Mukhopadhyay

The role of English in India has been controversial right from the time of its introduction, and several historical parameters testify to this fact. Controversies do exist even today at the socio-cultural level regarding the relative acceptability of English and its most formidable regional rival, now the national language of India—Hindi. Interestingly, language as a problem never emerged as a concern of the multitudes during a few thousand years old history of the country when by name it stood for a combination of large princely states and small empires. But with the onset of British rule, specifically after Macaulay's Minute[1] in 1835, English became the dominant language of communication among the educated classes in the Indian subcontinent. It is relevant to discuss here briefly the introduction of Western Education (i.e., English language and literature) *vis-à-vis* the prevalent conventional modes of education in colonised India.

To be objective, the introduction of English education had to steer ahead a quagmire of deep sociological repercussions right from the beginning. First of all, to think of the multilingual character of our country and her indigenous models of education, it led to the fragmentation of the traditional modes of Education in Tols, Madrasas and Maqtabs, which experienced an incompatibility with the emerging challenges posed by the

Western models of education. The incompatibility between the two ideals of education led to a distinctive cultural amnesia in the colonised people. To be honest, traditional model of education in India is seen to be breaking up bit by bit, since the mid-eighteenth century owing to its failure to negotiate the new challenges. The direct patronage of the Britishers began to establish, slowly and steadily, a new form of cultural elitism in colonial India. In accordance with the 1833 Charter of the British Government, the East India Company was directed to work towards the dissemination of English education. Macaulay's [in] famous *Minute* in 1835 served to give the imperial sanction for promoting the claims of English Education. It is also worth considering that following the Recommendations of Charles Wood, who was the Chairman of the Board of Control in England; the universities in Calcutta, Bombay and Madras were established. Moreover the Government Circular in 1844 made the knowledge of English compulsory in government jobs. Gauri Viswanathan in *The Beginnings of English Literary Study in British India* has asserted that the spread of English education led to Britain's ideological control over the people of India – 'maintaining control of the natives under the guise of a liberal education' (Viswanathan, *Literary review,* 17). In her *The Masks of Conquest* (1989), Viswanathan further observes that Britain's English Education Policy shrewdly furthered the colonial interests through the controlling tactics of imperial textuality: "A discipline that was originally intended in India primarily to convey the mechanics of language was thus transformed into an instrument for ensuring industriousness, efficiency, trustworthiness, and compliance in native subjects" (Viswanathan, *Masks* 93).

Taking cue from the historical perspective embryonic in the above quotation, one may take stock of the scenario of English Teaching in Free India that shows in course of several decades, a gradual paradigmatic shift from a multilingual to a bilingual encounter. It is significant that the attitude of the British to other Indian languages including Hindi was not biased as their colonialistic acumen made them realise that in a multilingual country like India, the knowledge and promotion of native, regional languages would help them to rule the land. However, Indians wanted English to continue even after the British have left the Indian shores and Hindi was declared as the national language. The subsequent story is well known. Eventually, the incorporation of the teaching of English language and literature in the Education policies of the country under colonial rule has opened up in course of several historical parameters, a new era where English language proves to offer a sesame to the entire world though at home, it continues to be a bone of contention at socio-political level of Indian life.

To be precise, post-Independence India notwithstanding her over all multilingual character, saw the arena of language teaching as a veritable welter of Hindi–English confrontation. Hindi is the national language of the country. In the context of the wide currency of spoken Hindi all over the country, it is undeniable that the Bombay film industry and the Hindi TV serials in hundreds of cable-channels with their super, mega stars have contributed as a great fillip to it. Their dialogues, the styles and delivery of speech have rendered much to the flamboyance of Hindi language in the common parlance of today's society These serials and movies reflect a cultural ethos with Hindi as a language deeply rooted to it. For the common people Hindi is the most favourite of all Indian languages which is easy to understand, brings people together and enables one to express all thoughts and feelings freely.

But in contrast to the 60 per cent of Hindi knowing people, only about a maximum of 5 per cent, as per the claim of *Hindiwallahs*, know English. According to them, some use it rather well, but the vast majority of people especially in Northern India and the Hindi belt of India, has a feeling of an [ir] reverential self-distancing from it chiefly because English is a language seldom used in the streets though a contrary picture is seen in South India. The national policies of the Government regarding the status of English language in Free India seem to suffer from some sort of indecision or the other. For example, Article 343(1) of the Constitution of India provided in 1950 that English as the official language of the Union would give place to Hindi by 1965. But in 1965, the Southern and North-Eastern states of India in particular, witnessed violent riots over language issue that led to the amendment of the article allowing English to continue as another official language till all the states and Union territories opt for the assigned role of English language. The first education commission headed by Dr. Radhakrishnan adjudged the contribution of English to the national cause and yet it stressed the need of its replacement from the status of state language on the ground of its being the language of the coloniser and creating a sense of cultural divide among people. Nevertheless, the commission recommends the study of English in high schools and universities so that, as Kudchedkar quotes from Kachru, "...we keep in touch with the living stream of ever-growing knowledge" (Kudchedkar 47). Subsequent education commissions also substantiated the policy of retaining English as a compulsory second language in the country.

However, the over all ELT situation in India does not project a very satisfactory picture. In many states, particularly in rural areas, perhaps the classrooms and the libraries are the only places where the language could possibly be learned. One may also take stock of other problems—differences in the socio-economic status of learners, their background (urban and rural), paucity of skilled teachers and the dearth of effective methodology of teaching and modernised teacher training programme that are responsible for the poor performance graph of English language teaching in India. Side by side, one notices with surprise and pleasure as well, that there has been a virtual proliferation of English-medium schools all over the country in accordance with the Government policy because of, as S. Kudchedkar has observed in his book *English Language Teaching in India,* " the global standards aimed at by educational institutions in India" (Kudchedkar 49). In India the National Curriculum Framework (NCF) 2005 prescribes that Basic English proficiency can be achieved in about four years. The NCF also recommends a multi-lingual approach to the use of the traditional, egalitarian 'Three Language Formula.' As R. Meganathan has pointed out, English is now being taught from Grade 1 in many states and union territories and some states are now offering a choice of English medium sections. He has further observed that "Twenty-six out of the thirty-five states and union territories (the provinces and the specially created regions) introduce English as a language from class I and the remaining states introduce the language either from class three or five"(Meganathan Para 2).

From a realistic point of view, R.R. Mehrotra has aptly detected a Janus-like attitude in the Government's policy regarding the status of English in Free India, a discrepancy "...clearly noticeable between pious official declaration and actual behaviour" (Mehrotra 163). He finds this attitude evidenced in the flurry of terms accorded to English in recent years such as–'the official language', 'the associate official language', 'the associate additional language', 'the tool language', 'the link language', 'the library language', 'the subsidiary language', 'the optional language', 'the additional optional language', the language of wider communication', 'the need-filling language', etc.

Furthermore, we notice recently a conspicuous drive in the IT sector to restore the original characteristics of Hindi in mobile phones, leading to a sort of bilingualism in e-mail and mobiles. This phenomenon practically necessitates it for us to study and discover Willy-nilly, some cross-cultural usability issues between Hindi and English. Information services like e-mail, news, market reports, Short Message Service (SMS), educational applications and other reading materials are now made available by cellular phone service. Significantly, mobile phones that are sweeping the Indian market are now becoming bilingual in so far as they support various services simultaneously in English and Hindi.

In a country where multilingualism forms the substrate of national spirit, its by virtue of its sheer strength of character that notwithstanding the dilly-dallying, indecisive and confused stand in the Government policy as well as a vehement oppositions from the champions of Hindi, English language has emerged as the compulsory second language in the native/vernacular medium schools and in English medium schools it is being treated with the status of First Language.

To return to the basic premise of the English-Hindi issue that this paper began with, it is relevant to quote from R.K. Narayan's essay "To a Hindi Enthusiast" where the writer deals with the question in his characteristic humorous way with an ostensible reference to the time limit stipulated by Article 343(1) of the Constitution of India in 1950 and the subsequent disturbances in 1965:

> Time alone can mature certain things. You feel fifteen years is a long gap of time. In a matter like the nation-wide adoption of a language you cannot fix a timetable in advance.... That the country should stir itself from the spell cast by a foreign language is a point that anyone, will readily grant, although personally I think it otherwise. For me at any rate, English is an absolutely *Swadeshi* language. English, of course, in a remote horoscopic sense, is a native of England, but it enjoys, by virtue of its uncanny adaptability, citizenship in every country in the world. It has sojourned in India longer than you or I and is entitled to be treated with respect. It is my hope that English will soon be classified as a non-regional Indian language. (Narayan: 26)

In a word, by dint of perfect resilience and adaptability, English today has shaken off its past colonial identity and merged in our national existence and voices the spirit of globalisation, so to speak, the call of the time which recommends the fusion of the local with the global.

Notes

1. The following is an extract from *Macaulay's Minute on Indian Education,* 2nd February, 1835 as discussed in Halsall, Paul's "Thomas Babington Macaulay on Indian Education." In his *Minute,* Macaulay exalts English language with a comparative inferiorisation of other native languages like Sanskrit and Arabic:

   All parties seem to be agreed on one point, that the dialects commonly spoken among the natives of this part of India contain neither literary nor scientific information, nor are, moreover, so poor and rude that, until they are enriched from some other quarter, it will not be easy to translate any valuable work into them. *It seems to be admitted on all sides, that the intellectual improvement of those classes of the people who have the means of pursuing higher studies can at present be effected only by means of some language not vernacular amongst them.*

   What then shall that language be? One-half of the Committee maintains that it should be the English. The other half strongly recommends the Arabic and Sanskrit. The whole question seems to me to be, which language is the best worth knowing?

   I have no knowledge of either Sanskrit or Arabic. But I have done what I could to form a correct estimate of their value. I have read translations of the most celebrated Arabic and Sanskrit works. I have conversed both here and at home with men distinguished by their proficiency in the Eastern tongues. I am quite ready to take the Oriental learning at the valuation of the Orientalists themselves. I have never found one among them who could deny that *a single shelf of a good European library was worth the whole native literature of India and Arabia.* The intrinsic superiority of the Western literature is, indeed, fully admitted by those members of the Committee who support the Oriental plan of education. (Paul para 1-3). Emphasis added.

Works Cited

Halsall, Paul. "Thomas Babington Macaulay on Indian Education." 17 Oct. 2007. <http://www.fordham.edu/halsall/mod/1833 macaulay-india.html>

Kodchedkar, S. (2002). *Readings in English Language Teaching in India.* Chennai: Orient Longman.

Meganathan, Rama. *English Language Education in Rural Schools of India: The Situation, the Policy and the Curriculum.* 30.10.2009. http://www.teachingenglish.org.para 1-6.

Mehrotra, R.R. (1977) English in India: the Current Scene, *ELT Journal* 1977 XXXI (2) : 163-170. London: OUP

Narayan, R.K. (1988). *A Writer's Nightmare Selected Essays—1958-1988.* New Delhi: Penguin.

The Beginnings of English Literary Study in British India. Oxford Literary Review, IX. London: OUP, 1987.

Viswanathan, Gouri. (1989) *Masks of Conquest: Literary Study and British Rule in India.* New York: Columbia University Press.

6

Surviving between English and Hindlish Swiftly: Shifting Paradigms of ELT in India

—Dr. Archna Bahadur Zutshi

The world is changing at a fast pace. We see a revolution in the field of media, and we see that the communication at all levels is reflecting the giant strides that the social networking has taken. Before we know it the social networking has spread its tentacles far and wide. There is 'Twitter', Facebook, Orkut, MSN and many such networks that are multiplying the available information into recipients' hands. The sites might be having the motivated agendas, and on the flip side accessibility to practically everything. People are not shy to seek and redeem old friendships so that they are a part of the teeming and growing milieu. Hence we see a new idiom that has evolved.

Hindlish is a well accepted phenomenon of our multilingual or bilingual society. The puritans too cannot hoodwink or overlook the growing impact of a bilingual communication, with the Indian community either in India or in diaspora. The Indians have arrived, we can see that at last the President of American too, Barrack Obama had to concede that Deepawali is a festival of lights and be celebrated with fervour at the White House. These master strokes of universalising the Indian ethos and culture cannot be ignored. For the Indians have been dynamic; they have also known the dynamics of change with each successive generation. The Indians have been both resilient the compromising by turn. There was a time when the Indian 'babus' or clerks, were phenomenally successful to take on the burden of their English master. There was an ascent on the Sanskrit and Urdu teaching centre; and the baton was passed on to Macaulay to motivate the Indians to generate world class English-speaking people on the subcontinent.

We see that India has seen a change in the field of English Language Teaching (ELT). The scene is completely altered even the expressions too in the communicative spheres. The classroom interaction between student and teachers too display that instead the being idiomatic-dependent, the vocabulary has evolved with current situational aspects. There is a subtle blend of the Indian responses that are perceptively evolved. We must study a situational instance in the Indian context; "touching the feet of the elderly in reverence" may be substituted with more commonplace vocabulary—"he respectfully folded his hands to greet" or may be substituted with "he greeted him with a namaste." "In salutation he raised his hand to an adaab." The room was completely in a state of disheveled disarray."It may be better substituted with: There was chaos, as though an upsetting 'andhi' had swept the room.

Here we must take stock of the situation and see what is the role of the ELT teacher in such a fast changing scenario. When the style and the communication is bang on the native, current flavor. ELT has survived in different set-ups and has the most profuse canvass to display the creative use of language. Whether it is every day situation or moments of exceptional exchange, wherein a person is set to face a panel of interviewers. We see a perceptive formality. This formality is crafted due to the impact of the print-media as well as the Internet jargon. The people are savvy and they adopt fast due to their fast connectivity and at all odd hours too.

An ELT teacher has changed scenes too to discuss with the core group, it might be a mall, it might be a metro-station, and it might be the visit to FM Radio Channel, a road show, a fashion programme. In each set-up the meticulous phrases are used in different jargon and the props described: Or furthermore a chance meeting with a person of the media or an icon from sports or films. At times even youngsters have the halo of fame, courtesy their programmes and successes on the National TV Channel. Some cases or programmes in point are 'The Young American Award'; the Busybee Spelling Contest is another teenage programme.

Subsequently, we see besides the shift to being formal, the communicative need is more focused to deal with competition and the competitive spirit. Cheerio! Yippee are the new interjections of applause. There the barrier of even restrictive body language has given place to convulative body thrusts. The speech has turned more of informal, display of emotions. Emoticons are more graphic, instead of saying Jubilant, or joking, or still sad or displeased we have faces propping up on the screen ands saying it all.

Between these shifts of fusion and remixes, of the Hindi Language leaving impact on the second language, giving it a different flavour, and furthermore reinventing the dialogue of progress. The urbanisation has left its makes even on the village folks, through the teaching innovations, through extensive computer usage. There was a projects undertaken by UNICEF under which they planned to make a serial to highlight the pressures in village communal life, it ran to stupendous success, with the winds of change being acknowledged by the governmental agents such as day care centre, anganwadis, of adult education and the blind beliefs of people against immunisation or safe drinking water.

The ELT teacher has to assume the role of the social change facilitator. Some of the agencies are grooming student for higher skills in language to increase their levels of employability. The Indians might lose their eminent standing of being versed in the English language better than the neighbouring Asian countries. The Chinese are committed to bring themselves to the vanguard of ELT courses and aim to capture the world trade and marked through outsourcing. ELT courses have survived in India, between English and Hindlish.

A major thrust of the shifting of the focus from English to native touch is due to the easy accessibility of the media convergence through the Internet and the radio transmission. English Language Teaching has shifted its focus to the available modes and mediums. The stylistic shifts have been from tradition to formal style. There is propensity to promote a typical repetitive jargon in colloquial English; the language is evolving through the paradigmatic searches of the young generation. At times there seems to be a globally accepted dialogue going on with the widespread presence of the BPO industry. The business and treading activities are cultivating a jargon, a well-defined strategic order wherein language has to evolve to be the tool of successive communicative enterprise. The global impact is evident and cannot be undermined or suppressed.

Therefore, we see that English Language teaching is done more in the commercial premises of language-teaching sectors with the labelling of 'American School of Language or the British School of Language', which try to cater to the market, the employability factor. We can come across a number of such institutions that promise of churn out the English-speaking hordes to fit the career-demand markets. There are business schools that also cater to this corporate demand. The onus is to create awareness that exists in the corporate sector, and English Language Teaching has to widen its curriculum base and manner in which it has to be imparted. So there are the testimonies to the swiftly shifting paradigms of English Language Teaching. Besides being bracketed as communicative English Language Teaching, it has to be interactive, and survive the pressures or demands of the computing generation.

There has been an apparent focus on ELT to celebrate different days, and events associated with them. To evolve about the locales that are current and in vogue Learning the Language and ELT is a hands-on experience, if it is the women's day the language capability of the learners should evolve around the issues related to gender sensitivity. Similarly the language keeps beats with the other ongoing processes of different times and situations. This creates the atmosphere and also the right involvement of the learner with the events and his surroundings, developing in him the requisite logical skills to develop an argument.

Nevertheless the scene is about some sessions of learning to drive the learner learns the vocabulary involving the procedure and its physical aspects. There is no artificiality involved in the situational dependent role-playing as ELT depends on lively and interesting hours devoted to a hobby, or an experience, something that is registered through the senses. There is a level of commitment, enterprise and creative satisfaction as learning is participative and is not merely a listless session of rote learning.

The English Language Teaching is no more confined to books the major role is given to the media and the Internet. Newspapers are all available in e-paper editions. There is a deluge of informative and interactive coverage, which is both formal and informal in form. Hence the very format of teaching is undergoing a swift paradigmatic shift. The links are informative we have to filter the information, with the help of awareness among the teaching community. They have to be guiding light to the Internet crazed generation. They can guide the reading tastes of the young minds by taking the Twitter sessions both seriously and functionally as mediums of expression and creativity.

There are sites and links, which have eminent knowledge banks, supportive tools to learning research, and even preserving and archiving the document. E-book seems to be the domain that charts the success of hardcopy sales; the authors find it convenient to download the e-version of the book before launching it in the commercial market for sales. We see the English Language Teaching has acquired very diverse dimensions. The story of ELT is becoming more complex and more interesting with cartoons and popups to illustrate the concept of a story. There are easy tools to aid comprehension and interesting ways to sustain the interest of the learner. There are blogs and many such interactive platforms where the distance between the learned and the novice is never emphasized on. The focus is on learning and acquisition of the skills of language.

7

Shifting Paradigms and Features of English Language Teaching (ELT) in India

—Dr. Ram Sharma

There are many languages in India. There are recorded a total of 1,652 mother tongues and over 190 recognised language varieties in the census of 1971, followed by languages with widespread currency (41 languages used for education, 58 taught as subjects and 87 used in media], Scheduled languages [Hindi, Telugu, Bengali, Marathi, Tamil, Urdu, Gujarati, Kannada, Malayalam, Oriya, Punjabi, Kashmiri, Sindhi, Assamese, Sanskrit) with Hindi at the top of the hierarchal order.

India's long history resulted in a multilingual situation and the basic structure of the Indian languages is thus made up of Aryan and Dravidian families. English after its origins in the fifth century has prospered in the different areas and colonies of the world. Its forays outside Europe began with the foundation of the American colonies and later in the sixteenth century during the Renaissance period. With the expansion of the British Empire in the nineteenth century 'with its Sun never setting', its language, i.e., English, emerged as a world language. It came to India as part of the colonial encounter between India and England in the second half of the eighteenth century.

English came to India with the English. Since the English had arrived here for the purpose of trade, in the beginning of the sixteenth century they focused their attention only on trade and they were not interested in encouraging the teaching of English. English teaching in India started by some missionaries who started schools where English was taught as one of the subjects. There was a reason why the English did not think of encouraging the teaching of English initially. It was that they feared that they might lose their colonies in India as they had lost in America. This can create a diversion so they focused their attention on trading and business. This fear was expressed by Randle Jackson, a member of the House of Commons, Who said, "We lost our colonies in America by imparting our education there; we need not do so in India too." However, after the Battle of Plassey in 1757, this situation began to change. The East India Company became the rulers of India. Now traders came in the position of ruling. In order to have full command over the people and to make them understand their language or to govern they decided to open educational institutions. Two such institutions were started for this purpose. Calcutta Madarsa was started in 1781 and the Benaras Sanskrit College was founded in 1791. In those institutions the teaching of classical learning was provided, but there was also the provision for the teaching of English. In this way, the British rulers began the teaching of English in India after the battle of Plassey (1757).

The importance of English in India went on increasing with the passage of time. A great demand for the spread of English education begun to be raised from different parts of the country. To meet this demand Raja Rammohan Roy established the Hindu College in 1817. Soon, thereafter the missionaries opened a number of schools and colleges in which the teaching of English was given utmost importance. Ironically, in 1823, one of our illustrious reformers Raja Rammohan Roy wrote a letter to Lord Amherst seeking replacement of Sanskrit and Arabic with English. The English were waiting for an opportunity, and within a decade, Thomas Macaulay found India suitable to implement English here. The letters of Macaulay's brother-in- law, Charles Travelyne, revealed that literature emerged a less abrasive means of controlling the colony. In 1835, Macaulay, in his famous *Minute*, strongly recommended that the spread of western learning could only be possible through the medium of English language. He argued that, "English is better worth knowing than Sanskrit and Arabic," that "the natives are desirous to be taught English" and that "it is possible to make natives of this country thorough good English scholars."

As a consequences, on February 2, 1835, the most controversial *Minute* was submitted to the Governor–General with an overt aim to create, "...a class of people, Indian in blood and colour, but English in taste, in opinions, in morals and in intellect... and to render them by degrees fit vehicles for conveying knowledges to the great mass of the population." (Biswas and Agrawal 1986:18). By 1837, the missionaries had begun to provide a significant part of the facilities for teaching English. English became the language of administration and judiciary in India even as the vernaculars continued to be used in several instances. Almost simultaneously subordinate level positions in the judicial and administrative institutions were thrown open to Indians by a government resolution. So the Indians got importance who were educated in English.

The Company's charter was renewed once More in 1853, under the pressure of government personnel to manage the widening domain of its, "India activities" the company decided to open up its highest Civil Service appointments to Indians. Now Indians can appear in Civil Services Examination and allowed them to appear for a competitive examination set up for this purpose.

Sir Charles Wood sent a dispatch to the court of directors on 9 July 1854. Anglicists like William White had no hesitation in equating spread of English with that of progress of the colonised. He declared, "As we link Calcutta with Bombay, and Bombay with Madras, and by roads, railway and telegraphs interlace province with province, we may in progress of time fuse India into unity, and the use and prevalence of our language may be the register of the progress of that unity" (White 1872). Consequently, three universities at three different port towns: Bombay, Calcutta, Madras were established, which was followed by two more at Lahore and Allahabad. As a result, the first generation of English knowing 'baboo' and 'brown sahibs' with colonised mindsets were produced.

The increase in the numbers of the centres imparting education in English intensified the importance of that language. But in our country that had become a colony under Queen Victoria, English was introduced in the universities established in 1858. Now the British could implement English language and literature here. In India they did not care for the opinions of the natives over whom they ruled. As a defeated society, Indians did not have choices. We were compelled to swallow English without being given a chance to think about the issue. The concept of lingua franca was for the first time introduced in India during the colonial period. However, the Indian Education Commission (1882) expressed its dissatisfaction at the extensive use of English as the medium of education. The Indian Universities Commission (1902) also raised its voice against the neglect of regional languages, and pressed on using the regional languages. The Calcutta University Commission (1917-1919) tried to strike a balance by observing that, "The educated classes in the various provinces of India will wish to be bilingual, to use their mother tongue for those dear and intimate things which form part of life and to use English as a means of inter-communication necessary for the maintenance of the unity of India, and of touch with other countries."

The Commission recommended in favour of regional languages, "We are emphatically of the opinion that there is something unsound in a system of education which leaves a young man, at the conclusion of his course, unable to speak or write his own mother tongue fluently and correctly. It is thus beyond controversy that a systematic effort must henceforth be made to promote the serious study of the vernaculars in secondary schools, intermediates colleges and in the university." As a result of this recommendation, the medium of English was restricted only to the colleges and universities from 1920 onwards throughout the country. India got independence in 1947. Since then Commissions and Committees and the leaders of public opinion took a close look at the value and use of English, and tried to strike a balance between gains and losses. There were many opinions and debates regarding use of languages. People like C. Rajagopalachari favoured the continuance of English, language, but there were persons who, under the influence of nationalism, advocated that English should go with the English as it had come with them. They argued that English being a foreign language was responsible for the waste of student's time and energy. They declared that students could learn and express their ideas more easily in their mother tongue; that English could not be suitable to the environment and culture of India; that could not comprehend or grasp it easily. Consequently, it was decided that regional languages should be developed and Hindi should replace English. Gandhiji had foreseen the consequences of the project of modernising India through English, for it created unbridgeable gulf between the English equipped and English unequipped. He said, "We are traitors to our mother by remaining under such a system—a gulf has been created between the educated classes and the uneducated class." Again he said on 15 August 1947, in an interview to the BBC, in English, "Let the whole world know that I do not know English." He had a clear-cut position regarding the presence and place of English language and literature in post-independence India. But the irony is that, English was firmly established as an official language of administration and a preferred academic language of India in the twentieth century. It not only displaced Persian but also changed the existing language hierarchy. Gandhiji very overtly deplored the situation by saying, "Of all the suppressions that affect India, none is so great as that a knowledge of the English language is necessary for imbibing ideas of liberty, and developing accuracy of thought" (1958; 5-6).

The University Education Commission (1949) suggested, among other things, that English be replaced, as easily as practicable, by an Indian language as the medium of instruction of higher education. The Constitution of India, adopted on 26 January 1950 provided for English to continue as the official language of the country for a period of 15 years to be replaced by Hindi at the end of that period. But the sad thing is that Parliament later decided to allow English to continue as the associate official language of the Union till such time as Hindi began to be used for administrative purpose all over the country. This shows the popularity of English language. During the fifties the three-language formula was created. It gives due importance to the regional languages and tries to promote national integration and national identity through a national link language that serves as a "Window of the World." An education commission was set up in 1964 to resolve the question of medium.

The commission discussed this question and proposed that the mother tongue should be used up to the highest level of instruction, but English should be taught both as a subject and as a library language at higher levels. After Hindi, English is the most commonly spoken or used language in India particularly in legal, financial, educational business and communicative systems. The Secondary Education Commission recommended introduction of English along with Hindi at the end of the junior basic stage, subject to the principle that no two languages should be introduced the same year. The University Grants Commission also stressed the promotion of learning of the English language as a positive instrument of knowledge.

In 1968, the National Policy of Education specifically emphasized the study of English and other international languages to keep pace with the development at the macro level. The Subsequent National Educational Policy proposals in 1986 and 1996 also accentuated the use of English for higher studies. One-third of the Indian schools had English as the first language.

Kachru in his survey (the population of which was a graduate faculty of English in the universities and colleges) found only 65.64 per cent has occasional interaction with native speakers of English, 11.79 per cent had no interaction and 5.12 per cent claimed to have daily interaction with native speakers of English.

English represents scientific knowledge, modernisation and development. As a result of the implementation of this proposal, the mother tongue got precedence over the English language, and a state of stability has prevailed for two decades afterwards. On one hand, a search for an alternative is going on, and some of the regional languages like Hindi, Tamil, and Bangali have grown enough to carry out communicative requirements; on the other side, a process of indianisation of the English language has already made its dent.

According to Rajendra Chetty, "English is getting assimilated them in turn, thus shaping a special identity for Indian English" (2004; 9). The Indian subcontinent in terms of members of speakers of English, ranks third in the world after USA and the UK. David Crystal estimated that 4 per cent of the Indian population used English in 1994, which comes to about 35 million. According to Kachru, "English functions in the Indian social context to perform social roles relevant and appropriate to the social, educational and administrative network." It is clear that

English in India bears peculiar ideology inscribed within its presentational codes it made the traditional uppermost caste monopolise learning and culture that raised a hue and cry against it. They were much worried about the standard of English, lack of facilities and what not.

English is recognised as the official language in the states of Manipur, Meghalaya, Nagaland and Tripura.

India is the third largest English book-producing country after United States and the U.K. in the world, and the largest number of books published in India is in English. Indian English writings have been now accepted as a part of Indian literary tradition, as Iyengar called it "one of the voices that India speaks'….it as the others."

We are the second largest English-speaking nation in the world and we are the third largest English books publishing country with its different varieties within Indian English. At the moment there are about 300 universities, excluding deemed universities, in our country and over 20,000 colleges and more than three lakh high schools where English is being taught either in the form of English medium or English as a major component where language or literature is taught. In short, much of what will happen to English we can only speculate about. Against the colonial and the post–independence policy regarding language or absence of it, M.K. Gandhi, Jawaharlal Nehru, Ram Manohar Lohia or Munshi Premchand had their own views. The situation has drastically changed, whether one likes it or not, and the fortunes of English have undergone radical change. It has come to occupy a unique place in our society. But let us not ignore a fairly well grounded reality that native speakers of English are already outnumbered by second language and foreign language speakers, and will be more heavily outnumbered as time goes on.

Works Cited

Bhatnagar, R.P. *Decolonising English Teaching in India.*

Biswas, A. and Agrawal, S .P. (1986). *Development of Education in India,* New Delhi, Vikas Publishing House.

Chaturvedi, A.K., "English Language Teaching in India." In *Indian Book Chronicle* (P.C. Mathur, Ed.]. Jaipur, Rajasthan. October 2006.

Chetty, Rajendra, Pier Paolo Piciucco [Eds.]. (2004). *Indians Abroad: The Diaspora Writes Back.* Johannesburg, STE Publishers.

Ghosh, R.N. *Indian Bilingualism and the Teaching of English* CIEFL, Hyderabad.

Kachru, Bajaj (1983). *The Indianisation of English; The English Language in India,* Delhi, Oxford University Press.

Mohanraj, Jayshree. *Spoken Conversational English,* CIEFL, Hyderabad.

Pathak, P.D. *The Teaching of English in India.*

www.chillibreeze.com/articles_various/Statusof English Teaching InIndia.asp

8

Shifting Paradigms and Teaching English through Hinglish: An Innovative Approach

—*Dr. Vikas Raval*

This paper aims to present the use of hinglish in India through focusing on special features of hinglish and how it differs from Standard English. It also aims to study certain common means of communication in Hinglish, e.g., advertisements, announcements, instructions, newspapers, etc. The researcher has also made experimental survey to find out the relevance of the above mediums as a means of teaching English in the Indian context.

Introduction

English, like all languages, is not static. It is ever changing and adopting new words and style. Global English has led to a crisis of terminology. The distinctions between 'native speaker', 'second-language speaker', and 'foreign-language user' have become blurred. English already finds itself in a different mix – nowhere does it enjoy complete hegemony. It is growing as an Asian lingua franca. The British Empire may have been responsible for the global colonisation of the English language, but much to the surprise of traditionalists the globalsing forces of commerce, technology, Hollywood and Bollywood mean that the 'purity' of the language has been invaded. This has not only been largely by 'Americanisms', but also by local appro-priations and reworking. Robert Birchfield once said, "Our language is changing slowly and America is leading the way now, not Britain." If he was present now he would have added "Asia" to his quote. Many countries, particularly Common-wealth countries such as India, South Africa and others, have made contribution to the English literature by creating novels, short stories and dramas. They speak and write English differently than the native English speakers and writers. Their English have some special features that are not found in the English, spoken and written, by British, Americans or Australians. The differences between these Englishes are not just on vocabulary level but from phonological to syntactical levels. Indian English known as *Hinglish* has its special characteristics.

Hindi-influenced Terms and Expressions in Indian English

India is a country of a billion people, and with two official languages. Hindi and English are designated as the country's national languages. This situation has lead to the spontaneous creation of "Hinglish," a hybrid language combining elements of Hindi and English. According to Professor David Crystal, Hinglish, spoken by 300 million Indians across the globe, is set to become more popular than English. There is a constant rise in Hindi words and expression used in Indian English. When Indians use English, it is often a mixture of English, Hindi and other languages. Even in "pure" Indian English, many Indian terms slip in frequently.

It became popular after the entry of satellite TV in India. Phrases like *Yeh Dil Maange More* and *We are like that only*, ushered in the rise of Hinglish by the advertising industry. Bollywood, the Indian film Industry, also plays a big role in the rise of Hinglish. Musicals is euphemism for Bollywood films. The phrase *bold scenes* substitutes as a description of risqué scenes in movies. "Rash driving" is a euphemism for hell-on-wheels motorists. *Take a Chill pill* stands for relaxing, *Supari* for contract killing and perhaps the most famous Don for an underworld boss and *Desi* for a local stuff or person are some of the terms coined by Bollywood. Perhaps the biggest euphemism given by this industry is the term *Gandhigiri* (following the principals of Mahatma Gandhi) for Gandhism. The usage of such lingo is often termed as *Gutka* (Indian Mouth freshaner) accent by the English press in India. Here are some more Hindi terms, which are generously used in Indian English:

— *achchaa* – good
— *array* – hey
— *bus* – enough
— *ek* – one (as a number)
— *masala* – risqué; spicy; hot (like a film)
— *pakka* – sure
— *yaar* – buddy; pal
— *neta* – leader
— *junglee* – wild, savage
— *bandh* – general strike
— *curry* – a spicy dish that signifies Indian cuisine to foreigners
— *Angrez/ firang* – a fair foreigner

Written and Spoken

The words and expressions in the following examples are found to be used both in written and spoken Hinglish. I was actually stumped when one of my British friends asked me what 'weightage' meant. I always thought it was English. So I consulted my *Oxford Learner Dictionary* and was dismayed to find that there was no such word as 'weightage.' More examples with their meaning are given below.

1. Weightage

Each question in the exam has equal weightage. The word, 'weightage' is specially used as an examination term. Its equivalent English word is 'weighting.'

2. Package

Training package. The word, 'package' means a 'parcel' or a box, bag, etc. in which things are wrapped or packed in English. Hinglish uses this word particularly in collocation with the word, 'training,' viz., 'training package':

3. Class-wise work

a) Area-wise distribution
b) Item-wise analysis

In Hinglish the morpheme 'wise' gives the sense of 'each' or 'according to' which is entirely different from English morpheme 'wise' which is used in the sense of 'in the manner or direction of,' e.g., clockwise.

Advertisements

Advertisements in English in Indian newspapers and signboards which are almost everywhere in the streets of Indian towns are even more interesting. Some examples with explanations are given below.

1. Vegetarian available here!

This was a signboard placed in front of a restaurant. It is most likely that the word 'food' was left out in the advertisement since advertising to get a vegetarian person in a restaurant doesn't make sense.

2. Abroad study programme!

This is an advertisement trying to allure young men and women of the country to further their study in overseas countries. In English it should be 'Study Abroad Programme!' rather than 'Abroad Study Programme!' It seems that Hinglish has this special feature of changing the word order because other examples of this kind were also found.

3. Marry your daughters for only rupees 50!

This advertisement might seem grotesque and even outrageous to an English native speaker's eyes; it might even be incomprehensible to them. However, this is neither outrageous nor incomprehensible for Indians. This simply means that you pay Rs. 50 and the person or the office that has put the advertisement will find a suitable groom for your daughter.

4. No entrance from the back side!

This funny signboard was found at the back of a hotel. Indians are very fond of putting up signboards. Every shop, office, school and hotel has its signboard. It's this enthusiasm which made the hotel management put this funny signboard, otherwise there was no need for a signboard, or just 'No Entrance' would have served the purpose. Educational advertisements in Hinglish have their own charm. Let us look at some examples.

1. Admission notice

> There will be 24 vacancies to enter class 1 and 24 to enter class VI, 1 & 2 vacancies to enter class VIII & IX respectively. The parents seeking admission to enter other classes may also submit the form....

The charm of this advertisement is in the last line. It might seem funny and amusing to foreigners but Indians have no problem in understanding the fact that parents who want their children to get admitted in this school should collect, fill, and then submit the forms. The fact that a well-known English medium school in New Delhi put up the advertisement makes it even more interesting.

2. *Required Doctors*

> A *multi speciality 100-bedded* Nursing Home well equipped with ICU/CCU, CT scan, 3D Ultrasonography & pioneer in the Laparoscopic Surgical field requires:
> 1. Candidate with good qualification & 2 Years Experience *may please apply* within 15 days.
> 2. Remuneration negotiable.

The most interesting feature in this advertisement is the construction '100-bedded' used to mean 'with 100 beds.' In English an adjective or modifier can be made out of a verb by making it participle, e.g., 'well-furnished rooms.' The same rule has been applied here. The questions, how a nursing home can be bedded and who beds it, are irrelevant since the advertisement is not meant for English speakers but for Indian speakers.

Morphemes: On the morphology level, English suffix was found to be added to Hindi words and Hindi suffix to the English words. Examples are shown below.

1. To a paisa*less* writer.
2. Sharam*less*...
3. Sharmaji, Rishiji, candidate*ji*

Idioms and Phrases

What is your good name?

A polite way of asking someone's name; it comes from a translation of Hindi phrase – *Shubh naam* (good name). 'May I know your name'? or 'Your name please?' is more appropriate in non-Indian settings.

Poor Joke (pj)

'Poor joke' is not a commonly used phrase; a more common way of saying the same thing is 'bad joke'!

Himalayan blunder

Very big mistake, a mistake of the size of the Himalaya Mountain. Blunder generally means 'big' mistake. May not need too many adjectives that are not commonly used overseas.

First-class

It means high-quality material and is used very broadly. 'Very good', or 'the best possible' is a better alternate description.

Seth ji and John ji

In India, we add 'ji' at the end of the proper name of a person to show respect. There is no equivalent translation. Mr/Miss is used in formal settings. Addressing by the first name, the tone of voice and communication style are better ways to show politeness.

Give me a ring

'Give me a call', is a better way of saying the same, when you want someone to call you. It has nothing to do with ring – the engagement ring, or friendship ring, or the wedding ring....

Innocent divorcee

It refers to someone who is forced to divorce with no fault of his/her own. Both sides probably feel that the fault lies with the other side, so the usage of word 'innocent' may not be understood.

English in common chat

Two days ago I was passing by a departmental store; two persons came out of the door of the store. I listened to their conversation very curiously.

> Isn't it? He's coming on Monday, isn't it?
> She is pretty, isn't it?
> Keshav knows everything, isn't it?
> Things are bad in this country, isn't it?

The tag question, 'isn't it?' is used for all kinds of structures as shown above for the purpose of seeking confirmation regardless of what kind of statement it has. This is also found in Hinglish.

Use of Hinglish in English Language Teaching Classroom

The foregoing scenario of Hinglish in India makes the researcher think about what sort of English should be taught in India's schools and colleges: the Standard English of the textbook, or the spicy mix-favoured Hinglish? The researcher develops certain research questions to find out the relevance of introducing Hinglish in ELT classroom:

> Can Hinglish be introduced in ELT classroom? To what extent?
> Is learning through Hinglish enjoyable?
> Are students aware regarding uses of Hindi words in English language?

Methods

Fifty students (25 boys and 25 girls) from VII semester B. Tech class were selected for the survey. They were given different exercises on four skills: Listening, Reading, Writing and Speaking, and were asked to perform certain work individually and in-group. Later on, the researcher received feedback from the participants regarding their experiences in language learning through the innovative method.

Exercise

Writing skill

Exercise			
Exercise No.	*Type of Letter*	*Read the Following Letter Carefully and Comment on the Use of Language*	*Participant's Comment*
1	Job application	This has reference to your advertisement calling for a 'typist and an accountant - Male or Female.'.. As I am both for the past several years and I can handle both, I am applying for the post.	
2.	Leave application	Since I have to go to my village to sell my land along with my wife. Please sanction me one-week leave.	
3.	Leave application	Since I've to go to the cremation ground and I may not return, please grant me half day casual leave	

Reading skill

Read the following railway instructions carefully and comment on the use of English language:

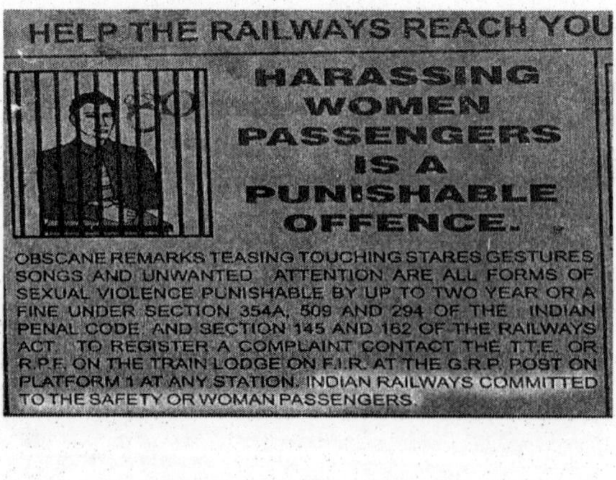

English in common chat

Two days ago I was passing by a departmental store; two persons came out of the door of the store. I listened to their conversation very curiously.

> Isn't it? He's coming on Monday, isn't it?
> She is pretty, isn't it?
> Keshav knows everything, isn't it?
> Things are bad in this country, isn't it?

The tag question, 'isn't it?' is used for all kinds of structures as shown above for the purpose of seeking confirmation regardless of what kind of statement it has. This is also found in Hinglish.

Use of Hinglish in English Language Teaching Classroom

The foregoing scenario of Hinglish in India makes the researcher think about what sort of English should be taught in India's schools and colleges: the Standard English of the textbook, or the spicy mix-favoured Hinglish? The researcher develops certain research questions to find out the relevance of introducing Hinglish in ELT classroom:

> Can Hinglish be introduced in ELT classroom? To what extent?
> Is learning through Hinglish enjoyable?
> Are students aware regarding uses of Hindi words in English language?

Methods

Fifty students (25 boys and 25 girls) from VII semester B. Tech class were selected for the survey. They were given different exercises on four skills: Listening, Reading, Writing and Speaking, and were asked to perform certain work individually and in-group. Later on, the researcher received feedback from the participants regarding their experiences in language learning through the innovative method.

Exercise

Writing skill

Exercise			
Exercise No.	*Type of Letter*	*Read the Following Letter Carefully and Comment on the Use of Language*	*Participant's Comment*
1	Job application	This has reference to your advertisement calling for a 'typist and an accountant - Male or Female.'.. As I am both for the past several years and I can handle both, I am applying for the post.	
2.	Leave application	Since I have to go to my village to sell my land along with my wife. Please sanction me one-week leave.	
3.	Leave application	Since I've to go to the cremation ground and I may not return, please grant me half day casual leave	

Reading skill

Read the following railway instructions carefully and comment on the use of English language:

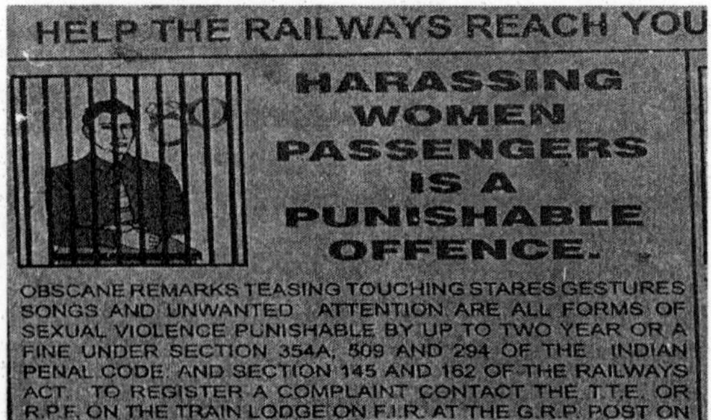

- Arrange the ideas logically.
- Use appropriate punctuation.
- Find out grammatical errors in sentence pattern and rectify them.
- Comment on the use of language.

Speaking skill

Read the following advertisements of Amul and discuss with your partners the creative use of Hinglish in advertisement:

Listening skill development

Listen to the following song from *Golmal*—then answer the questions that follow:

Let's get it on with, golmaal golmaal
Life goes on with, golmaal golmaal
Let's get it on with, golmaal golmaal
Golmaal golmaal

Oh aaye, *tum kwabon mein*
Oh aaye, mess up my brain
Oh aaye, I'm begging you
I'm right down on my knees
Is there a vacancy
For somebody like me
Cause I feel
Tu hi meri tu hi meri destiny
Is there a vacancy
I'm the best you see
Ke tu hi, tu hi meri tu hi meri destiny

Comment on the use of Hinglish in this song.

Turn the following Hindi sentences into English:

(A) tum kwabon mein (B) Tu hi meri tu hi meri

What is the exact meaning of "Golmal" in Standard English?

Language Development

Look at the Hinglish words in column A and find out their exact meaning in Standard English from column B:

A	*B*
1. *Badmash*	1. Uncultured
2. *Ganja*	2. Obnoxious man
3. *Bacha*	3. Naughty
4. *Haramzada*	4. Bald
5. *Jungli*	5. Child

Summary of the Findings

There is no doubt that a different kind of spoken as well as written English is emerging in India, and that could only be Hinglish. So far the summary of the survey can be given as follows: Hindi words are making their entries in English. Word order of English is changed in Hinglish. English suffixes are being attached to Hindi words and vice versa. To eliminate students' hesitation and make them feel relaxed, the English language should be used in the Indian context.

Works Cited

Corbett, J. (2003). *An Intercultural Approach to English Teaching*. Clevedon: Multilingual Matters.

Gurung, D.B. (2000). *Echoes of the Himalayas*. New Delhi: UBS Publishers.

Krashen, S. & Terrell, T. (1983). *The Natural Approach: Language Acquisition in the Classroom*. Oxford: Pergamon.

Mahal, Bajinder. K. (2006). *The Queen's Hinglish: How to Speak Pukka*. Harper Collins shrey27.wordpress.com/2007/01/30/amul-adsdfckr.com/archives/advertisement

Thapa, M. (2001). *The Tutor of History*. New Delhi : Penguin.

www.hindilyrix.com

www.eltweekly.com

9

Shifting Paradigms: Effective Strategies, Techniques and Methodology of Teaching of English in the Indian Context

—Dr. Arvind Kumar

With the spirit of globalisation and English becoming the global language, everyone has realised the inevitable, inextricable and multifarious role of English in the field of education, communication and for employment purposes. English has more than ever today become the most widely used means of international communication. Mass media has further enhanced the significance of English. It is not only an instrument of communication or even knowledge, but also an instrument of power.

English occupies an important place in our national life. It is being used as 'lingua-franca' for inter-state communication. It has enriched Indian languages and literatures, and has proved a powerful factor for our unity and national integration. It is inevitable for mobility, and for social and economic advancement. It is the language of opportunities because it takes one outside one's own community to such places where more opportunities are available for professional and economic growth. It is the language of modernisation. As a library language, English has already proved an asset to Indian scholars and as our window on the Western world. It has enables us to exchange our ideas with the outside world. In times to come, it will certainly continue to occupy a significant place in our national life, in our educational system and in the conduct of our national affairs.

Though the principles and methodology of English Language Teaching (ELT) in India right from the grassroots level to the university stage have undergone a drastic change over the last few decades, yet it still follows the traditional system, unmindful of the needs of different categories of English language learners. Now the system of ELT needs to be need-based and realistic. Communicative English has yet to receive the treatment it deserves. The emphasis in teaching has to be shifted from verbalism and memorisation to learning through purposeful, concrete and realistic situations.

During the past few years, there has been noticed a gradual lowering of the standards of English teaching owing to many reasons. Paucity of resources, shortage of trained and qualified teachers and the right kind of teaching material are some of the factors responsible for the decline. The traditional methods and conservative bases of teaching are incommensurate with the language needs of learners. Teaching of English at the college level is generally mistaken as the teaching of English literature only, while the linguistic interest is totally ignored. Although exposure to literature also results in the consolidation and sharpening of language skills, yet it is doubtful whether teaching at college level ever has had the aim of imparting language skills consciously.

In Uttar Pradesh, teaching of English language is in a pathetic state with policies and implementation at odds with each other. The profession suffers from a sense of frustration and helplessness. In all institutions, whether schools or colleges, the concentration remains on completing the prescribed syllabus and preparing the students for examinations. The handicap that an English teacher has to face is that the language part is practically given less time in schools as well as in colleges. Lack of proper environment also promotes aversion to English in the minds of students. The present system of teaching does not make any demand on the creative ability of the students. It is, therefore, imperative to find some stable and viable alternatives to the existing system of ELT.

The status of English has been changing with the changing face of time, which requires the teacher-learners' concern for its standard. Teachers and students are equally responsible for the loss of credibility of education in general and language teaching in particular. Two main reasons for the rapid decline in the standard of English in India are lack of positive attitude towards English and absence of adequate motivation. Another significant problem faced by the English speakers at the undergraduate level is the alienation of teacher from students because of the disinterest of the latter in classroom lectures. Inattentive students become a source of nuisance. Unsuitable books and faulty examination patters are some of other factors responsible for the sorry state of English in the country.

A close look at the English curriculum in our colleges would reveal that our English teaching is by and large purposeless. The present system is a continuation of the old one with minor modifications. There is a great confusion about objectives, methods and materials that have corroded the effectiveness of ELT in our country. The time has come for radical restructuring and sweeping changes. The efforts made so far have been peripheral and our resources and energy has mostly been misspent on theoretical importation. A few efforts that have been made to improve and ameliorate the situation have not been satisfactory. Teaching English in a country like India is both challenging and rewarding, and the success of the venture depends on the contribution of all concerned with the English Language Teaching profession.

Most of the problems in teaching English in India owe their existence to the following factors:

1. Large classes and insufficient infrastructural facilities.
2. Insufficient and untrained teachers.
3. Lack of reliable feedback.
4. Failure to go ahead with curricular reforms.
5. Impractical courses.
6. Total disregard of the learners' needs and aspirations.
7. Inadequate facilities for in-service training and subject up-gradation.
8. Undue interference with policies and matters pertaining to education in general and teaching of English in particular by those who are the least competent to do so.

9. Unthoughtful adherence to the traditional system of teaching English.

There is an urgent need to shift the focus from content to language. The courses are based on heavy textual matter where the emphasis is on textual analysis and theoretical part, developing a tendency of learning from notes. The result is that the students pass examination in English, but fail to write even a few correct sentences on their own. The ratio of periods to lessons is also not proper. The conventional methods of teaching elevate teacher to the position of a 'performer' and reduce the student to the level of a spectator and a passive 'receiver.' The student is expected to receive the right answers, memorise and reproduce them, using whatever methods he can adopt in the examination. The emphasis remains on literature only while the language part takes the back seat. Therefore, the provision will have to be made for specially designed courses and trained teachers. The time has arrived for the teachers of English to rise to the occasion and come up with new pragmatic approach to ELT. The courses have to be need-based and cognisant of the learners' expectations. The teachers need to be familiar with the cognitive processes in learners and the linguistic requirements of the students with thrust on the communicative aspect.

There is a crase nowadays for English-medium schools, but the effect it has on the young brains in particular and on the society in general, is disastrous. It curbs creativity and innovativeness of students. Therefore, adequate attention must be paid on learners from the economically and socio-culturally disadvantaged strata. We need to do certain things if English Teaching Learning has to become meaningful and purposive in India. We need to redefine the goals of teaching English in contemporary India, evolve alternative materials, methods and evaluation systems. We also need to induct professionalism in teaching so that the educators become accountable to society and recognise the rights of learners to demand quality education.

English Language Teaching through the communicative approach will give students some capacity for receptive and productive knowledge. While teaching English as a language, maximum emphasis should be laid on enhancing proficiency in communication skills. The textbook writers must rewrite the textbooks in such a way that the initiative may be transferred to students and communication skills are fostered in them. Team teaching from inter-disciplinary teachers has to be accepted, incorporated and made more effective. Efforts should be made to make teaching learner-centred. The student is not a passive entity, but an active mind that must significantly contribute to learning. For this, a sound methodology of language teaching is essential. Students should be drilled in linguistic routines.

Attitude and motivation are important factors in language learning. Successful learner of a second language must be psychologically prepared to adopt various aspects of behaviour. His motivation to learn is determined by his attitude towards the learning of language. If the student's attitude towards the teacher and his interest in language study are appreciated in a proper way, only then can the teaching of English be made more meaningful and rewarding.

Learner's errors are an inevitable part of language learning. The errors made in verb forms and patterns, auxiliaries, tenses, prepositions, articles, syntax, connectives, etc., are an evidence of the learning process itself. Pronunciation is the most crucial aspect of language teaching. It deserves more attention than appears to be given to it even by those who teach English and organise English studies in India. A systematic analysis of learner's errors would be of considerable significance in course designing and preparation of teaching materials. English may continue to be used almost indefinitely as an associate official language; therefore, the teaching of spoken English has become even more important. Efforts should be made to improve the quality of spoken English in India.

A good understanding of language is more or less connected with its good transmission. A faulty pronunciation will lead to a breakdown in communication or create misunderstanding and confusion. Grammar plays a crucial role in the teaching of English. A systematic study of grammar will help students to avoid errors, form correct speech habits and inculcate composing ability. Their strengthened confidence and increased sensitivity to the structural patterns of language will result in fluent and correct writing. A few lessons having ideal sentence structures and vocabulary may be chosen. A good command over grammar will facilitate a better appreciation of literature by enabling the students to resolve grammatical complexities and structural ambiguities of a literary text.

For good command over language, i.e., to increase the performance level of the students, a rich vocabulary is a necessity. It is often realised that the dearth of a good vocabulary hampers and handicaps their expression. A teacher of English should encourage his students to use, consult and refer to dictionary. He should motivate them to read newspapers, periodicals and magazines, not only for being updated in current affairs, but also to enhance their vocabulary. Dictation, vocabulary exercises, word usage assignments dealing with antonyms and synonyms, one word substitution, exposure to language labs, etc., need to be introduced to enhance the proficiency of the students in the use of language. In addition to the aforesaid, the courses should include learners' activities like listening to lectures, note-taking skills, taking part in discussions, public speaking, presentations and pronunciation activities, etc.

English being a living language has the capacity to change, to absorb and to expand. But the functional value of English deals with its communicative and pragmatic aspects. The English language teacher has always continued to occupy a central place in promoting his students' learning experiences. Now the teacher needs to put off his age-old mantle of preacher at the altar, and he has rather to create a learner-friendly environment in the classroom. Our aim as a teacher of English should not be to teach English for its own sake, but to motivate our students to speak and write language effectively, and not only to teach them theories about English, but also to make them proficient in the use of language.

10

Shifting Paradigms and Discourses of Blends: Commercial Values of Code Switching

—Dr. T.R. Muralikrishnan

This paper attempts to make an analysis and overview of code switching in English and Hindi, popularly known as 'Hinglish' as evident in the public discourses, with specific reference to advertisements. The paper proposes that the language in the public domain can get transformed with the active interference of such code switching among the young users of Hindi. The paper also attempts to see the ways in which code switching can be a motivator to mitigate resistance among the people for using the market product hence the language can be seen as a vehicle for promoting commercialisation.

Introduction

Bilinguals or multilinguals, with no change of interlocutor or topic, refer code switching to the mixing of two or more languages in discourse. This mixing can be at any level of linguistic structure, i.e., at the inter-sentential level or intra-sentential level. Early linguists treated these structures as deviant but structural approaches found the study of these as rewarding. Juxtaposition of two languages opens up the challenges for formally explaining the grammar of a new kind of syntax, which would have been simpler in case the linguist is dealing with monolingual structures. The morpho-semantic requirements are to be inclusive than exclusive. As it has been pointed out by Poplack, "the established loan words assume the morphological, syntactic, and often, phonological, identity of the recipient language," when it comes to lexical borrowing. The stock of linguistically and socially sanctioned loan words is available to monolingual users of the recipient language, who make use of them normally along with the remainder of the recipient language lexicon. Further the other category, viz., nonce borrowed words tend to involve lone lexical items which assume the morphological, syntactic and phonological identity of the recipient language. Like code switching, it requires a greater level of bilingual competence.

However the apparent similarities are questionable to a great extent when they are discussed in a broad perspective. As it is noted by Poplack (2001), the classification of lone items is the heart of fundamental disagreement among code switching researchers over:

- Whether the distinction between code switching and borrowing should be formally recognised in a theory of code switching,
- Whether these and other manifestations of language contact can be unambiguously identified in bilingual discourse, and
- Criteria for determining whether a given item was switched or borrowed. Researchers tend to identify two strategies, i.e. either an asymmetrical relationship (one dominating the other) or symmetrical one wherein which both languages play a meaningful role.

From English to Hinglish

English, which came as a colonial language, found a place in the educational setting even before the independence of the country. The administrative language at the formal level remained English, with a few exceptions in the southern states. Despite strong sense of nativism and nationalist exhortations, English survived in the country, thanks to the vision of the founding fathers of the country. With the advent of globalisation, liberalisation and privatisation, Indian people found the great advantage of learning

English. The new media culture has deep links with the Western counterparts and this has greatly influenced the people in their lifestyle, food, habits and approaches.

English in northern parts functions more as a professional language rather than that of mass use. Still, it is widely recognised for its commercial value. The educated elite prefer the twist in the language with appropriate connectivity with mass base and at the same time retaining the erudite features of expressions. The mass culture of the nation seems to prefer to bring the English language with the broad commercial appeal of the populated nation. Hence Hinglish is a viable alternative in the gen-next market.

The language in the public domain often gets transformed with the interference of code switching. This is evident in the Hindi ad campaign at the national level. English advertising is particularly effective for companies hoping to target the young professionals rapidly growing with money to spend. However, Hinglish works well with consumers in the mid- to upper-age brackets who have experienced the cultural transition that has reshaped India in recent decades. According to data released by the Population Reference Bureau, a scant 28 per cent of India's population lived in urban areas during 2003, and that the country's population density is a comparatively high 842 people per square mile. By the year 2050, India's population density should reach 1,280 people per square mile. According to the United Nations Population Division, in the year 2050, 20 per cent of population will be birth 0-14 years old, while 58 per cent will be aged 15-59, and 22 per cent of the populace will be 60 years of age and over. Many view the arrival of Hinglish and the influence of Indian words on English as a reflection (recognition?) of the rise of the Indian subcontinent as an economic powerhouse.

Illustration of Various Expressions

1) Retention of terminology after de-contextualisation:
   a) The expression *innit* was absorbed into British Asian speech via *haina* - a Hindi tag phrase, which got stuck on the sentences and with a meaning "is it not so?"
   b) The use of words such as *chuddies, bandana, pyjamas* have become popular.

c) Words such as *stepney, prepone, jungli* are part of accepted vocabulary.

In the given examples, the association is slightly asymmetrical as Hindi seeks an upper hand over the English counterpart. The words are accommodated in a new language after de-contextualising themselves from the natural roots. The connotation that is ingrained in the word *stepney* is not innocent, as it is understood in English.

2) Changing from one to another:

a) Yeh Dil Maange More!

b) Taste Mein Naya Twist

c) Just Munch Karo

d) Bacche logon ki party

e) Fun ke mood mein

f) Come on girls, waqt hai shine karne ka!

g) Ladki ko mari line, girlfriend boli, I'm fine

h) Life ho to aise,

i) Josh machine

j) Hungry, kya?

The relation that we find here is symmetrical as each contributes in its own significant way. The punch of the slogan gets intensified when juxtaposed with the other.

Mitigating Market Resistance

The Hinglish gets an extraordinary appeal among the masses as it combines the West and the East. The corporate world has shown great sense of imagination by spinning out unique catch phrases for incorporating the vibrant youth. The brand perception is a vital factor here. This concept would also create an acceptability of the brand within the lower age segments, which it definitely requires. The consumer market consists of mass base along with the South Asian diaspora's presence in the English-speaking countries, the spread of Bollywood through out the world, and the pervasive use of the internet with regional language features; make sure that the appeal remains constant. Linguists see this as a sociolinguistic tool. They see this phenomenon not as language interference on the basis that it supplements speech. It provides continuity in speech rather than presenting interference in language. It also does provide an opportunity for language development. According to Skiba (1997), when code switching is to compensate for a language difficulty, it may be viewed as interference and when it is used as a socio-linguistic tool it should not. Marketing, by corporate people, is done imaginatively where code switching is an absolute aid for promoting their product. A multilingual society like India can definitely appreciate the slogans in such fashion. In equating the West and the East, the product generates a cosmopolitan outlook. This syncs with the rationale of the post-liberalised India.

Conclusion

As any language, English is in state of flux in India. The tendency to globalise and to localise (*desi* variety) work together for commercial reasons and this opens up possibilities of code switching in English in India. The process is not linear always as it shapes the course of development in varied ways, enabling creativity and sometimes producing cultural shock. Code switching is now an acceptable method of communication. And it is only but appropriate that market forces exploit this facility to reach the masses for economic reasons.

Works Cited

Crystal, D. (1987). *The Cambridge Encyclopedia of Language*. Cambridge University Press: Cambridge.

Poplack, Shana (2001). 'Code Switching: Linguistic' in *International Encyclopedia of the Social & Behavioral Sciences*. Elsevier Science Ltd.

Sankoff, D. (1998). 'A Formal Production-based Explanation of the Facts of Code-switching.' *Bilingualism: Language and Cognition* I (1): 39-50.

Skiba, Richard (1997). 'Code Switching as a Countenance of Language Interference', *TESL Journal, Vol. III. No. 10. October 1997*. http://iteslj.org/, accessed on 15 Jan 2010.

11

Shifting Paradigms and the Future of 'Hinglish' in ELT: A Case Study

—Shubho Ray

The need of language emerges from the urge to communicate. And any dynamic language, like a river, after originating from its unique glacier, with maturity, gathers lot of foreign elements from the tributary 'langue(s)' and consequently enriches itself. That language which does not have this inclusiveness loses its vibrancy and with the passage of time becomes 'dead.' The flourish of any language is also correlated with the sociability of the race that uses it. It is then that the need to include words, expressions or word-phrases from other languages is genuinely felt. Talking of language Swiss linguist Ferdinand Saussure cited the following example:

> Why can a street be completely rebuilt and still be the same? Because it does not constitute a purely material entity; it is based on certain conditions that are distinct from the materials that fit the conditions, e.g. its location with respect to other streets.[1]

From the above quotation two significant notions come up: language can be "completely rebuilt and still be the same" and it is 'relational.' English is one such language, which has cherished its flexibility since its Germanic genesis. It is spoken or read by the largest number of people in the world for historical, political and economic reasons. It is a matter of great interest to learn that the dialects spoken by the settlers in England belonged to the

Germanic (or Teutonic) branch of the most important of the family of languages termed Indo-Germanic or Aryan. Indo-Germanic language, spoken in 3500 BC to 3000 BC, was split into eight dialects by 2000 BC. Each of these dialects with the passage of time developed into individual languages. Philologists are unanimous in bifurcation of the parent Indo-Germanic group into two subsets: Satem languages and Centum languages. While Satem languages comprised Indian languages like Sanskrit and Pali, the Centum group contains English along with Latin, Celtic and Scandinavian. Thus, the hypothesis of this paper that two versatile languages, English and Hindi, were connected by the womb since their inception, and therefore in future can intermingle to give birth to a more trendy 'Hinglish,' gains credibility. Saussure used two terms—'langue' and 'parole'—to connote "language as a system or structure on the one hand, and any given utterance in that language on the other"[2] respectively. Citing an example to illustrate this phenomenon Peter Barry writes:

> A particular remark in French (a sample of *parole*) only makes sense to you if you are already in possession of the whole body of rules and conventions governing verbal behaviour which we call 'French' (that is, the *langue*).[3]

Thus, 'langue' which indicates the system or totality of language shared by the 'collective consciousness' requires all the elements of a language along with the rules for their combination regarding grammar, syntax and so forth. Clearly, if Hinglish is to gain coinage concrete efforts should be made to form the Hinglish *langue*.

The History of Hinglish

With the diurnal rotation of the earth time elapsed and with that a gulf got created between the practitioners of the Satem and the Centum languages in two separate continents, Asia and Europe, respectively. Meanwhile, Hindi as a separate language was born of Sanskrit. And with the advent of the Muslim invaders across the Hindukush Mountains into northern parts of the Indian subcontinent, medieval India saw a meticulous blending of Urdu with Hindi. English language on the other hand experienced several 'influences' (Latin, Greek, Scandinavian and French) that not only changed the structure but also enhanced scope for other languages to make inroads into its domain.

The era of imperialism saw the intimacy between two modern, cosmopolitan and mature giants of languages: Hindi and English. This was more of a compulsion for the colonial power than choice. In order to carry out successful administration of colony India, and to practise the 'Drain-wealth' theory, the British rulers had to interact with and understand the native Indian culture. For this they needed knowledge of the major langue Hindi used by the inhabitants of the fertile north-Indian Gangetic plains. It is during this phase of history that we find the coinage of such words as "sahib" and "memsahib" in order to address the rulers. 'Sahib,' an equivalent of French 'monsieur,' indicates towards someone belonging to aristocracy. While the prefix 'mem' before 'sahib' in "memsahib" stands for the White/ Western/Aristocratic ladies, "laad sahib" was purposefully applied as a lampoon on those natives who tried to mimic the manners of the Englishmen, in the latter case the prefix 'laad' being the Hindi variant for 'lord.'

The Present Scenario

In a recent *English Today* issue David Graddol writing from India, in his article "Thoughts from Kolkata on English in India," writes:

> India is finally getting the infrastructure it so desperately needs, and road building is bringing more people into the cities, and allowing city-dwellers to commute from the city edges. Different kinds of people, from different social and language backgrounds, who all need to communicate. One of India's hundreds of languages has proved excellent for that lingua franca purpose it's called English.[4]

The first point to be noted here is that English is now established, even in the West/metropolitan centre, as "[o]ne of India's hundreds of languages." But, when someone like Graddol, "doing research for a British Council project – a sequel to *English Next*, which will look at the future of English [language teaching] in India,"[5] notes down his findings as "[d]ifferent kinds of people, from different social and language backgrounds, who all need to communicate" take refuge in English, there is a need to refute it because within North India communication can be successfully established with the use of Hindi only (even if it does not conform to the nuances of the dialect practised in the Hindi-speaking heartland). Therefore, since knowing English cannot be a pre-requisition to establish communication in commonplace activities, and that India has unanimously accepted Hindi as her national language in order to bridge the gap between varied languages, it becomes all the more curious as to what is the premise that led to the excesses of a cocktail vocabulary of 'Hindi + English=Hinglish' in contemporary India. Even more probing is whether 'Hinglish' can ever reach that pulpit where it can establish itself as a separate entity/language, or just be on the fringes with occasional brilliance tickling the cosmopolitan individuals with an illusion that they have mastered two most fertile languages of this world.

The seed of 'Hinglish' actually lies in postcolonial identity crisis of the natives. According to Homi K. Bhabha 'migrants, the colonised or political refugees' (Bhabha, 1994:12), could take on the task of unhousing received ways of thinking about the world and discovering the hybridity, the difference that exists within the periphery of identity. However, and importantly, these internal differences are displaced, existing beyond representation. Hence, rampant mushrooming of pseudo-languages, like 'Hinglish.' Cultural differences are figured as unrepresented, uncanny languages and presences, which bear witness to hybrid experiences, histories and lives.

India suffered the excesses of colonial rule for over two hundred years under the British. This has brought about a change in the psychology among the natives that anything 'English' or that which contains 'Englishness' is qualitatively superior to the native, as is the case here with India's national language Hindi. Frantz Fanon has noted his significant observations regarding the psychological shift among the native cultures in *Black Skin, White Masks* and *The Wretched of the Earth,* and looks at the psychosomatic effects on them (natives) because of colonial domination. While analysing these (psychological) effects of colonial domination and disempowerment on the colonised natives, Fanon in *Black Skin, White Masks,* points out that under colonial conditions the objective realm of material oppression involves the subjective realm (to make the native feel inferior). This phenomenon has been amply reflected in Graddol's article where he questions,

> But why do these [native] children need English? Why do their parents want it so badly that it has become an election issue? The answer to that helps us understand a remarkable change in India, which is recasting its relationship with the English language. All over India, private schools have been opening up to cater for the poor: in slums and for village Dalits (untouchables). In some rural and slum areas, half the children now attend small private schools, often just in a room in someone's house. It's difficult to get accurate figures because most of these schools are not recognised by the government.[6]

The researcher-critic is absolutely right to observe that:

> In India, private school means English-medium. Parents, however poor, desperately want better for their children, and for them better means English-medium. A survey, carried out by an Indian TV channel in summer 2009, found that 87% of Indians now 'feel that knowledge of English is important to succeed in life.' The dismal fact is that as far as English goes, these unrecognised schools are probably a waste of the family resources. But it underlines how success and English are tied together in the popular imagination across India.[7]

The inferences that can be drawn from this are that 'unrecognised' "private schools have been opening up," and even the poverty-stricken section of the Indian society "desperately want better [education] for their children, and for them *better* (italics are mine) means *English-medium* (italics are mine)" because ironically in the post-independent era those who know English have succeeded in every walk of life even though Hindi is the nation's national language.

At present two categories of speakers interact in Hinglish: first, those who have the minimum/basic knowledge of English and/as well as Hindi; secondly, those who know Hindi and with their insufficient acquaintance (and at times no acquaintance) with

English try to mimic the first group of users since they realise 'its trendy/fashion/ 'latest'/ 'cool.' While for the first group of users it is a strong way to write back to the empire by, say, "hindinising" English, for the second it is a 'fitness certificate' for survival in this breakneck competitive world of globalisation.

The Prospect of Hinglish

Kerry Maxwell in "New word of the month" classifies "Hinglish as a *noun*, meaning, 'a mixture of Hindi and English, spoken widely in India and by British Asians in the UK."[8] Pertinently, in June of 2005, the term 'Hinglish' became an issue to reckon with "when it was reported that more than 26 neologisms included in a new edition of the *Collins English Dictionary* were of Hindi origin" and it was all notably because of the "growing influence of the Indian subcontinent on the English lexicon."[9] The million dollar question is whether Hinglish has achieved for itself a credibility that it could be inculcated into English Language Teaching in India. For present it has definitely not. Hinglish has existed for decades in India, and the reason is not hard to decipher. Postcolonial India still suffers from the 'colonial hangover.' Indians are craving to mimic the language of the metropolitan 'centre.' And it is highly utopic for ill-learned practitioners of the language to long towards achieving credibility through the practice of such a pseudo-language like Hinglish. Unfortunately, owing to the special status long enjoyed by English language in India, because of the country's colonial history, and its prevalence in governance, media, and as a medium of education for many schools across the nation, it has become the language of choice among the youth. Over that, as Graddol observed:

> A few years down the line we will have to substantially revise our estimates of how many people speak English in the world – there are around 25 million children in each year group in India at the moment.[10]

What is disturbing is "teachers [...] are too rare [...]."[11] "Across India," Graddol points out that, "a new generation in primary schools is now expected to learn English, but there is a critical shortage of teachers who [even] speak the language."[12] It needs no research to understand then that the unrecognised schools will produce half-learned "Englishwallas" who would throughout rest of their lives struggle to master the language of their once colonial masters and write back to them. They would invariably fail and consequently seek refuge in a bastard langue Hinglish. Besides, the invasions of our bedrooms by cable television and the Internet have encouraged Hinglish, e.g., "Hungry kya?" or "Yeh Dil Maange More." These are punch-lines of Domino's Pizza and Pepsi respectively. It is anybody's guess that the purpose is to reach the target audience: the Generation-Y (i.e., the young generation) of India. The advertising world therefore adopts/adapts to the Hinglish because an average Indian would grasp the essence in "Yeh Dil Maange More" over "the heart wants more" for the simple reason that English language teaching in India has critical shortcomings, as discussed already.

But then can we close our eyes to this impending pseudo *langue*. Well we definitely cannot. Especially after David Crystal, a British linguist, "projected that at about 350 million, the world's Hinglish speakers may soon outnumber native English speakers."[13] Another area where Hinglish is being used regularly is Bollywood where even films are named in Hinglish for instance, "Morning Raga"(2004), "Jhankar Beats"(2003) or "Freaky Chakra"(2003). But till now we have appreciated Hinglish in snatches and that too with only business propositions in mind. In this way Hinglish could not be established as an authorised language of paradigmatic relevance.

We will have to undertake three substantial steps for achieving that:

1) archive the history of the origin,
2) research its development and relevance, and
3) suggest scopes for its flourish.

As pointed out in the previous section of this article, presently Hinglish is being spoken by a class of youth who have grown up watching music channels like MTV and Channel V. But majorityof India does not fall into this category. So inside a classroom—be it a rural school or the IITs—if the teacher as medium of instruction adopts Hinglish then it will raise the level of disparity

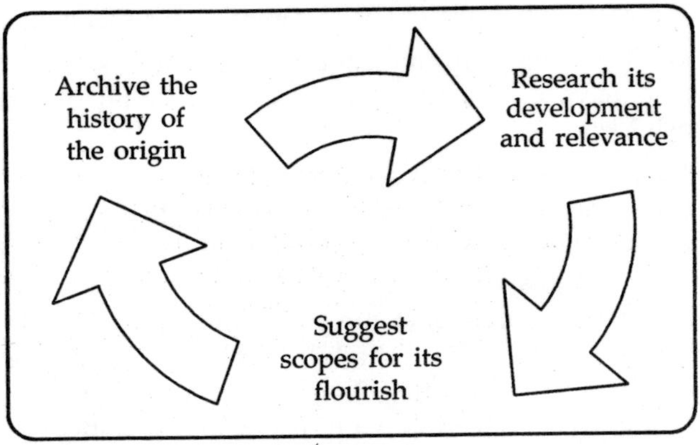

among students coming from varied socio-economic backgrounds. Those who could understand will enjoy this innovative teaching process while the rest will suffer from an inferiority complex.

This will never bring the desired results of ELT. What can be done at the earliest is:

a) Lexical documentation of Hinglish words with their meanings, and
b) Texts containing Hinglish vocabularies introduced in the syllabus uniformly across the nation. Howsoever Herculean the task may seem it will have to be that way.

There is no need to be baffled. One can start with Rudyard Kipling's *Jungle Book* and move on to R. K. Narayan's novels like *The Guide* and go on to the post modernist Salman Rushdie's fictions like *Midnight's Children*. According to Krishna Sen, "Narayan has created an unmistakably Indian ambience [...] even while using a non-native medium of communication."[14] A teacher can enlighten his students how Narayan:

> Makes no attempt to reproduce chaste British locutions, but employs a variety of linguistic devices to approximate the local idiom [...] [by] *code-switching* [...] [i.e.] the direct use of untranslated terms—*sadhu, swami, mahatma, devdasi, bonda.*[15]

He (teacher) can then interest his classroom by illustrating from contemporary writers' masterpieces and show how inclusion of the Hinglish terms by them, at free will, has enriched their works and may cite examples from the masterpieces of Rushdie, and the likes, who have coined terms like "chutnification of history," "funtoosh," etc.

India cherishes unity in diversity. It is this ideology that has kept her together since time immemorial. Language has an extremely critical role to play in this schema. No country in the world recognises as many as 22 languages, within its cartographical boundaries, as the government of India has done in "languages of the 8th Schedule" of the Constitution and bestowed them with the official language status. The vividness of mother tongues is noticed as we move from one state to another and find that lot of pride is taken by the speakers of a particular dialect or language claiming their exclusiveness. This creates fissure within the polity. The solution to these socio-linguistic problems is adoption of a pluralist approach towards language which will find some widely acceptable solutions. Hinglish has the potential of becoming a pluralistic lingo. Since a wide sea lies before us unexplored we are presently apprehensive. But, Come on *yaar* (friend)! Let us work together towards bringing true recognition for Hinglish. If clouds of doubt surround us then we just need to assure ourselves, the Obama-way, "Yes we can."

Notes

1. Saussure, Ferdinand de. (1983). *Course in General Linguistics*. Eds. Charles Bally and Albert Sechehaye. Trans. Roy Harris. La Salle, Illinois: Open Court. pp.108-9.
2. Barry, Peter. *Beginning Theory*, First Indian Edition. (2008). New Delhi: Viva Books Pvt. Ltd., 44.
3. *Ibid.* p. 44.
4. Graddol, David. "Thoughts from Kolkata on English in India" *English Today* 100, Vol. 25, No. 4 (December 2009). United Kingdom: Cambridge University Press, p. 21.
5. Ibid. p. 22.
6. Ibid. p. 22
7. Ibid. p. 23.
8. Maxwell, Kerry. "New word of the month." *MED Magazine*. Issue 32, (July 2005). 25 Feb. 2010 <http://www.macmillandictionaries.com/MED-Magazine/ July2005/32-New-Word-Hinglish.htm>.

9. Ibid.
10. Graddol, David. op. cit., p.22.
11. Ibid. p. 22.
12. Ibid. p. 22.
13. Scott, Baldauf (November 23, 2004). "A Hindi-English jumble, spoken by 350 million." *Christian Science Monitor* <http://www.csmonitor.com/2004/1123/p01s03-wosc.html>.
14. Sen, Krishna. "*Critical Essays on R. K. Narayan's The Guide.*" 2005. Kolkata: Orient Longman, p. 79.
15. Ibid. p. 79.

12

Shifting Paradigms and Second Language Acquisition in India

—Dr. Sarika Dubey

The theories of second language acquisition have traditionally been the offspring of general linguistic theory, sometime supplemented by insight from psychology. Our interest is in the language, learning process, whether it is comparatively recent and significant for general linguistic theory have own but it is language learning which is perhaps the litmus test for the worth and value of all theories of language. The linguists as well as the psychologists are interested in discovering what is universal in language and what general laws govern our acquisition of language. Their discussions are largely the learning of the mother tongue, but the moot point is if there are general language leaning principles involved, then they cannot also be without relevance to foreign language learning. The basic thing that requires serious and sustained consideration is whether or not language teaching procedures are based on general theories of language acquisition. These theories, by and large, suggest that the individuals are essentially the same in their language learning capacities; nevertheless, teachers are probably conscious of the diversity of language learning abilities that the pupils display.

General Theories of Language Acquisition

Behaviorism

This is a general language–learning principle, which enunciates that there is no difference between the way one learns a language and the way one learns to do anything else. The behaviourism is committed to admitting as evidence only that which the people make and the condition under which they are made. This may also be viewed as the stimulus–response phenomenon. The stimulus, to which the utterance forms a 'response', being physically present in the situation reinforcement does also play an important part in the case of behaviorism, particularly which regard to be child when he/she gets approval from his/her parents. Wilkins says about behaviourism that in this case "learning is controlled by the condition under which it take place:" "that as long as individuals are in the same way," that a "physical need in the child may be met as a result of his utterance" that parental approval "act as a powerful reinforcer" that the notice of "repetition is therefore extremely important" and that it is "the making of the response that is the learning process."

Mentalism

Mentalism, we find, goes against behaviourism almost wholesale, point. According to the mentalists, people learn a language, "not because they are subjected to a similar conditioning process, but because they process an inborn capacity which permits them to acquire a language as a normal maturation process." Language, they argue to say, is a very complex form of behavior, and perhaps can hardly be learnt in terms of external stimuli. In the view of these people, a learner has to be adequately exposed to the target language.

Language Environment

Language environment is something that the learner hears and sees in the new language. It may include a wide variety of situations as available in or through stories, conversation with friend, watching television, and reading street signs, newspapers or book. There are two kind of language environ-ment: macro environment and micro environment.

Macro Environment

When the focus of the learner or speaker is on the form of the language, then the language environment is formal. The formal language environment focuses on a conscious learning of rules and forms, however, when the focus is on the content of the communication, and then the language environment is natural. The natural language environment seeks to enhance the development of the communication skills are both the foreign and host situations. There are three types of communication in which the learner participates: one way; restricted two ways and full ways.

One-way Communication

The learner listens to or reads the target language, but does not respond. The communication is one way; it is towards the learner, and not form him her.

- *Restricted Two-way Communication:* The learner responds orally to someone, but he/she does not completely use the target language.
- *Full Two-way Communication:* The learners are both a receiver and send messages. Most of the research works emphasize the usefulness of one-way and restricted two–way communication during the early period of learning process.

Micro Environment

While the macro-environment factors are the board, general characteristics of the language environment, macro environment factors point to the specific structure of the language the learner hear of sees, e.g., the induction of yes/no question into the learners' environment. Three micro environment factors have been individual factors have been identified from the perspective of their effect on the quality and pace of language acquisition. These are salience, feedback and frequency.

- *Salience:* It refers to the ease with which a structure is heard or seen. As, for example, people and hear or seen. As for example, people can hear or see the English article, 'the' more easily than the past tense ending–ed, e.g., talked. Psychologists have defined salience by referring to those characteristics, which seem to make others. Such characteristics, besides other, do also include phonetics substance. In the sentence, *She does not want anything, does* not and *want* receive greater salience or prominence than *she* or *anything*.

- *Feedback:* It points to the listener or reader's response to the teacher's speech or writing. One kind of feedback is correction; another is approval, which is also known as positive feedback. Still another kind of feedback consists in expanding or modifying the learner's speech without making them unduly conscious of modification. This is known as expansion correction.
- *Frequency:* In the language acquisition procedure frequency refers to the number of times a learner hears or sees a given structure. The typical example in this regard is the recurrence of WH–question involving what, who, which, where, when, whose and whence. The count of such question should be considered as the basis of frequency in the given language environment. It has generally been assumed that the more a learner tries to acquire a structure, the sooner will he/she learn the language.

Micro environment factors have their impact on second language learning only when the learners have reached a certain level in their L2 development, the level at which they are in a position to internalise a given structure. The salience or frequency of the structure may increase the probability that they would steadily notice the structure and acquire it.

Internal Processing

Language learning, essentially speaking, occurs or materialises in the mind of the learners, where mental structure or mechanism processes and organises the language to which they are exposed. A systematic study of the discrepancies between the languages that the learner produce and the language they hear or read provides the basis from which we can infer the attribute of an otherwise invisible mental structure. Researches in the concerned are suggested that three internal processing factors play a substantial role in second language acquisition:

Filter – organise – Monitor – the learners' performance

Filter

It is that part of the internal processing system, which subconsciously screens incoming language, based on what the psychologists call affect. It conditions the learners' native needs, attitudes and emotional states. Filters are the first main hurdles that the incoming language date has to encounter before they are processed further. It determines:

- Which target language model will the learner select?
- Which part of the language will be attended to the first?
- How fast can learner acquire language?
- When should language acquisition effort cease?

Organiser

It subconsciously processes data, which the filter lets in. it is chiefly concerned with the learners' ability to organise gradually the new language system. Its subconscious functioning is cognitive in nature, the functioning of the organiser may be seen in terms:

a) The Systematic progression the learners acquire before a structure is finally acquired.
b) The errors that systematically occur in the learners speech.
c) The common order in which mature structure are learned and analysis of these aspects of the learner's participation in L2 system reveals different facets of the operation of the inner processing that governor acquisition of language.

Monitors

It is that part of the learners' internal system, which controls conscious linguistics processing. As and when conscious linguistics processing takes place, the learners may be set to be using the monitors. When a learner performs a drill, it requires conscious attention to linguistics form; when he memorises a dialogue, conscious processing is ininevitably taking place, and a monitor is being used. The degree to which the monitor is used or may be used depends on at least:

- The learner's age
- The amount and quality of formal instruction
- The focus on verbal task
- The personality of the learner.

Within the same language environment, the learners have mostly the same innate language processing mechanism, and yet there are some learners who learn second language better and faster then others. It is, therefore, proper to identify those individual factors that affect a leaner in acquiring a language.

- *Personality:* It signifies and aggregates of trades or characteristics of a particular individual. One has to see or perceive whether an individual. One has to seen or perceive whether and individual is an extrovert on introvert, impulsive or reflective, authoritarian or submissive, intelligent or dull. There are several other simpler qualities that constitute and reveal an individual's personality. The operation of personality is quite evident and crucial in second language. Those who have done research work on personality in relation to language learning do also include such aspects as those of the label of self-confidences, ability to emphasize, and the degree of logicality or the power to analyse.
- *Empathy:* The dictionary meaning of the word 'empathy' is so plain and clear, and yet so telling; it is the ability to share someone else's feelings or experiences or the capacity for participating in another's feeling or ideas. It has been pointed out that one might expect a strong relationship between an individual's capacity for empathy and his L2 performance. It is unlikely, though, that someone 's capacity for participation in another's feelings or ideas would be measured in linguistics manipulation task; nevertheless if empathy is an important factor in L2 learning, then it is likely that empathy manifests itself in the participation in another's feelings and ideas from more effectively than linguistic manipulation.
- *Age:* Scientists sport the belief that children are better at language acquisition than adults. Children acquire second language in natural environment learned initially.

> Children under ten experience enough natural communication in the target language and do always succeed in attaining native–like proficiency, while those over fifteen find it difficult to be able to do so. Various concerned studies confirm this very view saying that children may not learn second language faster than adults, but they do learn better.

A number of suggestions have been made regarding the nature and causes of child–adult differences in respect of second language acquisition. However, no single suggestion is adequate for explaining the differences between the child and the adult in learning the second language. The first suggestion involved in this connection is biological in nature, and, quite naturally, it seeks to examine the problem whether or not the child and adult brains are fundamentally different.

In his book *Biological Foundation of Language*, H. Lenneberg says that the development of specialisation of functions on the left and right sides of the brain (cerebral dominance or lateralisation) begins in childhood and is completed by puberty. Puberty marks the time when automatic acquisition from more exposure to a given language seems to disappear. It is because, after puberty, the left and the right hemispheres of the brain develop specialised functions, and the organiser ceases to build up a new language subconsciously. That is why, Lunenburg says that the transfer of language functions in one part of the brain while another is related to the plasticity, that is request for learning a language naturally and completely. Piaget maintains that in spite of all children-adult differences in respect of the language learning operation, the adult's cognitive superiority should eventually place them better than children in language learning process.

Reference and Transfer

The first language has been considered to be the cause of major problems in the course of learning second language. However, of late L1 (first language) is not usually asked upon as annoying interference in a learner's part to acquire L2 (second language). According to Contrastive Analysis Hypothesis, the automatic transfer L1 structure to L2 performance is negative when L1 and L2 structure differ and positive when the two structures are the same. Negative transfer results in wrong, while positive transfer results in correct construction. Such negative or positive results are due to the influence of L1 habits on L2 production.

Interference refers to a distinct linguistic phenomenon. Psychological interference refers to the influence of old habits on the new ones that are being learned. Sociolinguistic interference takes us to language interactions, to linguistic borrowings and shifts that occur when different language communities are in contact. The behaviourist who first defined transfer says that technically speaking transfer is a process involving an automatic, uncontrolled and subconscious use of learned linguistic behaviour in the attempt to produce new response.

It is not infrequently that the term 'inter-language' is used to suggest the intermediate stages observable in the learners' language between the native and the target language. The assumption is that there are psychological structures talents in the brains, which are activated when one attempts to learn a second language. It is this stimulus that produces inter-language, a language system different from that of L1 and L2. Moreover, five aspects of inter-language performance are also mentioned, and these are:

1) Language transfer
2) Transfer of training
3) Strategies of learning
4) Strategies of communication and
5) Over generation of target language materials.

This interslanguage approximate system is spoken of at times also as approximate syllabus. This term has the advantage of implying or pointing to the developmental nature of language learning. The learner's system keeps on being modified as new elements are incorporated into the learning and become evident in terms of the learners' errors. The errors committed by L2 learners are important for a proper understanding of the process of second language acquisition and also for planning courses. A contrastive study of contact languages may be fragmentary and so inadequate, and our attention is thus necessarily drawn to those sources of error, which are independent of L2. The factors responsible for or causing these errors are:

i) Learning strategy
ii) Teaching technique
iii) Folklore in L2
iv) Period over which L2 has been used by the speech community, and
v) The learners' sociolinguistic situation.

There seems to be a system in the learners' error, and this system does have its own significant. It is believed that second language acquisition is strongly influenced by the learner L1. The most obvious evidence in this regard is the accent of the speaker. The L1 utterance does also affect other aspects or levels, including syntax and morphology. It is believed as well that the role of L1 in second language acquisition is a negative one, i.e., L1 gets in the way of or interferes with the learning of L2 in such a way that the features of L1 are the transferred to L2. Really speaking, learning L2 means overcoming the effect of L1 and steadily replacing those features of L2. According to the behaviourist learning new habits, the grammatical apparatus programmed into the mind for the first language interferes with the smooth acquisition of the second. The notion of interference has its own centrality in the behaviourist account of L2. Interference results in proactive inhibition, and in order to develop new linguistic habits, the learner has to overcome these inhibitions.

Theories of Second Language Acquisition

There are several theories relating, in particular, to second language acquisition, and these theories do have their own important in the field of research. In fact, they reflect a variety of perspectives with regard to second language acquisition. These theories are (i) the acculturate model (closely associated with the nativisation model); (ii) accommodation theory; (iii) discourse theory; (iv) monitor theory; (v) the variable competence model; (vi) the universal hypothesis and (vii) the neuro function theory. And though it is neither possible nor perhaps desirable to discuss all these theories or model in detail, one may try to identify and understand the real aim of these theories as well as the role of the second language acquisition research.

a) Second language acquisition research may be described as a search for an appropriate level for description of the learners system of the rules. The main goal is description, i.e., characterisations of the linguistic categories, which constitute the learners' inter-language at any point of development.

b) They seek what really motivates the learner to learn and what forces them to stop learning.

c) A reference is made to two types of second language acquisition: assembly mechanism and power mechanism. The difference is important because some theories focus on how, while other on why. It is only a comprehensive theory that would explain both assembly mechanism and power mechanism.

   The two approaches to the theory of building are:

   i) Theory then research and
   ii) Research then theory.

   The theory then research approach involves five stages:

   i) Developing an explicit theory
   ii) Deriving a testable prediction from the theory
   iii) Conducting research to test prediction
   iv) Modifying the theory if the prediction is unconfirmed
   v) Testing the new prediction if the first prediction is confirmed.

   The research then theory approach has four stages:

   i) Selecting a phenomenon for investigation
   ii) Measuring its characteristics
   iii) Collecting data to look for systematic patterns
   iv) Formalising significant pattern as rules.

d) One has to look as discourse in order to be able to study how language learning evolves out of the strategies used to carry on a conversation. The types of conversation depend on who the learner is— child or adult.

Discourse analysis considers the teachers' as well as the learners' contribution. It describes not just the function of separate or isolated utterances but also the utterances combined for larger discoursal units. A three–phase discourse consists of exchanges between the teacher and student in the course of which the former initiates and supplies the feedback, while the latter responds. For example.

Teacher: I the clock there on the wall?

Student: Yes.

Teacher: Good, the clock is there on the wall.

e) It is both pertinent and useful to consider the kinds of classroom interaction. Three basic kinds of pedagogic goal are:

   i) *Core goal:* It points to the explicit pedagogic purpose of the classroom.

   ii) *Framework:* It focuses on the organisation requirement of the lesson

   iii) *Social goal:* It involves the use of language for more than personal purpose.

Second language acquisitions follow a route in syntactical development. Native speakers adjust their speech in order to negotiate meaning with non-native speakers. The conversation strategy influences the pace of the route of second language acquisition in a number of ways. Conversation, articulate conversation, is at the very centre of second language acquisition.

Works Cited

Britton, J. *Language and learning* (penguin edition, 1972).

Emig J.A. (Ed.). (1966). *Language and leaning*. New York, 1966.

Fletcher P. & M. Garman (Ed.). (1977). *Language acquisition*. Cambridge.

Lado. R. (1957). *Linguistic Across Culture*. Ann Arbor: Michigan.

Long. R.B. (1961). *The Sentence and it Parts*. Chicago.

Linneberg, E.H. (1967). *Biological Foundation of the language*. New York

Menyuck, P. (1971). *The Acquisition and Development of Language*. Englewood Cliftis: New Jersey.

Piaget, J. (1960). *The Language and Thought of the Child.* London. Translated from Frensch by M &r R Gabain.

Powell, L.S. *Communication and Learning* (London, 1969).

Stock E.C. & JDA. (1974). *Widdowson: Learning about Linguistic.* London.

Skinner, B.F. (1957). *Verbal Behaviour.* New York.

Wilking, D.A. (1982). *Linguistics in Language teaching.* Landon. p.162.

13

Shifting Paradigms and Combating Hinglish: Cartographing English (Sharing ESP-Law Experience)

—Alka Singh

"More Indians speak English than any other language, with the sole exception of Hindi. What's more, English speakers in India out number those in all of western Europe, not counting the United Kingdom. And Indian English-speakers are more than twice the UK's population," reveals the census 2001 data on bilingualism and trilingualism in India (*The Times of India,* New Delhi, March 14, 2010). This data not only reveals the impact of English in India, its impact on Indian psyche and thus its popular outreach, but it also brings cold waves for the other Indian languages. It is really a matter of debate and serious discussion but we may keep it for some other day keeping the propriety of the theme in question.

Introduction

The present paper attempts to underline the scope, purport and prospects of the so called Hinglish. I have analysed it with regard to very common experiences of a ESP teacher especially in a classroom and the academic milieu of English teaching for Law.

Hinglish to me is a hybrid construct, it is a postmodern grafting of two major languages—English and Hindi. While discussing this sociolinguistic construct with my friend R.P. Singh of the University of Lucknow, we inferred that it's a unique mating of two unknown entities in the same way as G.B. Shaw devises in his theory of Life Force. If we use the expressions like "Just chill *yaar,* Idea to *wakai* bumper *hai, Bada* fantastic *hai,* Sweetu, I was willing to complete your assignment in Holi vacations but *kya karen yaar, ghar jao aur itne dino baad* to time *hi nahi* spare-*ho paata,*" we reach the funky world of English where everybody is Bindaas and every girl is a *Bandi*. The following sentence may also fall in the category of Hinglish, "When I speak *aiyyeai* speak, when you speak *youayyai* speak, no speak in middle." We may assert that Hinglish is the fusion of Hindi and English which is very easily discernible in the college canteens, and on the campus of academic institutions. Ashish Tripathi writes on this form of language, "It's *jhakas* and *bhaukal.* Keep aside grammar because this lingo is full toss. Some may find it bizarre at times beyond comprehension – but if you have been or are campus *ka keeda*...oops we mean a regular campus creature, this funky jargon is the right way of expression." (*The Times of India,* Lucknow, Jan.11, 2009). Neelam Raj comments on it, "It is definitely not the Queen's English. Call it Maharani's English if you will. There is nothing royal about it though, it is about the masses" (*The Times of India,* Lucknow, Jan.11, 2009). The following statement of columnist Gur Charan Das makes clear the force and flow of English. He writes:

> ...two trends that are likely to determine our linguistic future. One is the rapid spread of English across India; the second is the unprecedented popularity of Hindi. The collision of the two we call Hinglish, but should, in fact, be called Inglish because it is increasingly pan India street language and borrows from all vernaculars. Mixing English with our mother tongues has been going on for generations, but what is different this time around is that Inglish is both aspirational language of the lower classes and the fashionable idiom of the upper class drawing rooms. Inglish is the stylish language of Bollywood, FM radio and national advertising. Advertisers in particular have been surprised by the terrific resonance of the slogans such as, 'life ho to aise', 'josh machine', and 'dil mange more' (*The Times of India,* Lucknow, July 16, 2006).

What is Legal English?

Legal English is a significant form of ESP. It undertakes English to shape for a ready made use of the legal professionals. For meeting such requirements the ESP practitioners prepare a specific Programme of Action (POA). The following objectives are common while planning and taking up of any such programme:

a) Background Sensitisation

To improve students' ability to;

i) develop an understanding of the political, social and legal environment and the related issues.

ii) feel the legal and civic concerns and the basic issues involved in the peaceful human life.

b) Meeting Inguistic Abilities

i) To make the learners able to use accurately and appropriately the cohesion and coherence devices, particularly rhetorical markers of logical relations between clauses and sentences, so as to communicate commonly occurring propositional functions in legal discourses.

ii) To make the learners able to demonstrate the appropriate lexical choice at both the word and phrase level in conformity with the stylistic and collocation conventions of the related discipline.

iii) To enable them to display grammatical accuracy and rhetorical skills in taking up different moves in the field of legislation and laws. In particular it may expose the skills of embedding reporting clauses in issue statements articulating clause relations in compound conditional sentences distinguishing between general principles and their particular application to the problem facts, and applying modal, adverbial, nominal and other strategies in legal language.

iv) To make them able to display accurate control of punctuation and spellings specially in the usages of Latin maxims.

v) To strengthen the vocabulary and usages with a study of: Foreign words and phrases (specially used in the field of

Law) & Common errors made in term of using English language for various purposes.

vi) One-word substitution.

vii) Words often confused with reference to spelling, their pronunciation and meaning.

viii) Antonyms and synonyms.

ix) A session to be allotted especially for reading and listening comprehension. For this purpose the practice may be made from simple paragraph to long articles dealing with various social, political and economic issues. Selected excerpts and passages from legal texts may be used.

x) Knowledge of different type of composition and writing skills. Paragraph development, skills of paraphrasing, forming story and analysis on various situation based themes and evidential circumstances, précis writing, etc.

xi) Report writing, making business and other research proposals, dissertation, project, etc.

xii) Public and business interaction, meetings, presentations, taking notes and references.

xiii) Business correspondences: notices, messages, circulars, official and business letters, etc.

xiv) Essay writing with special reference to legal essays.

xv) Interfacing judicial styles with reference to a study of leading judgements.

xvi) Understanding self effectiveness: interpersonal skills, self-esteem, meaning, importance, components of self-esteem, high and law self-esteem, measuring self-esteem.

xvii) Emotions: meaning, characteristics, types, related facts on emotion, handling of some emotional states – anger, anxiety, depression, fear, etc.

xviii) Emotional intelligence – meaning, importance and relevance.

xix) Appreciation of electronic media for legal and social cause may be included to sharpen their skills in communi-cation.

xx) Imparting the training of documentary film making.

Besides, as part of their co-curricular activities they must practice: oral presentation, group discussion, role play, quizzes, etc. They should be given assignments like writing a message or a formal formatting, framing of sentences, etc., in order to invite the expected delegates, the chief guest and other official people to a seminar or a conference with all specific details of venue, timings and other necessary items to be included, in a concise and clear manner with an eye to time limit. They should also be asked to submit a project pertaining to any aspects of communication or management as a part of their course under the guidance of a faculty concerned.

The above-mentioned broad objectives are based on developing the following abilities, along with brushing up the finer sensibilities of a human being:

- Comprehensions
- Demonstration
- Co-relation
- Developing syntactical and structural knowledge of language, and
- Analysis

Possessing communication skill is an art. It is an important qualification for a person who aims at offering anything to society. In case of preparing a sensitive legal personnel, its importance becomes manifold. When such a person is on work in the field different jostling problems and circumstances appear to be managed by him, and for this, communication skill, be it oral or written, is the backbone. On the Language of Law V. Sasikumar writes:

> The language of law is characterised by precision and complexity. The interpretation of legal language calls foı an indepth understanding of its specialised 'register' of vocabulary and a wide range of complex language structure. Its effective use in speaking and writing demands an even greater mastery of the varied resources of the English language (qtd. in Myneni, *English II for Pre Law,* VII).

Prof. L.N. Mathur, in a personal interview, states that, "Students of Law in general have been found more careless and callous in their attitude towards common spelling error, sentence construction and in appropriate citations of cases." Giving an illustration with reference to the word 'will' in the case of a transfer of property he says, "a person who makes such a will is a 'testator'; the one to whom the property is transferred, that is the receiver of the property is named as 'legatee'; and the subject matter of the will, say the property to be transferred is called 'legacy.'" Hence, a student of law is required to be careful while writing the word/words like legatee or legacy. It may also be seen here that for a common man 'will' is simply 'consent' or may be 'knowledge', but for lawyers, judges and law students, the word is needed to be understood in its proper and specific content. For instance, they are required to know whether this 'will' exists in that particular legal document with reference to the transfer of property or it is a will regarding the custody of a 'minor' child or it is a will regarding something else which may be/may not be recognisable in any court of law. Thus, whether it is an oral or written form of communication, the language to be used by the people associated with legal discipline is very peculiar and specialised in terms of its meaning and content. It is, therefore, suggested that a person writing a legal document or any legal writing requires appropriate grammatical knowledge in order to construct appropriate sentences with all necessary punctuation marks, appropriate tenses, verbs and the right word in a right way at the right place. The writing must be simple and concise without missing any of the important point/points of the content or the subject matter dealt over there. Legal writing should follow the dictum, "brevity is the soul of wits."

Thus, legal English is based on accuracy. Even a small lapse of punctuation mark can mar the drafting and purpose of the document. It has a strong base on propriety of the academic discipline. In such a scenario and unwritten commandments, we may find that the use of Hinglish in written documents and oral communication is injurious and nasty sign not only for the Legal profession but almost for any field of ESP because ESP normally caters to the professional communication, and the professional setting is more articulate and disciplined than the literary or general framework of human and linguistic affairs. On this *chutnified* English Rashmi Roshan Lall's comment is worth mention who doubts and feels frightened with the increasing inclination of Indians towards Hinglish. She writes, "The boneheaded and the brashly patriotic rejoice at the formal induction of words like 'chuddies', 'change', 'aloo', and 'theek' into the *Oxford English Dictionary* (OED). But patriotism does not exonerate us from linguistic infantilism. The Mera Bharat Mahan brigade cheers Hinglish as the emerging linguistic superpower. But it reckons without historical precedent. Latin may be a good example of lingua franca throttled by its thriving vernacular offshoots." She further writes, "As one of the largest hubs of non-native English speaking peoples of the world, it may not be in India's interest to casually murder standard world English, nor to cease speaking it. Where would we be if Hinglish were the only 'English' we knew? Perhaps less fluent and an assured communicators on a world stage that has at least 1.5 billion speaking English as a second language (*The Times of India,* New Delhi, January11, 2009).

Legal profession includes different groups and strata of human life and so it becomes very realistic. Aparna Singh who teaches Law opines that, "a student of law should be the jack of all trades and the master of legal issues.... A practitioner in legal and judicial field should know every ins and outs of society, and should prepare oneself as a master reader of human psyche as well. When it contextualises the cause of language, I feel the mastery over each and every nuance and the rock and bend of it is the prerequisite for the making of any legal professional ("Personal interviev", Lucknow, 3 March, 2010). Therefore, keeping in mind the prerequisites of making a successful legal professional and also that of its diversified nature, I am of the opinion that a legal language course should also include a small functional module on different issues of sociolinguistics with some discussion of Hinglish.

Works Cited

Bush, Donald W. and Charles P Campbell. *How to Edit Technical Documents.* Hyderabad: University Press, 2000.

Chemenviro. Lucknow: *BBDNITM,* Vol. 2, 2006.

Day, Robert, A. (2000). *Scientific English.* Hyderabad: University Press.

Myneni, S.R. (2006). *English for Pre-Law.* Hariyana: Allahabad Law Agency.

Kalam, APJ Abdul 'Legal System and its Dimensions.' *University News*, New Delhi: Association of Indian Universities. 41(49) December 8-14, 2003.

Proceedings of the National Seminar on Environmental Imbalances: Hazards and our Role. Lucknow: BBDNITM, 20 March, 2004.

Singh, R.P. (2005). *Functional Skills in Language and Literature*. New Delhi: OUP.

_____________ . (2002). *Professional Communication*. New Delhi : OUP.

Stevens, Anne M. Finding (2002). *Reading and Using the Law*. New Delhi: Thomson.

14

Shifting Paradigms and Eng(Hing)lish: Officialese or Globalese or Glocalese!

—*Dr. Anshu Surve*

It has become a cliché to say that English is the lingua franca of the globalised world. English is a legacy from the British who colonised countries to establish their supremacy on the 'Orient', to form "a class of persons, Indians in blood and color, but English in taste, in morals and in intellect." The colonial influence is still present with the persistence of English language but the global spread of English has resulted in the emergence of a diverse range of postcolonial varieties around the world. English language has undergone an unprecedented change from the situation when "Many native speakers cherished an image of themselves as the custodians of English language and therefore assumed that their discursive and pedagogical norms merit universal transfer."

To a fascinating new picture depicting the growth and evolution of various Englishes across the globe, the socio-cultural system in India has undergone tremendous change in the past ten years. India's transformed status from a Third World nation into a fast developing nation, from a dormant and static economy to the new emerging economic superpower has brought major changes in the socio-cultural fabric of India in terms of democratisation of education, infrastructural developments, social cohesion, availability and exploitation of the resources and consequently India, Indian being redefined with a separate identity of their own, not on the margins but leading the world from the forefront even when the entire world was engrossed in desperate attempts to counter recession. The linguistic consciousness of the nation propelled by modernisation and globalisation engaged the non-native speakers of English to make English their own. Now has emerged a class of people, already Indians in blood and colour, also Indian in their treatment, acceptance and utilisation of English. This had led to the emergence of new varieties of English with all regional and local peculiarities in the form of Indlish, Hinglish, or even Gujlish. Exploring the hegemonic status of postcolonial English, the social, cultural polities that direct its sustenance provide a clear and original account of the evolution of these varieties. These Englishes have developed unique and diversified properties as being localised, regionalised.

The initial seeds of English's ingress were laid more than 500 years ago on December 31, 1600, when Queen Elizabeth I granted the charter of the East India Company. It granted a monopoly on trade with India and the East to some merchants of London. And at that time English had no meaningful presence in India, as Sanskrit and Persian were the languages of social and administrative functions. Gopal and Mishra point out that "One cannot speak about the hegemony of English language in India without putting it in a continuum with Persian and Sanskrit." Mishra further adds that all the three languages were imposed on Indians "in order to conduct the business of the state or the hierarchical region."

It is generally supposed that Lord Macaulay imposed the study of English on Indians. Macaulay believed that the dialects commonly spoken among the natives of India contain neither literary nor scientific information. They are, moreover, so poor and rude that, until they are enriched from some other quarter, it will not be easy to translate any valuable work into them. He reiterated that the intellectual improvement of those classes of the people who have the means of pursuing higher studies could be effected only by means of a non-native language. They actively sought to impose British culture and language on the "natives," so that some of them can be converted into "civilised" Englishmen. The reasons of introducing English in the colonial India can be interpreted on the grounds of Said's Orientalism. Said defined Orientalism as:

> Orientalism is fundamentally a political doctrine willed over the Orient because the Orient was weaker than the West, which elided the Orient's difference with its weakness. . . . As a cultural apparatus Orientalism is all aggression, activity, judgment, will-to-truth, and knowledge (Orientalism).

Said outlines how Orientalist discourse was transferred from country to country and from political leader to author through the four elements: Expansion, Historical confrontation, Sympathy and Classification, in the eighteenth and nineteenth century. Macaulay, a true believer in the superiority of the West (occident) over the East (orient) declared that: "I have never found one among them who could deny that a single shelf of a good European library was worth the whole native literature of India and Arabia. The intrinsic superiority of the Western literature is, indeed, fully admitted by those members of the Committee who support the Oriental plan of education."

Macaulay's imposition of the education and subsequent English language can also be interpreted on the grounds of imperialism. Imperialism ascribes dual interpretation, one in terms of an action and the other describing an attitude. It is understood in relation to empire building, as the expansion of a nation's authority by territorial conquest establishing economic and political powers in other territories or nations, and when such encompasses non-contiguous "colonies" or "protectorates" then the term also subsumes colonialism. In that sense, most European seafaring powers were at one time or another colonialist and therefore imperialistic, regardless of their exploitation or benevolence toward their colonial possessions and people. The second connotation of the term describes the imperialistic attitude of superiority, subordination and dominion over foreign people—a chauvinism and comportment relegating foreign people to a lesser social and or political status. The British held the view that the natives of India cannot be educated by means of their mother tongue but by a more intelligible foreign language. Macaulay reiterated the claims of English as it stood preeminent even among the languages of the West and the vast intellectual wealth, which English hoarded is of far greater value than all the literature which 300 years ago was extant in all the languages of the world together.

Another reason for introducing English in India was that it was the language spoken by the ruling class; by the higher class of natives at the seats of Government and also that English was likely to become the language of commerce throughout the seas of the East. Moreover, a letter of Raja Rammohan Roy, addressed to Lord Amherst in the year 1823, is a profound evidence of local demand of English. Therefore it can be asserted that Indian speakers of the English language appear quite early in its colonial history, promising to fulfil the role of mediators between the East India Company and the markets over which the company sought control (Stein, 264). During the British Raj (1765-1947) Indian education was anglicised and English became thoroughly entrenched in an alien linguistic, cultural and administrative environment.

India, Post-colonialism, and the Global Hegemony of English

"The significance of Anglicism was not in determining educational policy in Britain's colonies, but rather in developing a discourse about English as the crucial medium for the purveyance of knowledge.... The effects of...the colonial Anglicist discourse were far less significant within colonial language policy than they are today within global institutions of support for English." (Alastair Pennycook, 94).

The various micro-practices of (cultural) power have helped to construct English language hegemony in multiple postcolonial contexts. English's complex and often paradoxical hegemonic status within the contemporary Indian context is mirrored on the global level where it has become the language of the world's political and economic elite. Among other domains, English is the either the *de facto* or official working language of: international organisations and conferences, scientific publication, international banking, economic affairs trade, global international politics, advertising for global brands, audio-visual cultural products (e.g., film, TV), international tourism, tertiary education, international air/sea traffic safety, international law, technology transfer, and internet communication (Graddol 8). According to David Crystal, it is the first language for 400 million people, most of them in the United States, the United Kingdom, Australia, New Zealand and South Africa. Furthermore, he reports that it has achieved "special status as a 'second' language in more than 70 countries," many of them ex-colonial countries such as India and Singapore where English is estimated to be spoken by at least another 400 million people. He further reports that English has become the most widely taught foreign language in schools around the globe with an estimated 1 billion students taking English ("English in the New World").

Pennycook attempted to apply a Foucauldian-inspired postcolonial critical theoretical analysis to the historical rise of English in the global context. His core argument is that colonialism has historically been, and continues to be, a crucial site of cultural production. He argues persuasively that English has also been, among other things, successfully—though problematically—cast as a great borrowing language, as a superior purveyor of reality, as paradoxically grammatically sophisticated and easy-to-learn, and even as a language embodying the masculine ideal (143-146). English; he contends, continues to be "indelibly linked with the reproduction of colonial relations" (214). In other works examining the global hegemony of English, Pennycook asserts that the colonial language policies of the past have "powerful continuity" with the present in terms of the ways in which they construct particular views about language.

Raj Dua predicts that English will only continue to strengthen its hegemonic position within the Indian linguistic configuration of power. The expansion of education, the momentum in the spread of English, the perpetuation of sociolinguistic inequality, the dominance of the English educated elites and intellectuals and their control of the state apparatus, and finally, the inertia of the Indian languages, elites and masses–all seem to reinforce the hold and spread of English for many more years to come, if not forever.

The term "desalinisation" seems to be of particular importance while talking about post-colonialism. In this case it means an intellectual process that persistently transfers the independence of former colonial countries into people's minds. The basic idea of this process is the deconstruction of old-fashioned perceptions and attitudes of power and oppression that were adopted during the time of colonialism. First attempts to put this long-term policy of "decolorising the minds" into practice could be regarded in the Indian population after India became independent from the British Empire in 1947. The co-existence of English and Englishes can be explained by a single underpinned process, which builds upon the constantly changing communication needs of the colonisers, the colonised and also those who are decolonising adapting to the global market demands. The influence of the colonial education on the culture and identity of the colonised; the impact of the developments in science and technology, global economy on the existing knowledge systems, and the efforts of the colonised to decolorise contribute to the symbiotic existence of English (of the native speakers) and the Englishes (of the non-native speakers).

English is a corpus driven by its own contradictions. English in India, one must properly foreground and contextualise English's historic role as the language of the cultural and administrative elite, its ideological and material connection to socio-economic stratification and upward mobility, its historic relation to other languages in India, particularly Hindi, and its status as an ever expanding world language which has become deeply imbricated in hegemonic notions of modernity, progress, and liberal (late) capitalism. The politics of English focuses on the ideological, material and political linkages between "global" English and global capitalism. English-contends Holborow, has become "the language of capitalism at the turn of the twenty-first century." For Holborow, as an essential human social practice, language is deeply implicated in the relations of power that collectively constitute the human social totality. Capitalism is at the heart of the contemporary totality. It therefore must "be the backcloth to the examination of the role of English today." In short, there continues to exist a complex– though unequal– mutually constitutive relation between the linguistic practices of (former) colonisers and (post) colonised.

As language is a poignant tool in the transmission of a specific culture not in its universality, but in its particularity as the language of a specific community with a specific history, written literature and orature are the main means by which a particular language transmits the images of the world contained in the culture it carries. "Language as communication and as culture is then a product of each other.... Language carries culture, and culture carries, particularly through orature and literature, the entire body of values by which we perceive ourselves and our place in the world.... Language is thus inseparable from ourselves as a community of human beings with a specific form and character, a specific history, a specific relationship to the world" (Ngugi). During 300 years of its existence in India English has immersed itself in the cultural fabric of the nation. Either as a 'link language', or 'utilitarian language', or 'the language of choice', 'language of opportunity', or 'the language of upward mobility' English with all its myriad varieties plays an important role in constructing human social, cultural world smiling in economic prosperity.

With the acceptance of India as an 'economic tiger', and the recognition of Indian prowess to mobilise the global resources, there is an obvious shift in the attitude of the world towards India, Indian culture and Indian languages. Vaishna Narang, a professor of linguistics at Delhi's JNU University, said the shift was noticeable. She too attributed the change to the country's growing prosperity. "There is a much, much greater sense of confidence in ourselves and our language. People no longer look at Indian music and culture and language as in any way substandard or vernacular." This pride in the Indian ways has influxed a confidence to transform and mould English the Indian way. The phenomenon is summed up by Ms Pamela Philipose, a senior editor with *The Indian Express* newspaper: "We are independent-minded and are speaking English like we are speaking Hindi-Vindi, Tamil-Shamil, and all.... We are moulding angrezi (English) and scolding it, we are mangling it and strangling it, under-mining it and over-mining it." Thus, making it our own-Indlish, Hinglish or even Gujlish as the distinct features of one corpus, i.e., Indology.

David Crystal, an honorary professor of linguistics at Wales University and the author of more than 50 books in the English languages, states that the growing popularity of the Indian culture implies that Hinglish will be a spoken language beyond the continent. According to him: "The certain phrases of Hinglish are to be global, since most Indians are engaged in the sphere of information technologies, use the Internet and send e-mails. This is still the language of the government, elite and mass media." The advance of outsourcing and especially the concentration of the foreign firms in Bangalore have resulted in the evolution of new words in English like "Bangalored" or "bangalorian." For instance, in 2005 a new edition of the *English Collins Dictionary* included 26 neologism of Indian origin... Jeremy Butterfield, the chief editor of the *Collins Dictionary* says, "The trend towards penetration of words belonging to different cultures will grow all the time. If new words are to be used widely enough, they are included in the dictionary and become English words." Scott Baldauf, staff writer of *The Christian Science Monitor* said that "Hinglish, a portmanteau of the words Hindi and English is more commonly seen in urban and semi-urban centers of India, but is slowly spreading its root into rural and remote areas via television and word of mouth, slowly achieving vernacular status."

Many speakers do not realise that they are incorporating English words into Hindi sentences or Hindi words into English sentences. This highly popular mixing of both the languages in most parts of northern and central India has grown from the fact that English is a popular language of choice amongst the urbane youth who finds itself comfortable in its glossary. It is already the medium for imparting education in many schools across the nation.

The advent of cable television and its pervasive growth has seen the masses exposed to a wide variety of programming from across the world. Bollywood has been instrumental in popularising Hinglish through the worldwide penetration of Bollywood movies.

Newspaper journalism and its enthusiastic appropriation of a foreign language by progressive local culture is another factor contributing to its localisation. Clearly newspapers imagine themselves as channels in the unstoppable flow of globalisation, and also localisation of global language. Explaining the phenomenon, Ajay Upadhyaya, former editor of *Hindustan Times* says, "They are targeting a reader who, even if not at home in English, wants to get into that mode, for joining a decent educational institution, for social status, cultural transformation, for employment and business" (Puri: 2007). By using Hinglish or Indlish or other varieties people are trying to normalise it within the landscape of unique economic and sociological conditions that force English and Hindi speaking people (professionals) to work together leading to the emergence of a unique language.

Hinglish, a lively hybrid is the outcome of Code Switching or Code Mixing. For instance:

> "That eve-teasing man thinks he's such a ranjha, but he's really a badmash. Chi-chi."
>
> In proper English it is expressed as: "The man who sexually harasses women thinks he's such a Romeo, but he's really ill-mannered. Ick."

Another example from Gujlish stands as:

> *Emna pappa January maa off (read 'o' as in own) thai gaya.*
>
> In Standard English it is expressed as: "His father passed away in January."

What we call as hybridisation is Code Switching and Code Mixing for academicians. Code switching is a term in linguistics (the scientific study of natural language) referring to using more than one language or variety of language in a conversation. Bilinguals, who can speak at least two languages, have the ability to use elements of both languages when conversing with another bilingual or multilingual. Code switching is the syntactically (syntax is the study of rules and principles to study the construction of sentences in natural languages) and phonologically (phonology is the use of sound to encode any spoken language) appropriate use of multiple varieties. Code switching can occur between sentences (intersentential) or within a single sentence (intrasentential). On the other hand, code mixing is the use of two languages at the same time or rather changes of language at the same time. Let me give you example of for both to make it clearer.

Example of Code-Switching

> Hey, there how are you?
> I am fine, long time no see, *aur bolo kya haal chal*?
> *Sab thik hai yaar, bas* am a little busy these days.

Okay, how's your work life?
Cool yaar, sab thik hai, acha hai.

When written in English it takes the shape as:

Hey there, how are you?
Am fine, long time no see, so what's up?
Everything is fine, but am a little busy these days.
Okay, how's your work life?
Cool buddy, everything is fine.

Example of Code Mixing

Yeh train *ka* time change *ho gaya hai kya*?
In proper English it becomes as: Has the train timing changed?

Code mixing has given rise to new languages like Hinglish (Hindi + English), Benglish (Bengali + English), Tanglish (Tamil + English), even across the border as Chinglish (Chinese + English), Pinglish (Pakistani+ English), Arabizi (Arabic +English) and so on.

David Crystal, a British linguist at the University of Wales, predicted that the world's 350 million Hinglish speakers might soon outnumber native English speakers in the United States and United Kingdom. English either as a first language or as the second language has survived through the centuries by marrying with different dialects, by borrowing words and phrases from almost every single language in the world now has a new and a long term alliance with local languages in this case Hindi. And this time it is market forces; global culture and the economics of globalisation that have given English a new global as well as local identity. Thus, from *Officialese* in the colonial period, from *Globalese* in the postcolonial period, English is fast gaining the status of *Glocalese* (a combination of global and local English) during the years of decolonisation.

Works Cited

Ahmad, Aijaz. (1992). *In Theory: Classes, Nations, and Literatures*. London: Verso.

Chatterjee, Partha. (1993). *The Nation and Its Fragments: Colonial and Postcolonial Histories*. Princeton: Princeton University Press.

De Swaan, Abram. (2001). *Words of the World*. Malden, MA: Blackwell Publishers, Ltd.

Dirks, Nicholas B. (2001). *Castes of Mind: Colonialism and the Making of Modern India*. Princeton: Princeton University Press.

Fanon, Frantz. (1959). "On National Culture." *The Wretched of the Earth*.

Ghosh, Partha S. (1996) "Language Policy and National Integration: The Indian Experience." *Ethnic Studies Report* 24.1:49-72.

Goldberg, David Theo Ato Quayson. (2002). "Introduction: Scale and Sensibility." *Relocating Postcolonialism*. Malden, MA: Blackwell Publishers.

Gopal, Sarvepalli. (1989). "Of Skylarks & Shirting: The English Language in India." *Encounter* 73 : 14-20.

Graddol, David. (1997). The Future of English: A Guide to Forecasting the Popularity of the English Language in the 21st Century. *The British Council*.

Holborow, Marnie. (1999). *The Politics of English: A Marxist View of Language*. London: Sage Publications.

Kandiah, Thiru. (1995). "Foreword: Centering the Periphery of English: Towards Participatory Communities of Discourse." *De-Hegemonising Language Standards: Learning from (Post) Colonial Englishes about English*. New York: St. Martin's Press.

Laitin, David D. (1989). "Language Policy and Political Strategy in India." *Policy Sciences* 22.

Mishra, Pramod K. (2000). "English Language, Postcolonial Subjectivity, and Globalisation in India." *ARIEL*.

Naz, Rasool. (2007). "Global Issues In Languages, Education And Development: Perspectives from Postcolonial Countries." Orient Longman.

Parakrama, Arjuna. (1995). *De-Harmonising Language Standards: Learning from (Post) Colonial Englishes about English*. New York: St. Martin's Press.

Pennycook, Alastair. (1998). *English and the Discourses of Colonialism*. London: Routledge.

Phillipson, Robert. (2000). "English in the New World Order: Variations on a Theme of Linguistic Imperialism and 'World' English." *Ideology, Politics and Language Policies: Focus on English*. Ed. Thomas Ricento. Amsterdam: John Benjamin Publishing Company.

Poddar, Prem. (2002). *Violent Civilities: English, India, Culture*. Denmark: Aarhus University Press.

Rahman, Tariq (1999). *Language, Education and Culture*. Oxford: Oxford University Press.

Rajan, R.S. (1993). "Fixing English: Nation, Language, and Subject." *The Lie of the Land: English Literary Studies in India*. Ed. R.S. Rajan. Delhi: Oxford University Press.

Raman, R.S. (1996). "The Future of English in India." *Contemporary Review* 268: 16-21.

Ramanthan, Vai. (1999). 'English Is Here to Stay': A Critical Look at Institutional and Educational Practices in India." *TESOL Quarterly* 33.2 (1999)

Romaine, Suzanne. (1997). "World Englishes: Standards and the New World Order." *World Englishes 2000*. Eds. Larry E. Smith and Michael Forman. University of Hawaii Press: Honolulu.

Said, E.W. (1978). *Orientalism*. London: Routledge and Kegan Paul.

Tully, Mark. (1997). "English: An Advantage to India?" *ELT Journal* 51.2:157-164.

Viswanathan, Gauri. (1989). *Masks of Conquest: Literary Study and British Rule in India*. New York: Columbia University Press.

E-references

http://www.cia.gov/cia/publications/factbook/geos/in.html

Crystal, David. "English in the New World." British Council Website. <http://www.britishcouncil.org>

15

Shifting Paradigms: Technology as an Effective Language Teaching Tool

—Dr. Anju Bala Agrawal

Computing is a radical new way to process and organise information and as such it represents a new form of language. Teachers can help English language learners by using computers and its various implications like software, e-mail, world wide web, etc. They need to be aware of the changes that may affect them in the future because technology will affect classrooms in developing language skill, vocabulary and other components of language learning. English language learner (ELL) students need a variety of language experiences. They need to hear language, write language, speak language and read language. We believe that computers can play an integral part in providing ELL students with valuable language experiences as they learn a new language. Verbal interaction and the use of a variety of language functions by English language learners can be facilitated by the use of the computer. This paper focuses on the use of computers, e-mail, world wide web, etc., in teaching.

Computer assisted instruction can be a supplemental teaching tool for teaching English language learners. Computers can provide rich and contextual environment. To learn vocabulary context and visual clues allow students to become active learners. Computers can incorporate various learning strategies as well as accommodate a variety of learning styles. One way to use computers for English Language Learners is to teach vocabulary. Kang and Dennis (1995) write, "Any attempt to treat vocabulary learning as learning of isolated facts certainly will not promote real vocabulary knowledge."[1] Students need to learn vocabulary in context and with visual clues to help them understand. Computers can provide this rich, contextual environment. The computer also allows students to become active learners in a one-on-one environment. Computers can incorporate various learning strategies as well as accommodate a variety of learning styles.

There are several ways in which technology can be used to improve reading ability. Most simple reading texts are also very primary in content. Older children may consider themselves too old to be reading such primary content books. Computers however can increase the interest level for older students while keeping the text simple and easy to read. Another benefit of using computers for reading instruction is that the computer offers immediate feedback on performance. They also can provide added practice when necessary. According to Case and Truscott (1999), students have been able to improve their sight word vocabulary, fluency, and comprehension. Computer-based reading instruction also allows for "increased interaction with texts, attention to individual needs, and increased independence through an ability to read texts they would not otherwise be able to read."[2] Technology can also be used to improve parent involvement in their child's education while improving the parents' literacy as well. Computer software and games provide many fun opportunities for students to practice literacy skills. There are numerous software packages for improving spelling, phonics skills, grammar, and sight word vocabulary. When English Language Learners are learning their second language, any and all language experiences are valuable to assist in reading ability.

Computers and software can help English language learners develop vocabulary skills and knowledge. They can also help ELL students develop their writing skills. Composition for beginning learners should be a guided activity so students do not become frustrated. Writing paragraphs in a language that is still somewhat unfamiliar to students can be difficult. When using a computer, however, the use of graphics can make this much more enjoyable. Using clip art can also help students to convey their thoughts more clearly.

Using electronic mail (e-mail) as a supplement to the classroom curriculum can be effective. The students voluntarily used the e-mail. They were self-motivated to use their new language in a new and creative way for them. One of the benefits of using electronic mail included the scrolling feature that allowed the students to view the incoming message and use its structure as a model for creating a response. The scrolling feature also allowed students to easily edit and revise. The major benefit of using e-mail as a language learning activity is the fact that students are using meaningful language and authentic text. Grammar skills can also be demonstrated and reinforced using computers. The teacher can direct students to somehow highlight a specific part of speech (e.g., nouns) throughout their writing. To highlight, students have a lot of choices, such as underlining, italicising, or changing the font size, colour or type. Using a computer as a medium for studying grammar is much more motivating for a student as opposed to writing with a pencil.

E-mail, a sub-part of computer is one of the easiest ways to the language teacher interested in e-learning. By creating an e-mail account, homework and feedback may be provided to students. E-mail story writing, information gathering, proof-reading of students' document and other such activities may help better teaching and learning of English language. Another aspect of technology is world wide web that constitutes an incredible resource material. One can use online material for use with activities and exercise type. One may open website into website in search of a better to best material.

It is our role to prepare English language teachers today who will be the classroom and school leaders of tomorrow. These new teachers must be ready to step into the status quo as well as to advance the profession by infusing technology into their teaching. If we want new English language arts teachers who can accomplish this feat, we as their teacher educators must be models of that process. We offer the following seven principles as touchstones for infusing technology into English language teacher preparation programs.

The first principle is the principle of introducing and infusing technology in context. It is the *sine qua non* of the list. Technology should be a naturally supporting background for both the content and the pedagogical content knowledge of English language. Teaching and learning English language is our goal; technology is a means by which we can reach that goal. To infuse this technology, we must build on what we know from research and practice—that is, "what we know about reading (and literature), writing, speaking, listening, viewing and visually representing" within our classes we can build the instructional scaffolds for students to advance as technology users while staying focused on teaching English language.

In a "Teaching Writing" method class, for example, the teacher educator, aware of the literature on peer response and student writing, asks students in class to post their drafts on the computer screens. Students then move from one computer to another, first reading classmates' rough draft and then offering revision suggestions in writing. Students continue to move from one computer to another, stopping at each to read and then write responses and suggestions. When the authors return to their own computer, they find on the screen a wealth of responses to consider as they set about revising the draft. After the students/ preservice teachers experience the activity, they reflect on the process, determine its rationale based on "what we know" about teaching writing, and then articulate that rationale. The discussion then turns to how technology aided this experience, how it is different from a similar paper-and-pencil activity.

To carry this experience to the next level of learning, Carol's writing methods students engage in ongoing email correspondence with students at a local middle school. The methods students help the middle school students with their writing, offering suggestions for revision and serving as a real, appreciative audience. The middle school students get substantial, individualised help with their language, and the methods students get to know middle school students while learning the instructional revision approaches and communication skills beneficial for young adolescents

The second principle is focus on the importance of technology as a literary tool. The impact technology has had on our language—how we read, write, view and visually represent information. Words used everyday such as windows, files, menu, and mouse have new meanings and mental images; headlines include such prefixes as cyber, and hyper; media ads and discussions include such terms as dot com, url, and www. Clearly, ad creators, writers, editors and producers assume that members of the reading public understand this new language. These vast lexicon changes reflect not only a vocabulary shift but also a thinking shift. We have new "pictures" in our reading and listening memories, pictures that have moved into our daily communication. Just as technology is influencing language and reading, it has already had an impact on writing and teaching writing. As students use computers more (pen and paper less) to compose, the way we teach writing is greatly affected. Seeing a student's writing drafts in process will be harder because they will embed and internalise their own recursive writing process. In turn, instructionally guiding students through their writing process will be more challenging. However, we do not need to abandon our awareness that both oral and written discourse contain like elements and follow processes that teachers need to understand in order to help students develop and extend communication skills. We need to acknowledge that technology has enlarged these processes to include visual discourse, which is closely linked with oral and written discourse. To help preservice teachers see the impact of technology texts on reading.

The third principle is model English language teaching and learning while infusing technology. One of the critical lessons to learn as a teacher in a technologically rich environment is that we will never be completely caught up; we will never know everything. We will constantly learn with and from our students. As a result, the English language arts classroom will necessarily become learning-centred and learner-centred, with both teacher and student functioning in both roles. To ensure that our soon-to-be teachers understand this shift, we need to create and model how this kind of classroom looks and functions. At the same time the teacher and students are using technology to aid their own writing processes, the teacher demonstrates the MOST important element of modelling technology integration—taking risks, trying out new technologies with students, and relying on the students to supplement their instruction.

The fourth principle is to evaluate critically when and how to use technology. Teacher educators, as well as our students, need to be critical consumers of technology, to be thoughtful users who question, reflect, and refract on the best times and ways to integrate technology. To be models of this process, we need to be critical evaluators in our own methods classes and involve our students in that process. The goal of this critical analysis of technology integration is to articulate and internalise a process for questioning and probing both the why and how of infusing technology through various applications, programmes, websites, methods of teaching, or communication tools. If teachers use this process, they will become teacher-researchers in their own classrooms. They will systematically pose questions, examine when it is appropriate and useful to integrate technology and when it is not, and follow through with the implementation and evaluation of the technology use. In such a process they will be informed, adjusted, or validated by systematic classroom observation. They will seek to discover "where the truth lies."

The fifth principle is to provide a wide range of opportunities for using technology within the content. According to Bertram Bruce, students should "learn technology, learn through technology, learn about technology."[3] To provide diverse experiences and perspectives, we can infuse opportunities for students to learn to work the technology itself and to develop those technological skills through the study of English language content pedagogy. For example, by saving drafts of their writing in individual e-folders, which are situated within the class e-folder on a server, students learn a technology skill while also using the technology as writers who save their texts in process. As they then consider how and why they might use this class folders set-up and process when they become teachers, they are reflecting about technology and its real application. Possibilities abound for the integration of technological opportunities that relate to English language arts content. Students can create web sites, "read" the Internet, participate in online discussions (List Serves, real-time chat rooms, asynchronous discussions, videoconferences), and use all kinds of writing process skills on computers, create texts, add content and pedagogy merge in such experiences.

The sixth principle is to examine and determine ways of analysing, evaluating, and grading English language technology products. Technology products are new genres for most of us, and they require a new set of process skills. Understandably we may be uncertain about how to evaluate the students' process, the quality of the work, and the product itself. When we infuse technology into our English language teacher preparation programs, we as teacher educators come face to face with these challenges. We are pushed to examine and think about these newfound forms, genres, and products. With our students we can work to determine the best ways of evaluating and grading them. We can make these kinds of decisions by:

- Keeping the content up front—that is, what is the content of the product?
- Determining the objective for the project itself—that is, what was the goal of the process and the product? What were students to learn?
- Using that information to create rubrics and evaluation descriptors. One way of finding appropriate evaluation and grading processes for technology products is to have students locate a variety of web sites on a subject and analyse their parts and effective.

The seventh principle is to emphasize issues of equity and diversity in technology accessibility. English language teachers should be sensitive to student needs so that all students, regardless of differences, receive encouragement, support, and opportunities to learn. We need for our soon-to-be-teachers to both witness and understand the diverse accessibility to technology their school and their students will have. And they must consider this variability in their class assignments, opportunities for use in the school day, and homework expectations. In our teacher preparation programmes we need to reference this challenge in our own assignments, classroom work, and expectations. We have also learned that computers cannot be understood simply as tools, considered in isolation from the social, political, or economic contexts in which they are developed and in which they continue to be used. Technology is a richly embroidered artifact of a culture and as teacher educators our future teachers and we need to acknowledge that fact. We need to devise ways of responding and coping with the inequities the division of computer access will be between poor children and the middle and upper class children.

The increased use of the Internet and the proliferation of websites have brought about a new set of basic skills for students (and even adults) to master information literacy skills. Paul Gilster, in his book, *Digital Literacy* defines this kind of literacy as "the ability to understand and use information in multiple formats from a wide range of sources when it is presented via computers."[4] This shift to a learning-centered classroom does not mean, however, that the teacher is obsolete. Instead, it demands that the teacher's role change from that of an "information-giver" to one of "designer" and "director" of instruction. Teachers need to design worthwhile problems for students to solve and worthwhile projects for students to pursue. As students work on these activities, the teacher "directs" the students, offering suggestions and serving as a respondent for their emerging insights.

Using the principles we offer above, we suggest that English language methods classes can infuse technology in a way that does not interfere with the content pedagogy but supports it in a way that actively involves students and prepares them with the technical and pedagogical skills for creating the new learning-centered classroom. The teaching strategies are needed to accommodate the computers. As students' access to information improves so that they can go beyond what the teacher or school provide, and can locate information much closer to its source, the relationship between teacher and student inevitably changes. Some students may have a much stronger practical knowledge base and operational under-standing of computer technology than their teacher does. Recognising this, we need to work out how to acknowledge and use their skills and bring our own teaching expertise and critical awareness to bear in choosing appropriate ways of working with computers.

To sum up, computer-assisted instruction has been shown in a range of studies to facilitate learning in a variety of ways. Computers can be used to aide in teaching English Language Learners in core academic subjects, such as reading and writing.

Computers can aide in vocabulary development as well as verbal language development. Ultimately, however, it is important to recognise that computers are not a substitute for effective teaching. Computers are a tool—they are simply one type of supplement to the regular curriculum in teaching English Language Learners as they develop their English language skills.

References

1. Kang, S.H. & Dennis, J.R. (1995). "The Effects of Computer-enhanced Vocabulary Lessons on Achievement of ESL Grade School Children" *Computers in the Schools*, 1999, 25-35.
2. Case, C. & Truscott, D. (1999). "The Lure of Bells and Whistles: Choosing the Best Software to Support Reading Instruction." *Reading and Writing Quarterly: Overcoming Learning Difficulties*. 361-369.
3. Bruce, B. (1998). Dewey and Technology. *Journal of Adolescent & Adult Literacy*, p. 222.
4. Gilster, Paul (1997). *Digital Literacy*. New York: John Wiley & Sons.

16

Shifting Paradigms in English Language Teaching in India: Ruminations on Hinglish

—*Dr. Ravindra Pratap Singh*

Noted Indian critic C.D. Narsimhaiah suspected in 1990 that "we hardly have any standards of our own-so much of work is derivative-this so even with regard to our own literature–the reason why it is hard to tell an Indian critic by his work. We write now on the model of Leavis, Trilling, Northrope Frye: and now like a Sunday Supplement reviewer and cover the entire gamut of critical activity as it obtains in England and America. We have, if one way says so, a circumference, hardly a centre." Although the statement was made with reference to critical and creative writing in English yet it has some bearings on English language also. The current scene of English in India reminds me the statement of B. N. Singh, when he states that "the role of English in colonial domination on the one hand, and its reception by Indians on the other, are being frequently questioned even within the English Departments of Indian universities." English, today in India, has become as popular as western attire. In the phrase of CEM Joad we can say that so many people in so many ways that it has started losing its shape are wearing English. The Hinglish is a result of this trend. I quote Gurucharan Das who finds:

> ...two trends that are likely to determine our linguistic future. One is the rapid spread of English across India; the second is the unprecedented popularity of Hindi. The collision of the two we call Hinglish, but should, in fact, be

> called Inglish because it is increasingly pan India' street language and borrows from all vernaculars. Mixing English with our mother tongues has been going on for generations, but what is different this time around is that Inglish is both aspirational language of the lower classes and the fashionable idiom of the upper class drawing rooms. Inglish is the stylish language of Bollywood, FM radio and national advertising. Advertisers in particular have been surprised by the terrific resonance of the slogans such as, 'life ho to aise', 'josh machine', and 'dil mange more.'
>
> (*The Times of India,* Lucknow, July 16, 2006)

So Hinglish or Inglish is a special dish that we may call *Lapsi* turned out of that flour which some unskilled bakers were trying to bake into fine breads. Anyway, we cannot ignore the existence of Hinglish in the same way, as we can't help snatching Western outfits from Indian bodies. Expressions like *Woh to tensaniyay gaya,* "Sir I wanted to complete the task but sir *kya karta masla hi aisa fans gaya...,*" "*kal din bhar* busy *tha,* night *me* assignment complete *kiya,*" "*Ama kya* gorgeous top *tha*" are common expressions today. In contemporary *Desi* popular communication pattern we should not startle even listening one friend asking another not to interrupt the communication flow, by saying "When I speak *aiyyeai* speak, when you speak *youayyai* speak, no speak in middle."

English in India has not always offered a bed of roses; it has faced many a shocks and jerks. With every bend and stride, it has faced scorching strokes from regions, ethnic centers, and native languages *but* with its mercantile forces and lovey-dovey nature it has assimilated with the Indian language. While flaunting Hinglish we should not understand it baseless or something brought to the board by a magical wand, it has a long and solid ideology-a constant effort of the *Desi* Anglicans.

It should be taken as the postcolonial assertion in culture and language. Before focusing the modes and patterns of the Hinglish or Inglish, I feel it an urgent task to briefly introduce postcolonialism. Post-colonialism, in literature, is a discourse that reacts to the discourse of colonisation. It concentrates on the writings that deal with the issues of de-colonisation or the political, social and cultural independence of people who were formerly colonised and subjugated during the colonial rule. 'What makes a literature, a postcolonial literature?' is an issue of debate? I personally feel that the postcolonial literature emerges out of the identity of the self, the sense of self importance, social or cultural change or erosion, voice against the misuse of power, voice against exploitation, colonial abandonment, alienation, gender analysis, gender identity, racial identity and nationalism. Robert J. C. Young writes on the nature of post-colonialism:

> Post-colonialism names a politics and philosophy of activism that contests that disparity, and so continues in a new way the anti colonial struggle of the past. It asserts not just the right of African, Asian and Latin American peoples to access resources and material well being, but also the dynamic power of their cultures, cultures that are now intervening in and transforming the societies of the west.

Post-colonialism, starting from the days of the vanishing of colonies to the advent of globalisation has seen different shades. A serious debate is seen in academic gatherings, and read through the pages of the academic journals and books but there seems to be a great deal of uncertainty on the denotation of the term. Many of the debates among postcolonial scholars centre on the fact that which writing should be included in the postcolonial canon. Much of the discussion among postcolonial scholars involves the criticism of the term "postcolonial" itself. In addition, it is seldom mentioned but is quite striking that very few actual authors accept and use the term to label their own writing.

It should be taken into account that postcolonial theory functions as a sub-category under the nomenclature of "cultural studies." It is mostly undertaken as an alliance of the leftist radical literary theory and criticism generally comprising the Marxist, Gramscian, Foucauldian, and various feminist schools of thought, among others. All these ideologies aim at analysing and evaluating the inequitable and inappropriate power structure as expressed in culture, literature, film and art etc. In general the exponents and followers of it assert themselves as politically engaged and committed to some variety or the other of the liberation process.

Post-colonialism may be seen as a freshening shower on the

piercing and scorching colonial hangover. Along with different political means of assertions and agitation against colonialism, language seems to be the most obvious and pervasive tool, especially in countries that have been under alien/foreign dominion. In this context Homi K. Bhabha writes:

> The creation content in the invisible but insistent structure of linguistic difference does not lead us to some general, formal acknowledgement of the function of the sign. The ill-fitting robe of language alienates content in the sense that it deprives it of an immediate access to a stable or holistic reference 'outside' itself. It suggests that social significations are themselves being constituted in the very act of enunciation, in the disjunctive, non-equivalent split of *énoncé* and *enunciation* thereby undermining the division of social meaning into an inside and an outside. (*The Location of Culture,* 64)

So language "provides the terms by which reality may be constituted" and "the names by which the world may be 'known'" (Introduction, *Post-colonial Studies Reader,* 283). The effects of language in a colonised country transcend the basic function of speech as communication and acquire a more cultural significance. Ngugi Wa Thiong'o writes in this context, "Language carries culture, and culture carries, particularly through orature and literature, the entire body of values by which we come to perceive ourselves and our place in the world" (Ngugi, "The Language of African Literature," *Post-colonial Studies Reader*, 290).

With reference to imperialism vs. native language Ngugi further writes: "What is the difference between politician who says Africa cannot do without imperialism and the writer who says Africa cannot do without European Languages?" (*Decolonising the Mind,* 1986, Ngugi, 'The Language & African Literature', *Decolonising the Mind,* 26)

In his view, Language was, "the most important vehicle through which colonial power fascinated and held the soul prisoner. The bullet was the means of physical subjugation; Language was he means of spiritual subjugation." (Ngugi. *Decolonising The Mind,* 09)

Such importance given to language raises the great political/

linguistic debate: How English language should be treated in the commonwealth nations? Should it be accepted, rejected or re-oriented? Does writing in English suggest the betrayal of the mother tongue or the assumption of a new post-colonial identity? Is English a "postcolonial anomaly, the bastard child of the Empire" (Salman Rushdie, 'Introduction', *Mirrorwork: 50 Years of Indian Writing, 1947-1997*) or has it evolved to fit the need of its speakers in the post-colonial world?

Englishmen have left the territories but English language still pervades among classes. Even in the literary world, English bears the mark of socio-economic distinction. "The English language is a tool of power, domination and elitist identity and of communication across continents" (Braj. B. Kachru, "The Alchemy of English," *Postcolonial Studies Reader*, 291). Two of the major responses to the pervasiveness of English in postcolonial writings include rejection and subversion.

Being afraid of the encroachment of English on the indigenous culture and traditions Ngugi Wa Thiong'o, calls for the complete rejection of the imperial language and concludes, "The bullet was the means of the physical subjugation, and Language was the means of the spiritual subjugation" ("The Language of African Literature, *Post-colonial Studies Reader*, 287). He believes that the retention of the colonisers' language prevents a nation from achieving the true independence.

Working on the ideology as mentioned above, the soil of Africa and that of India produced special varieties of English with more earthy and local smell. In a traditionally oral culture of Africa, English in its written form is not only an alien language but also a foreign concept. I find it a suitable place to cite references from some of the African postcolonial texts. Vera Ibwe, in his novel *Nehanda* writes in favour of retaining orality:

> Our people know... power of words. It is because of this that they desire to have words continuously spoken and kept alive. We do not believe that words can become independent of the speech that bore them, of the humans who controlled and gave birth to them... The paper is the stranger's own peculiar custom. Among ourselves, speech is not like the rock. Words cannot be taken from the people who create them. People are their words.... (*Nehanda*, 40)

Further it is significant when he writes, "words must be kept alive. They must always be spoken." (*Nehanda,* 42) It gives the feel of a 'Return to Nature.' Language is one of the most important issues in postcolonial studies. During colonisation, the colonisers usually imposed their language over the countries and countrymen they colonised, checking the natives from speaking their mother tongues and vernaculars. It is evident in the context of India. In some cases the colonisers diplomatically banned the native languages. Literature is replete with the illustrations that how students were demoted, humiliated, or even beaten for speaking their native language in the colonial schools. In response to the systematic imposition of the colonial languages, some postcolonial writers and activists advocate a complete return to the use of the indigenous languages. Others see the language (e.g. English) imposed by the coloniser as a more practical alternative, using the colonial language both to enhance inter-nation communication.

The practice of decolonising the mind by language is very vehement in Africa. Chinu Achebe explains the dectonising the mind by the weapon of language, in the following words:

> The price of a world language must be prepared to pay in submission to many kind of use. The African writer should aim to use English in a way that brings out his message best without altering the language to the extent that its value as a medium of international exchange will be lost. He should aim at fashioning out English, which is at once universal and able to carry his peculiar experience..., But it will have to be new English, still in full communication with its ancestral home but attend to suit its new African surroundings. (Chinue Achebe. 'The African Writer and the English Language' in *Morning Yet on Creation Day,* 61-2)

In India, Indian English in its different shades gives the pure Indian smell. Moreover we can say that English has been Indianised. It may be seen as an Indian language. The following features of the Indianisation of English as enumerated by Archana Burde are significant here:

a) The Indianness in Indian English is the result of the acculturation of English in the linguistically and culturally pluralistic context (of India).

b) Acculturation is language change and language adaptation determined by the parameters of Indian Culture.
c) Indian English is the result of the institutionalisation of an interference variety of English.
d) Interference is indicative of linguistic changes caused by pluralistic language contact situations.
e) Indianisms are deviations.
f) Indianisms in Indian English are linguistic manifestations of pragmatic needs for appropriate language use in a new linguistic and cultural context.
g) Deviations refer to the linguistic and cultural nativisation of a variety of English.
h) Nativisation is the result of new 'unEnglish' linguistic and cultural setting in which English is used as a tool of communication.

(Krishnaswamy and Burde, *Linguistic Colonialism*, 31)

On the form and feature of Indian English, Keki N. Daruwala says in his 'Mistress':

> You can make her out the way she speaks her consonants bludgeon you; her argot is rococo, her latest 'slang' is available in classical dictionaries... She will not stick to vindoloo, but talks of roasts, pies, and pomfrets grilled. She speaks of contreau and not cashew arrack, which her father once distilled. No, she is not Anglo-Indian... She is Indian English, the language that I use. (Keki N. Daruwala: *The Keeper of the Dead*)

Kamala Das, another doyen of Indian Writing in English, also has something to reflect on the Indianisation of English and related issues:

> I am Indian, very brown, born in Malabar; I speak three languages, write in two, and dream in one. "Don't write in English," they said, English is not your mother tongue. Why not leave critics, friends, visiting cousins, every one of you and me alone? Why not let me speak in any language I like? The language I speak becomes mine, its distortions, its

> queernesses, all mine, mine alone. It is half English, half Indian, and funny perhaps, but it is honest, it is a human as I am human, don't you see? It voices my joys, my longings, my hopes, and it is useful to me as cawing is to crows or roaring to the lions... ('An Introduction' reptd in *The Arnold Anthology of Post-colonial Literatures in English* (ed.) John Thine: 717.)

Language is, therefore, one of the very potent means of bringing out revolution in a very peaceful way. Words have greater power than guns and they wield greater impact than the orders of the sovereign. Hindi folk wisdom *Jahan Na jaye Ravi wahan jayen Kavi* speaks volumes on it.

In the countries like India and Africa where Indian English and African English have shaped themselves into specific and equally potent varieties of the British English (Received Pronunciation), it has become clearer that re-shaping the Language is a potent means for strong thinking against colonialism and it should be there. We can further illustrate it in the words of Dennis Walder:

> Whatever the generalisations, suspicions and admonitions of critics, politicians, theorists and legislators, the writers are eager to go on writing, whether in their new, 'borrowed' tongue or in the old original. Their specific histories decide their position for them as much as they themselves feel they have done. Yet the forms of language, of English, adopted are very varied, and one best thought of, in terms of continuum, upon which different positions are defined in terms of usage and status–themselves varying over time of space. (*Post-colonial Literatures in English: History, Language, Theory*, 1998).

The postcolonial English reflects 'a semiotic system of modernity' and a vernacular language. I have suggested the term 'Junta English' for it. The Junta English emanates out of an interaction between the King's English and *bhasha;* the vernacular. It also represents the Indian national culture for a receiver of it across the seas. The introduction of postcolonial English is mainly a blend of nationalist pride and the aspiration and need of a cross-border communication. It is a pattern of grafting the local aspiration to the global segments and settings. On the nature of the post-colonial world, Robert J.C. Young's statement may be cited:

> The postcolonial world is a place of mixture. Since Mc Luhan invented the concept of global village in 1968, the cultures of the world have become increasingly interlayered, mixed and juxtaposed. Largely a product of technology, of instantaneous media systems by means of which anything that happens in the world can instantly be seen everywhere else. (p.129)

This trend of globalisation has also produced a special kind of forward and backward flow of communication and related segments in language. The following statement of Barrie Axford is discernible here:

> The effect of global processes and institutions is to relativise national and local identities and practices and to establish transnational and post-national forms that marginalise or bypass local rules and values. At the same time many global practices are subject to an implicit, but sometimes an explicit, 'localisation', to fit local tastes but also to protect local identities. (554)

We have adapted English in a special way in India, chiselling it as per our need. "India is the most talkative country in the world, it often seems, and it comes at you in almost 200 languages, 1652 dialects and a million signs and slogans screaming out of every store and taxicab." Citing the above statement of Pico Iyer, Neelam Raaj writes:

> In this linguistic mélange, if there is one language that's making itself audible across the country, it is countrified English. Used by everyone from cabbies to CEOs, it is fast becoming the country's best –loved (and most hated) characteristic. It is inventive, witty, colourful, and uniquely Indian because we speak like that only. If someone is a big bore, you can tell him to stop pukkaoing you. If you don't want to work, you can chill yaar. If you want to show appreciation, you say it s kiskass maga (in Kannada English) (p.10)

She further writes, "It is definitely not the Queen's English. Call it the Maharani's English if you will. There is nothing royal about it though, it is about the masses." It is that which I propose as Junta English. The orientation of English in Indian context is not the act of common man only. The great masters of language like Salman Rushdie, Raja Rao, Mulk Raj Anand, Amitav Ghosh, etc., have added much to it besides the contribution of the poets whom I have illustrated earlier. Raja Rao writes in the Preface to *Kanthapura:*

> We are all instinctively bilingual, many of us writing in our own language and in English. We cannot write like the English. We should not. We cannot write only as Indians. We have grown to look at the large world as part of us. Our method of expression therefore has to be dialects, which will some day, prove to be as distinctive and colourful as the Irish or the American. Time alone will justify it.

Neelam Srivastava cites the following passage from Salman Rushdie's *Midnight's Children* and mentions the transformation of English in Indian context:

> He wallops me in the back, toppling me forwards into Mary's arms. 'Hey little wrestle! You look fine!' 'But so thin Jesus! They haven't been feeding you properly? You want cornflower pudding? Banana mashed with milk? Did they give you chips? And Hanif booms, 'Yes, tickety-boo! The boy is really ship-shape! Come on phaelwan: a ride in my Packard, okay?' And talking at the same time is Mary Pareira, 'Chocolate cake,' she is promising, 'laddoos, pista-ki-lauz, meat samosas, kulfi. So thin you got, baba, the wind will blow you away.'...Your Pia aunty is waiting! My God, you see if we don't have a number one good time!'(p. 239)

G.V. Desani has a great impact on Rushdie. His novel *All About H. Hatterr* has already created a landmark in molding English in Indian context. Rushdie has not only used the expressions like, 'Lovely Lassi, Funtabulous Falooda and Bhel-Puri Bombay Fashion' (215), he has also used the literal translations of the typical vernacular speech and expressions. The following passage is worth mentioning here, "Mother raper! Violator of your daughters! ... Rapist! Arre' my God they found the badmaash! There he *is*!'... 'So, mister: is it you? Mister Hindu, who defiles our daughters? Mister Idolater who sleeps with his sister?" (pp. 76-77)

Why and how this all happens with language, with English– is a complex question, although I have already fccused on it. As a rejoinder to it, Neelam Srivastava cites Bakhtin and writes, "Heteroglossia, namely the dialogic interrelation of different registersand dialects that gravitate within the orbit of a national language, is in constant tension with the tendency towards linguistic centralisation and unification" (Bakhtin1981: 272-73). In India, rather than a national language, there is a "national linguistic system, composed of a variety of different languages." (p.140)

All the above discussed facts, and circumstances have produced a variety of English in India in the postcolonial phase which is running side by side the already established Indian English and, therefore, I find the expression–Junta English more suitable for it. On such an English Neelam Raaj writes, "call it Hinglish, Binglish, Punglish, Tamilish... Everyone's mixing it up. Chutnified English is uniting India as never before" (*The Times Of India*, Lucknow, January 11, 2009, 10). The following list of expressions given by Neelam reflects the spirit and flavour of the Junta English:

Binglish (Bambaiyya English)

Timepass: A national pastime.

Item: Refers to a sexy damsel. ("Kya item hai")

Filmi: means melodramatic like a Hindi film. ("Don't be filmi")

Yaar: A friend. ("Where's the party yaar?")

Fully faltoo: Condemning something as utterly useless.

Panga: Never take issue with someone bigger and stronger.

Kanglish (The Kannada Version)

Aa?: It's the universal question tag which can transform any English into Kannada. ("Leftaa?, Righta?")

Adjushtu: Adjust. Originates from the accommodating nature of all. Bangalorians. ("Sir, one more banana buying means it will adjust within 10 rupees.")

Beautifully chu-chumbe: An idea that is laudable.

Seas go salty: When you add salt to the sea, you question the authenticity of a pro.

Kick-ass maga: To express appreciation

Tamilish (Tamil + English)

Machan: The equivalent of the Hindi *yaar* and the Australian mate, it's used only about a thousand times every day. ("What's up machan?")

Da: Term of address for friends and those younger. Feminine: *din*. ('I love you, da' was the title of a Tamil film)

Punjlish (Punjabi-Speak)

Backside: Rear of a building. ("Backside pe entry hai").

Tension: Everybody has it. ("I am having so much tenshun these days!").

Hazaar: Upamanyu Chatterjee used hazaar f*****d hazaar times in *English August* and it slipped into everyday coinage.

Fundas: Short for fundamentals. ("*Tumhara funda hi galat hai*").

(*The Times of India*, Lucknow, January 11, 2009, p.10)

Hinglish or Inglish is smoothly gaining strong foothold in our speech communities. Mohd. Tariq, a student of MA semester II at Lucknow University, comments on the popularity of Hinglish, "Hinglish or Inglish, which is an upcoming trend in North Indian speech pattern, is a linguistic and cultural interface. A debate has been started in the print and electronic media because somehow it has accepted it." Mohd. Ahmad, his classmate, finds the use of Hinglish as "the most fascinating trend among the youngsters." The reference books and established dictionaries are very easily and smoothly incorporating these popular Hindustani expressions in their body and content. Hesitations in accepting it is shattered in the postcolonial milieu. Willingly or unwillingly people are getting attracted to it. With such gestures, Hinglish merrily moves on, and this democratic trend and all-inclusive nature of English have spanned English as a universal language.

Works Cited

Axford Barrie etal. (2002). *Politics: An Introduction,* London: Routledge, 2002.

Ashcroft, Bill, Griffiths, Gareth and Tiffins, Helen (Eds). (1989). *The Empire Writes Back: Theory and Practice in Post-Colonial Literatures.* New York: Routledge.

Bhabha, Homi K. (1991). *The Location of Culture.* London: Verso.

Chinua Achebe. (1954). 'The African Writer and the English Language' in *Morning Yet on Creation Day.*

Das, Kamala. 'An Introduction' reptd. in *The Arnold Anthology of Post-colonial Literatures in English,* ed. John Thine.

Deleuze, Gilles & Féllix Guattari. (1987). *A Thousand Plateaus: Capitalism and Schizophrenia.* Vol. 2. Trans. Brian Massumi. Minneapolis: U of Minnesota. p. 1987.

Gandhi, Leela. (2007). *Postcolonial Theory: A Critical Introduction.* New Delhi: Oxford University Press.

Kachru, Braj. (1983). *The Indianisation of English: The English Language in India.* New Delhi: Oxford University Press.

Daruwala, Keki N. (1982). *The Keeper of the Dead.* New Delhi: OUP.

Krishnaswamy N. & Burde Archana S. (2004). *Linguistic Colonialism and the Expanding English Empire: The Politics of Indian's English.*

Narsimhaiah, C.D. (1990). *The Indian Critical Scene: Controversial Essays.* Delhi: BR Publishing House.

Nayar, Pramod K. (2008). *Postcolonial Literature: An Introduction.* Delhi: Pearson Longman.

Ngugi wa Thiong'o. (1981). *De-colonising the Mind: The Politics of Language in African Literature.* Portsmouth, NH: Heinemann.

Raaj, Neelam. "Jab we Speak." *The Sunday Times of India.* Lucknow. January 11, 2009.

Rao, Raja. *Kanthapura.* New Delhi: Oxford University Press.

Rushdie, Salman. (1992). *Imaginary Homelands.* New York: Granta.

______________ (1981). *Midnight's Children.* London: Picador.

Singh, B.N. "Indianising English Studies: A Postcolonial Project" *Lucknow Journal of Humanities.* Vol. 1. No. 2. July-Dec. 2004.

Srivastava, Neelam (2008). *Secularism in the Postcolonial Indian Novel*. London: Routledge.

The Times of India. Lucknow. January 11 2009.

Walder, Dennis (1998). *Postcolonial Literatures in English History, Language, Theory*. Malden: Blackwell.

Young, Robert J.C. (2007). *Post-colonialism: A Very Short Introduction*. New Delhi: Oxford University Press.

17

Shifting Facets of English Language Teaching in India: Oscillating between English and Hinglish

—Dr. Manju Ojha

As it is said that literature is the mirror of society, in the same approach films are also the mirror of society. Films are the means of entertainment to the people in the world. Television is the means of support to the people in the worlds, which shapes their attitude, opinion, and make them to think before they start doing a particular work. The most beautiful aspect is it helps the people to know about different religions, places, and important things to do about the past and the future.

The media makes billions of dollars with the advertising they sell and that we are exposed to. We buy what we are told to be good, after seeing thousands of advertisings we make our buying decisions based on what we saw on TV, newspapers or magazines, to be a product we can trust and also based on what everyone else that we know is buying and their decision are also based on the media. These are the effects of mass media in teenagers, they buy what they see on TV, what their favourite celebrity advertises and what is acceptable by society based on the fashion that the media has imposed on them. There are some positive and negative influences in young people. Last year released movie Ajab Prem ki Gajab Kahani left a great impact on youngsters when the hero of the movie conversed in Hinglish. Youngsters who are weak in English started using this language. Nowadays you see on TV and in this ad:

> Models use nice *khushbu* [fragrance]. My daughter who is in 3rd standard taking convent education and good at English still liked this ad very much. In the modern scenario Hinglish has become very popular in India and definitely it is also influencing the English language teaching, and teachers are becoming habitual to use this language in classrooms. Even English medium students are also fond of using Hinglish words and enjoy it.

Hinglish may be called a hybrid of English and now Hindi which has its own dictionary. Is it really a pukka way to speak? Hey! "badmash" where are you coming from? Are you a "badmash"? And if you had to get somewhere in a hurry, would you make an "airdash"? Maybe you should be at your desk working; instead you're reading this as a "timepass." These are some examples of Hinglish, in which English and the languages of India overlap, with phrases and words borrowed and re-invented and leave a great influence on teaching.

Hinglish is also used on the Indian subcontinent, with English words blending with Punjabi, Sindhi, Urdu and Hindi, and also within Indian families to enliven Standard English. Nowadays many words of Hindi have got absorbed into English. Really English is oscillating between English and Hinglish.Even many scholars have collected words for a dictionary of the hybrid language.

In the global world where we are living today, the whole world is dependent on effective means of communication. Language is the medium of communication; it is radical that a certain degree of perfection be achieved in the language. Acquisition of language requires the development of the vocabulary and comprehension powers of the learner. Unless the student is placed in an atmosphere that helps him/her to imbibe and develop these skills, language learning will pose a problem. For a learner to be proficient in the language, nuances of the language need to be learnt. In place of enhancing vocab youngsters are using Hinglish. Much of it came from British rule when it was ruling in India. The exchanges of words among the British white population and the Indians started. It's also sometimes a secret language, which is being used by many Indians. For the young are linguistic magpies, borrowing from any language, accent or dialect that seems fashionable. Other words are "haina" - a Hindi tag phrase, stuck on the sentences and meaning "isn't it?" Balti - bucket, "Balti" will probably be taken to mean bucket in India rather than a type of cooking, as this cuisine owes more to the West Midlands than South Asia.

A hooligan is a "badmash" and if you need to bring a meeting forward, you do the opposite of postponing—in Hinglish you can "prepone." Mobiles have modernised Hinglish and made it popular in India. Nowadays SMS are in full swings in Hinglish and are liked by people of all ages.

Hinglish has also become the globalised language. Many people speak English in India than anywhere else in the world because English has become an international language. English is also the language of commerce and satellite television, movies, mobiles, and the use of Internet signifies that more and more people in the subcontinent are exposed to both Standard English and Hinglish. Some flavoursome phrases have been generated due to this collision of languages. If one is feeling "glassy" it means one wants to drink wine. And a "timepass" is a way of distracting oneself.

Some evocatively archaic phrases are also used, such as "stepney," literally illiterate people speak 'stepney' which in "Asian part is used to mean a spare part, as in spare wheel, spare mobile or even, in some insulting words also to use rough language. The word 'Stepney' originated in eastern London, a popular brand of spare tyre was once manufactured in Wales.

Hinglish has been given a modern, fashionable spin by its use on music channels, In Asia and in advertising. And in some music programmes such as Goodness Gracious Me and the Kumars at Number 42, with a catchphrase about "chuddies" (underpants) have got a lot of popularity using Hinglish in English. Pundit, thug, pyjamas, caravan, and bungalow and many other words which has been imported from India are being spoken comfortably over the world with great ease. Language expert David Crystal has described India as having a "unique position in the English-speaking world." "[It's a] linguistic bridge between the major first-language dialects of the world, such as British and American English, and the major foreign-language varieties, such as those emerging in China and Japan." The exporting of words into English from Hindi has been an old tradition. *The Waste Land* a poem by T.S. Eliot the phone *Om Shanti Shanti Shanti* was used, catching the attention of using Hinglish in English. *The Times of India* reported: "Brand India has shaken, stirred and otherwise Bangalored the world's consciousness." Yes, "to Bangalore" is another Hinglishism, meaning to send overseas, as in call centres.

The arrival of Hinglish and the influence of Indian words on English are also a reflection of the rise of the Indian sub-continent as an economic powerhouse. But there are much older crossovers between English and the languages of the Indian sub-continent, with many words imported from the soldiers and administrators of the British Raj. These borrowed words include "pundit," originally meaning a learned man; "shampoo," derived from a word for massage; "pyjamas," meaning a leg garment and "dungarees," originating from the Dungri district of Mumbai.

Even the suburban-sounding "caravan" and "bungalow"—and the funky "bandana" and "bangles" — were all taken from Hindi words. Hinglish is being used for commercial promotion, like Domino's Pizza "Hungry kya?" asks one Domino's Pizza advert, while in another ad, Ford has sold the Ikon as the "josh car" (meaning full of energy and excitement) and the very popular restaurant McDonald's has propagated this slogan "What is your bahana?" (meaning "What's your excuse?"). Advertisers in the Far East use a form of fractured English too, as much for its visual impact as its meaning.

Not only Hinglish has been fused with English to take on a new identity but also so many other South Asian languages have been mingled in English. There is Spanglish, used in parts of the United States where people shift seamlessly between Spanish and English, and where hybrid words are created, such as a sign "No hangear" meaning "No hanging around."

It is natural and inevitable that languages will adapt and change to whatever is around. But this pick and mix approach should be embraced, not resisted." There might be puritans in any culture who say you can only be the master of one language, and that you shouldn't try to cross two languages. But do we only have one fixed identity? I don't think so, I think we can step in and out of different identities—and we can do the same with languages. "People might say this is my language, this is way it has always been. Well, it hasn't. Shakespeare's English was different from Chaucer's. The evolution of language is never going to stop."

As George Orwell wrcte in *1984*, "the fewer words we have, the more restricted our thinking becomes." With this in mind, I embrace the evolution and expansion of any language (especially the one I use). Adding words to your language, allows for more freedom of thought and expression. However, it does also mean you need a better spellchecker. We have always used a mix of English, Gujarati and Swahili in our everyday language. It is so embedded that we do not realise it. So all this is natural and continues to evolve as more mixtures of languages occur. It's great listening to people in Kenya and those here as well those from India. We just mix more as we expand the use of the Internet as well.

"I love the integration of foreign languages into the English language. It's one of the reasons I studied it, and one of the reasons etymology was my favorite subject. Let's face it; English is a mish-mash of foreign languages with added dodgy pronunciation and spelling! This is gruntling news—a most disappointing story for anyone who enjoys flirting with language. And let's not overlook the claims of Honklish and Singlish too, lah! All those dynamic Chuppies (Chinese-speaking upwardly-mobile people) can't be wrong...!

The latest fashionable version of Thai also contains a lot of English words. To the with-it crowd, 'chill chill' now means relaxing and 'hiso' (from high society) posh. For example, a commonly said phrase 'pai nang chill chill kan' translates to 'let's go and lounge around.' I would query the origin of 'innit' as from 'haina.' My father told me off for saying innit in the sixties, it is from 'isn't it,' especially around Bristol. Check Dirk Robson's books, *Krek waiters peak brissle,* and *Eurekal.*

As a British Asian, I grew up in West London in the late Sixties/early Seventies, whilst my cousins grew up in the West Midlands. The origin of the word, 'init' is pure Brummie—and we (in the South) adopted it after listening to our cousins. I agree with Dave Gibbs about the origin of 'innit.' In rural Gloucestershire I was being corrected by my parents well before 1950 for using innit istead of isn't it. The previous comments about 'innit' being from 'isn't it' are indeed correct, but your respondents have missed the point being made. English has many forms of these so-called "tag questions" depending on the sentence: 'isn't it,' 'aren't we,' 'weren't they,' 'don't you.' Hindi has just one ('na' or 'hai na'), just as French ('n'est-ce pas') and German ('nicht wahr') do. The usage being described is that these English speakers now use 'isn't it' (reduced to 'innit') in ALL cases, and not just where you would expect it grammatically. The suggestion is that it's the way it's being used that has been influenced by other languages, not the etymology of the word itself. To Dave Gibbs and Les Giles: The article doesn't claim 'innit' comes from 'haina.' It only states 'innit' was introduced into Hinglish as an invariant tag (in the same way 'haina' is used in Hindi), i.e. a tag that can substitute any other kind of English tag (English: 'We've seen this movie before, haven't we,' Hinglish: 'We've seen this movie before, innit'). Very good article. You can also add other Indian words like cash (From *kasu*-Tamil), catamaran (*Kattu maram*-Tamil), mango (*mangai*-Tamil), and juggernaut (*jegannath*-Sanskrit). Another example of the erosion of Britishness. Why isn't there an article on how Asians that come to Britain are becoming more British, instead of the locals becoming more foreign? Why is the BBC so terrified of Britishness?

I had always wondered why there is a pub in Southall called 'Glassy Junction.' Now I know. Thank you for enlightening me! Hinglish? Sounds good to me. Language should be alive. And to Mr. Alexander of Portsmouth - I might live in Quebec but I still consider myself Brit. It's just that my concept of 'Britishness' includes using local French argot terms in my everyday speech. Learn to live with it. It is the greatest strength of the English language that it adopts anything it can use to enrich itself. This is one of the reasons why English is such dominant language internationally and why it is supremely well suited to the production of poetry and literature of so many varieties. Hinglish is a wonderful example of a living language in action, evolving to meet the needs of its speakers. I can't wait to call somebody at work and 'prepone' a future meeting!

A very good article indeed. Indians have no doubt got their language embedded into English but in doing so they have also made their language (at least spoken one) 'corrupt.' You would see more and more of younger generation speaking English rather than their mother tongue (which could be one of the hundreds of languages India has). Let us take the case of Kashmir (where I am from). Kids are actually discouraged to speak Kashmiri (their native language) by their parents/elders, which I feel is disgusting. No doubt English is a must in today's world but not at the expense of one's mother tongue. This has reached to the point in Kashmir where over 95 per cent of people cannot write Kashmiri and a slightly smaller percentage cannot read their language. By the way, I can read Kashmiri to some extent but cannot write it, which I really feel sad about.

Well, I am originally from Wales, and can certainly vouch for the strong existence for a 'Wenglish' (mixture of Welsh and English). Great fun to use and just another way of expressing oneself.

It is all well and good enriching languages, but I think the Indians have gone one step too far to try and destroy their own language. If you listen to Indian news broadcast, one in Hindi and the other one in English, you will find that the news in Hindi uses a lot of English words and the news in English is pure English. This applies to all programmes, whether it is in England or India.

English is so rich because it has never been crystallised like German or French. As long as it keeps growing and developing it will remain predominant as the most democratic language of all. However, people in Britain must accept that it is no longer our language and that we will one day be simply speaking a dialect of a much wider common tongue.

Fascinating! I was checking out the BBC take on our election and found a new source of interesting news stories. We do not say 'Innit' here in the US, but the use of the word 'like' cannot be, like, described, like, you know?

On the derivation of 'caravan,' does this have Indian roots or Arabic? There is a city in Tunisia named 'Kairouan/Qairouan.' Arabs may have borrowed it from the Indians like the numerals though. This is a truly delightful piece. English, whilst basically a Germanic language is already a glorious concoction of French, Nordic, Latin and Greek with trace elements of Celtic and much else besides. I see no reason to be other than grateful that we have such a wonderful language and additional Hindi elements will only add to its richness. English is a prime example of Saussure's principle of diachronic change. Long may it be so. Don't forget Franglais, Chinglish, Konglish, Janglish, Singlish and Texmex. These dialects will always appear where main languages meet. Sam Alexandroni listens in at a Mumbai espresso bar:

> A: *Kya Bataoon Yaar*. I'm *thoda* bored. Need some *masti* in my life. Getting really *pukkaoed*. (What say, dude? I'm a little bored. Need some excitement in my life. Getting really bored.)
>
> B: Chill man. *Chal* let's go for a *picchar*. (Chill, man. Come on, let's go to a movie.)
>
> A: No *rey*. Don't have any *paisa*. (No, dude. Don't have any money.)

In India, English has long been the language of the government and the educated elite, and anyone who mixed Hindi and English was jeered at. Now that is changing. Hinglish has become the hep voice of urban India, and thanks to the spread of cable TV and the popularity of Bollywood films its influence is reaching far beyond the cities. In a country with 16 national languages and more than 1,000 dialects, Hinglish is turning into a common tongue.

Businesses have been quick to catch on. "Hungry kya?" asks one Domino's Pizza advert, while Ford has sold the Ikon as the "josh car" (meaning exciting) and McDonald's has come up with the slogan "What your bahana is?" (meaning "What's your excuse?").

A fad of no importance? Wrong, according to David Crystal, professor of linguistics at the University of Wales in Bangor, who suggests that, given India's huge population and its industrial and cultural influence, Hinglish could soon become the most widely spoken form of English in the world.

18

Shifting Paradigms: Decolonising Indian English

—*Dr. Sharda Iyer*

Identity has been defined as the process of creative realisation. It has been said that to create an identity is a part of the essential business of an artist. Identity and 'identity crisis' have become the 'Semantic' because of our time. A sense of identity is a perennial sustaining creative force in a writer and the loss of identity is the root cause of all problems, it could culminate in the deadening of life and automatisation of man. A creative writer's sense of identity, his efforts to seek it, and the challenges that he faces while exploring and affirming them are issues of considerable significance, especially in a newly developed art or literature in a new language.

Creative writing in itself is a quest for identity. The quest became hazardous and takes a powerful dimension when such a creative spirit finds expression though the medium of a powerful alien language—as with the Indian Writing in English which came into existence during the British Colonial rule. An accident of history brought us into contact with English which was seen as a gift of Goddess Saraswati by Sri Rajagopalachari and as a Surz Canal to East and West by Sri Aurobindo. Indians first learnt to comprehend and then to read and write, and later used it for creative purpose, which began as a purely utilitarian prose. It gradually developed to the most ambitions form—poetry, fiction, drama, political tracts and even epics. In fact, it was a literature that had sprung on a hospitable spirit from a seed blown by a random breeze from afar.

The French historian, N. Taine, said that literature is a creation of three factors: the race the, milieu and the moment. As regards the Indian Writing in English the 'race' is the mixed Indian race, a result of invasions conquests and occupation extending over thousands of years, the 'milieu' the variegated Indian subcontinent comprising every kind of extremes and hints to a geography and cultural heritage all its own, and the 'moment' is the meeting of the West and India. It was, as Sirinivas Iyengar describes, "to be Indian in thought and feeling, emotion and experience, yet also to court the graces and submit to the discipline of English for expression in a novel experiment in creative mutation."

The history of Indian Writing in English is a long history of endurance assimilation and integral transformation. Negotiating the rough passage between Indian diffidence and the Englishman's indifference, condemned as a parasitic literature, looked at as a misdirected effort and a miscarriage of talent, it has been struggling to affirm its identity through the spiritual and imaginative odyssey by its exponents. The task before them was not an easy one, for on the one hand they have been criticised by the West for being too Indian "A sterile tradition which blight even major talents," as Burton remarked, and by the Indians who looked down upon them for catering to the West.

The Indian writers have made serious efforts to create their identity and prove that they are part of Indian literature and not aliens. "English is one to the new voices in which India speaks, it is a modern facet of that glory which commences from the Vedas." To demolish the impliability of conditioned reflexes of the British hangover, cease being imitative and derivative, and make Indian Writing in English authentic and relevant not only in subject matter but also in reshaping English to express the Indian experience. The aim, as Raja Rao said, is not to adopt but adapt English and bring about de-colonising and create an Indian English.

A truly Indian work is one which is about India and Indian, presents an Indian print of view, and is written in a language and style which fits well into the matrix of Indian cultural ethos and way of life. One touch of nature makes the whole world kin but it is in literature that the heartbeats of a nation are heard.

Language is a supremely humanising influence, through which there is instituted in man a second human nature. Language is the means by which the setting of the human being is immensely enlarged. It is through the sentence patterns we use, the idioms, words images that the categories of thinking, feeling, valuing which they imply are incorporated into the stuff of our being. Language is both the creation and the expression of what is most deeply and peculiarly human in us. Indians have experimented with the English language to mould it, to give an Indian flavours to suit the Indian mode of feeling and expression.

Prof. Srinivasa Iyengar expresses the difficulties that an Indian writer faces when he writes in English, "To be Indian in thought and feeling and emotion and experience yet also to court the grace and submit to the discipline of English for expression is a novel experiment..." There are peculiarities in Indian life, experience and speech that don't admit translation into English. What is written has to be recognisably India to Indian writers and English to the English readers. English in Indian is conditioned by its geography, grammar and speech habits in different linguistic areas, but it cannot go very far from the Standard English. The need for expressing the values, verities and heartbeats of one culture in the language of another is different. But language at a deeper level transcends mere translation, the medium is the message, and the soul charged piece of writing acquires its own meaning.

Nissim Ezekiel said "Historical situations create cultural consequences." An accident of history brought us into contact with English nearly more than three centuries ago. When a language has had a spell of centuries and the best of our thinking, founded new ideas through the thought and literature that came to us through the English language and a pattern of our experience made it in that language, an expansion of it is the same medium must be taken as a necessary result not a forced exercise. In certain circumstances a language chooses a nation, but in India, the people have chosen the language. In India English has blended itself into the cultural and social complex of the country, and hence cannot be treated as alien. Indian has been using English for communicating and for artistic expansion if necessary or necessarily in an Indian way.

Multilingualism is a feature of our socio-cultural and religious left matters, and an awareness of linguistic and literary variety is embedded deep within us. Once we accept English as a natural part of our palimpsest, that is Indian culture, we do not have to enter into the irresolvable argument, whether English is an Indian language or not. In India, English occupies an inevitable place in the layer upon layer preservation of different cultures and traditions. In fact, English is the latest linguistic cultural spectrum like Persian or Urdu. Though English is not strictly an India language, it can neither be dismissed as an alien, but as Raja Rao said, "it has to be adopted and adapted to the Indian conditions."

William Walsh recognises that Indian Writing in English has been 'creating' not 'catering,' (to the West), with an originality of experience, thought, imagery, idiom, consciousness of their county's milieu, and with their personal experience transformed the material "into literature that is universal in its appeal."

The Indian writers' choice of English has been mourned, admired and at times been barely tolerated. The underlying assumption has been that in all Indian Writing in English there is a hiatus between the cultural experience that is expressed and the language chosen to express it, though Indians have not been the first to use a language other than their own. Leonard Forester in *Poet's Tongue* has effectively demonstrated that writers have used languages other than their own from the Middle Age down to the present. Multilingualism has existed as a relatively unrecognised tradition in literature and life all over the world.

Mulk Raj Ahand observes that most of us in India mix casually, even in ordinary conversation, a good sprinkling of English words, phrases like, Have you finished your khana? Or, Don't act like a jungli. More than a thousand Indian words have been added to the *Oxford English Dictionary*. Mulk Raj Ahand makes a difference between the bazaar English or higedly-Pigegdly English and the pidgin English used for creative writing. It is this zeal of acceptability which has made him use Indianised English in his novel *Untouchable*.

But it was Raja Rao who, in his preface to *Kanthapura* (1939)—which may be taken as an important critical document and a manifesto of the critical creed—highlights some of the problems faced by the creative writers in English, and has tried to resolve it, "...we cannot write like the English, we cannot and should not. We should adapt and not adopt English so as to make it a suitable instrument of expression of the Indian sensibility." He makes a powerful plea for the adaptation of English language to Indian needs. In this way one would develop a new dialect, a new species of Indian English. There is nothing wrong in it, since this has been done in other countries too. This has resulted in American, Australian, Canadian and Caribbean English, to mention a few. English is not to be rejected but adapted and Indianised as he has so successfully done in *Kanthapura*. It is not even the English of the educated but the natural language of the rural folk.

As the woman begins her narrative one can almost hear the grandmother talking, "our village—I don't think you have heard about it—Kanthapura is its name and it is in the province of Kara." Describing Murthy, the hero, she tells "...he was a cow, quiet, generous, serene, Brahmanic, a very prince I tell you. And if only I had not been daughter her widow, I should have offered him a granddaughter if I had one."

Writers of Indian English fiction have tried to evolve a personal language by maturating the English language. More recently Salman Rushdie and others including Amitav Ghosh, Amit Chaudhari, and Arvind Adiga have made serious efforts Rushdie's "to conquer English." R.K. Narayan observed that the English language through sheer resilience in endangering a process of Indianisation; it cannot be said whether the process of transmutation is an enrichment or debasement of the English language, but it has definitely served the purpose admirably of conveying unambiguously the thought and acts of characters who flourish in a small town named Malgudi.

In the field of poetry, poets like Nissim Ezekeil, Kamala Das, R. Parthasarthy Ramanujan, Arun Kolatker have blazed the new trait and have made Indian English poetry—Indian first and last. They are no longer deterred by their ancestors' linguistic timidness, nor apologetic for writing in a language that is not their own, and are no longer enthralled by foreign culture or sensibility they make free use of English, not mechanically, but effortlessly out of a natural in inward-ness.

The question whether Indian writers can successfully wield English as a medium of creative expression is of no relevance. Now Kamala Das's answers to all those who advised her not to write in English must silence all doubts about Indian writers' capability in this regard. In her poem *Introduction* she writers:

The Language I speak
Becomes mine, its distortions, its queerness
All mine, mine alone. It is half English, hall
Indian, funny perhaps, but it is honest
It is human as I am human
Is human speech, the speech of the mind, that is
Here not there
A mind that sees and hears and is aware
Not the deaf blind speech.

Joseph Furtado was the first to use Pigdin English or bazaar English in poetry in 1920. But he did so only in a few humorous poems and did not seem to be aware of the possibilities of its emergence as a powerful vehicle for poetic expression. Ezekiel has made more serious efforts to bring the idiom of poetry close to the spoken language. No other poet has no successfully explored the resources of Indian English and its nuances as he has done in his *Very Indian Poems*. English has undergone radical changes in his hands, especially in poem like, *Goodbye Party for Miss Pushpa T.S, Irani Restaurant, Instruction the Railway Clerk, The Profession, The Patriot, Soap,* and others.

Some people are not having manners
This I am always observing
For example other day I find.
I am reading soap
For ordinary washing myself purpose
So I am going to one small shop
Nearly in my lane, and I am asking
For well known soap brand

The shop man is giving me soap
But I am finding it defective version
So I am saying very politely
Thought in Hindi, is not so good as my English...

In his *Very Indian Poems,* he has succeeded in creating the authentic impression of Indian people and places and in giving the peculiar flavour of the language as used by the English loving, status conscious Indian belonging to the middle class Indian society. In a poem like *Patriot* he writes:

> I am standing for peace and non-violence
> Why world is fighting, fighting
> Why all people of the world
> Are not following Mahatma Gandhi
> I am simple not understanding.
>
> Pakistan behaving like this
> China behaving like that
> It is making me very sad
> I am telling you
> Really most harassing me.

R. Parthasarthy's task in *Rough Passage* and more so in 'Home Coming'—the third section of *Rough Passage*—is to acclimatise the English language to on indigenous—in his case Tamil—tradition. The poet is conscious of the hiatus between the soil of the language he uses and his own roots. Parthasarthy: "Even though I am Tamil speaking and yet write in English there is the overwhelming difficulty of using images in a linguistic tradition that is quite other than that of your own." Thus there is a need to return to our linguistic tradition.

> How long can foreign poets
> Provide the staple of your line
> Turn inwords, scrap the bottom of your past

His stay in England had made him realise:

> There is same thing to be said about exile.
> You learn roots are deep
> That language is a tree loses colour
> Under different sky.

Ramanujan, an expatriate in USA, Professor in linguistics, writes, "English and my discipline give me my outer form...and my first thirty years in Indian and my frequent visits, my profession and pre-occupation with Kannada, Tamil, and folklore give my inner substance, my inner form, image and symbols." *Striders* and *Relations* reflect an interior landscape. "Ramanujan's deepest roots are in the Kannada and Tamil past, and he has repossessed that past, in fact made it available in English language, an achievement without parallel in the history of Indian English poetry," notes Parthasarthy. Ramanujan has successfully conveyed what is the subtlest and most incantation is locked up in another linguistic tradition. He said, "I must seek and will find my particular hell only in my Hindu mind." In an obituary he writes:

> Father when he passed away left dust
> On a table full of papers
> Left debts and daughter
> A bed-welting grandson
> Named by a toss of
> A coin after him.

Described by Ruth Wilde Schuler, the editor of *Prophetic Voices*, USA, as one of the finest writers in India today, P. Rajan's poetry draws its sustenance from his knowledge of his basis in English poetry, his awareness of his Indian heritage and his deep grounding in Tamil tradition. His poetry never degenerates into the faded echo of the Western masters. His use of the English language is distinctly Indian.

In the field of Indian English Drama bold experiments have been made in the use of language and technique. Girish Karnad strongly believes if Indian English Drama wishes to go ahead, it must go back first. Asif Currimbuoy, Gurucharan Das, Ezekiel, Mahesh Dattani have boldly experimented with Indian English. Guru Charan Das remarked, "The English Theatre in India will have to project the kind of hybrid English we speak with Indian expressions." Das uses the Indianised form of English words and expressions in "larin sabib larins" for Lawrence, *Kya yar chalo Bai, Argrey Badshah, Sat Sri Akal* and transcriptions of India expression in *larin sahib* imparts naturalness, crispness and an Indian flavours to the dialogues, and succeeds in capturing the typical local flavours.

The Indian English writers have established the truth that the Western model is on more for them. They are original in treatment, form and content. As Indian dance, music, architecture are uniquely Indian, we can evolve a system in which India English writing need not take its bearing from the West. There is no more justification for the century-old accusation that we Indians are a nation of mimics, victims of English education which has conditioned the faculties of our perception so much so that we have failed to respond to the immediate situation. Indian English writing has come to stay as literature of India because it is based on English adapted and transformed as an Indian language, namely, Indian English.

Works Cited

Das, B.K. (1992). *Modern Indian English Poetry.* Bareilly, Prakesh Book.

King, Bruce. (1987). *Modern Indian Poetry in English.* Delhi, OUP.

Reddy, G.A. (1979). *Indian Writing in English and its Audience,* Bareilly, Prakesh Book.

Iyengar, K.R. Srinivasa (1982). *Indian Writing in English.* Delhi, Sterling.

Pathak R.S. (ed.), (1992). *Quest for Identity in Indian English Writing (part II) Poetry.* Delhi, Bahari Pub.

19

Shifting Paradigms and English Language Teaching Methods: Historical Perspective and Present Problems

—*Dr. Sunil K. Rai*

India is a country with a mixed population of different languages. In northern India, the common language in use is Hindi and in southern India, four different languages are used, namely, Tamil in Tamil Nadu, Telegu in Andhra Pradesh, Malayalam in Kerala and Kannada in Karnataka. English is the common language for communication in India. Teaching here, then, is a multi-cultural, multi-religious, multi-language experience and can be very challenging. This is urban India. Rural India has its own challenges. Realising that learning English makes all the difference and that the only way to bridge the economic gap is to learn English, many state governments have introduced English at level/class one. One hundred and fifty years of intimate contact has made English an integral part of our education system, and we can neglect its study only at the risk of loss of ourselves.

There is no doubt in my mind in making this statement that today English is an international language, spoken in many countries both as a native and as a second or foreign language. It is taught in the schools in almost every country on this earth. It is a living and vibrant language spoken by 100,300 million people as their native language. Millions more speak it as an additional language. English is spoken habitually in the United States, the British Isles, Ireland, Canada, Australia, New Zealand, the Republic of South Africa, Liberia and many territories under the United Kingdom and the United States of America. It is estimated that 300 million people speak English as a second language, and an additional 100 million people use it fluently as a foreign language. As a rough estimate, 1,000 million or one billion people around the world have some knowledge of English, either as a native language, as a second language, or as a foreign language.

English is the associate official language of India which has over 1,000 million (over billion) people not even that but our neighbours like Pakistan, Bangladesh who were ruled by Britain continue to use English both as an optional medium of instruction in their schools and as one of their official languages.

English is learned everywhere because people have found out that knowledge of English is a passport for better career, better pay, advanced knowledge, and for communication with the entire world. English is also learned for the literature it possesses, and for the variety and rich experience it provides. English has replaced French as the language of diplomacy. In this computer age, English is bound to expand its domains of use everywhere. Everyone wants to appropriate English as their own. It is important that the students are given ample opportunities to practices English in the class as well as outside the classroom, even as it is important for them to have time and freedom to digest, reflect and analyse what has been exposed to them. Internalisation of the linguistic structures and their ready and easy retrieval for communication are achieved in many ways.

As we are using this language as the second language so the following rules surely help in getting better hand to the language:

1. One should prefer the shorter word to the longer one.
2. While writing or speaking use simple, everyday words rather than fancy ones.
3. Preference should be given to verbs over nouns and adjectives.
4. In attempting a short composition, preference should be given to the short sentences with an average of no more than 20 words.

5. Remember always that use of the active voice is always better than the passive one.
6. Avoid as much as possible the usage of compound and complex sentences and try to communicate in simple sentences.
7. Business letters or articles should be divided into three paragraphs.
8. Write with the ear. A sentence may look good on paper but its modulation may be grating. Listen to your sentences in your head as you write, and do not write anything that you could not contentedly say.
9. Write for the eye as well as the mind. Prepare an overall design, positioning understandable headings, sub-headings, and captions for each segment, showing the organisation of the text. Make the whole document visually appealing to its reader.
10. Use margins between sections or paragraphs, and lines to make the document look good.

Asia had a long tradition of teaching and learning foreign languages. Memorisation of vocabulary and translation of sentences often formed the major part of such learning processes in the past. Ancient languages such as Sanskrit and Pali were mastered in Asia through the process of memorisation of texts and vocabulary lists and in most of the rural parts of the country the same old tested format is still applied to make students learn the nuances of the language. There are various methods applied to acquire proficiency in the language.

Language Teaching Methods

Grammar translation: This method emphasises reading, writing, translation, and the conscious learning of grammatical rules. Its primary goal is to develop literary mastery of the second language. Memorisation is the main learning strategy and students spend their class time talking about the language instead of talking in the language. The curriculum requires the memorisation of paradigms, patterns, and vocabulary, with translation being used to test the acquired knowledge. In most of the rural areas, the schools teachers are following this method only which some or other ways hampers the fluency of the language in the personality of the student.

The Natural Method: Since children learn naturally to speak before they read, they imbibe the sound from the surrounding and then gradually pick those words which are spoken by their family members. A great deal of pantomime accompanies the talk. With the aid of gesture, by attentive listening, and by dint of repetition, the beginner comes to associate certain acts and objects with certain combinations of sound, and finally reaches the point of reproducing the foreign words or phrases .

The Phonetic Method: This method emphasized "oral expression as the basis of instruction, stressing pronunciation, avoiding grammatical rule giving, and seeking to impart a practical mastery of language forms for use in-country; cultural information was also provided. The teacher would read a passage aloud, explaining unfamiliar words as students followed along. After discussing questions on the passage, students would paraphrase the story aloud. Next would come written answers to questions, phonetic work on new words, and ultimately recitation. Gestures, pictures and interesting contexts were to be used in making applications of familiar material. Graded reading would come later." This method demanded "heavy requirements for linguistic expertise on the part of the teachers."

The Direct Method: Adult learners can learn a second language in essentially the same manner as a child. Therefore, if possible, the teacher should try to create a natural learning environment within the classroom. Instead of explicit grammar instruction, the major emphasis is on communicating. Classes are carried out totally in the second language with absolutely no reliance on the first language or on any form of translation. The expectation is that through question and answer dialogues, the second language will gradually be acquired.

Teaching of receptive skills (listening and reading) rather than teaching of productive skills (speaking and writing) was encouraged as the first step. Contrastive analysis of the native language of the learner with the target language was done. Teachers were required to have a good knowledge of the phonetics of the language they teach, but they would use it to teach pronunciation and not phonetics. This method was indeed an extension of the Natural Method, with greater emphasis on and sophistication of knowledge of linguistics.

Teachers have to say so many things simply to organise the lesson – starting or stopping an activity, getting students to do or not to do things. Much of this language consists of simple commands and instructions which are repeated lesson after lesson. If you say these in English, students will quickly learn what they mean. The following are some simple classroom commands in English, which you should continually use in your class:

Stand up (please).
Sit down (please).
Look! Look at me.
Listen!
Repeat!
Again! Open/Close your books.
Stop talking!
Come here, please.
Come to the front.
Be quiet, please.

Most of the language we need for organising the class consists of simple expressions which can be used again and again. However, teachers may often need to use more complex language, for example, when explaining a new word or a grammar point, or explaining how an activity works. In such instances also, make your explanations as simple and clear as possible, so that the students understand.

Use simple, short sentences; use gestures to show each of the action you want them to understand. Use simple blackboard drawings; give difficult words in the language known to the students. Giving explanations in English is worthwhile if it can be done successfully and without too much difficulty. However, there are many occasions when it is best to use the students' own language—either because the language needed is too complex, or because it is easier, quicker, and more convenient.

An explanation in English could be very confusing, especially if the concept or words are unfamiliar to the students. It would be better to give examples in English, and then to give a translation of the word. By using the students' own language, we can give a clearer and fuller explanation, and refer to equivalent expressions in their language. It is best not to rely only on explanations in either language. It is more important to give plenty of examples and a chance for students to practise. An advantage of using the students' own language is that the situation can be given more quickly and easily, leaving more time for practice. However, an advantage of using English is that it provides useful listening practice, and helps students by giving them some of the words they need.

While teaching in the classroom teacher must use visual aids which are very important because showing visuals focuses attention on meaning, and helps to make the language in the class more real and alive; having something to look at keeps the students' attention, and makes the class more interesting. Visuals can be used at any stage of the lesson, to help in presenting new language or introducing a topic, as part of language practice, and when reviewing language that has been presented earlier; good visual aids can be used again and again and shared by different teachers.

You can use the following as visual aids in your class: yourself, the blackboard, real objects, flashcards, pictures and charts. The teacher can use gestures, facial expressions, and actions to help show the meaning of words and to illustrate situations. You can use the blackboard to draw pictures, diagrams, maps, etc. You can use real objects in the classroom and bring other things into the class – food, clothes, containers, household objects, vegetables, etc.

Listening is an Important Ingredient of Learning English: Listening is necessary to develop the speaking skill. The student listens to oral speech in English, then separates into segments the stretch of utterances he hears, groups them into words, phrases, and sentences, and, finally, he understands the message these carry. In the classroom, students listen in order to repeat and to understand. In listening to repeat, students imitate and memorise linguistic items such as words, idioms, and sentence patterns. It is very unfortunate that the listening skill is the most neglected one, both in first and second language teaching. Teachers tend to focus on the rudimentary elements of listening briefly, and pass over to other aspects of language teaching. Discrimination of sounds and intonations often form the major part of listening practice in the classroom. Listening for content is often assumed. In reality, the listening skill is fundamental to the entire process of mastering and using a language, whether first or second or foreign.

Listening is like painting, like colour, in day-to-day environment. You don't notice, but it is always there in every linguistic activity. Listening is important for casual chats, face to face encounters, and telephone messages, for enjoyment of radio and television programmes, formal lectures, and many other activities.

In the early stages of listening, the students may have to be taught and exposed to discrimination of sounds used in English in isolation as well as in combination, not simply as sounds in themselves in isolation, but as units of meaningful words. Listening helps also to understand and act according to the emotional state of the speaker.

First of all, you should be clear about your goals in teaching a lesson for listening comprehension. These goals must be made explicit and explained to the students so that the learning process becomes meaningful to them.

Secondly, you should plan for a careful step-by-step progression in the material and, in teaching the same in the class. You should give direction to the students as to what they should listen for, where to listen, when to listen and how to listen.

It is important that students develop consciously their memory span while listening to a message. Their auditory memory span must be strengthened and expanded in progressive steps in English.

While personality factors play a very important role in deciding how successful a listener a student could become, the learners need to have some minimal competence in listening to the speech of the native speakers. In due course they should be able to listen and remember relatively lengthy sentences and phrases.

Communicative Classroom Activities

There are several types of exercises one could introduce here.

i) Ask the student to listen to a short passage (an excerpt of a lecture for which internet or cassette player or DVD may be used) and then ask students to answer a few questions. This is to test the listening comprehension of the students.

ii) Another exercise is called cloze dictation. This takes the form of asking the students to listen to a paragraph and to write the missing words. Leave the first few sentences as they are so that a proper context is established for subsequent blanks in other sentences.

iii) Further the teacher can demand some inferential skill from the listener: Listen to the lecture and then evaluate the following statements as true or false. The student is not only asked to listen but also think over the matter and make inferences in this type of exercise.

iv) Listening to radio plays and advertisements is yet another interesting activity.

v) Story telling or story reading. Follow this with questions, asking for factual information and inferential state-ments.

If a teacher's life history and testimony of the student is a good topic for the purpose, he will focus upon his birth, family, childhood, school, work specialisation, marriage, travel, present activities, plans, etc. Note that practising this as part of speaking skill will help develop the writing skill later on. In writing, this will take the form of guided composition. Subsequent assignments can include oral reports on other subjects, and may lead to debates between class members (Bowen et al. 1985).

Oral reports, telling anecdotes, or jokes are some of the activities you should incorporate in every class. The ability to talk about an incident, tell an anecdote, joke, etc., is a valuable social skill. Presentation should always be followed by a question-answer session in which the class will raise questions and the presenter will answer. Some assistance from the teacher may be required at this stage.

Learning rhymes, poems, songs, proverbs, sayings, etc., brings the student a little closer to the culture. Additionally, the rhythms learned along with the poems and even the songs are usually valid examples of the different elements in the language. You should expose them to popular literature, ask them to imitate and repeat after you, and use these as interludes for fun and learning. A lot of learning does take place when students get involved in enacting the content of the rhymes. Intonations are easily acquired in a chorus drill.

To conclude, it is generally agreed that the continuation of study of English is both desirable and necessary. Knowledge of English has become essential for intellectual, cultural, economical and political relations with the rest of the world. Its study is indispensible for higher legal, technical and scientific education and technological progresses. And, therefore, it is extreme important for us to understand and adapt the flexibility of this language, and to help our students to imbibe its nuances as easily as possible.

20

Shifting Paradigms: Need of Remedial Teaching for Promotion of Students' Communicability in English in Rural Colleges

—*R. K. Mishra*

Teaching of spoken English in general has been eclipsed in colleges due to certain faults and lapses in the application of recommendable pedagogic skills and strategies. Teaching of English at the college level has practically degenerated into mere interpretation or lecturing without skill. The stereotypical explication of the prescribed topics makes teaching of English not only monotonous and insipid but also ineffectual and unproductive to students who are hardly benefited in learning the skills of writing as well speaking. The present pedagogic method of imparting teaching of English language in colleges does not cater to the needs of students in as much as it fails to provide adequate exposure of language learning to them.

In the present system of teaching the teacher of English goes on interpreting a topic perfunctorily and monotonously in his own language without facilitating students to discuss the subject taught or to interact with him in that regard. This system of teaching on the other hand provides motivation to the teacher to gain the advantage of promoting his own skill of communication in English by lecturing. His teaching is comparable to a one-way traffic along which vehicles run in a particular direction. The students have to learn the language silently and passively as a result of which they become practically dormant and speechless in spoken English. Thus, students' incompetence in speaking English is attributable to this unsound and faulty system of teaching of language in colleges.

The rural colleges adversely suffer from these defects and shortcomings as they are deprived of many scopes and opportunities available to students of urban colleges. A contrastive picture of the facilities available to students of rural colleges and those of the urban colleges is presented below to highlight the superiority of learners of English in towns and cities in their acquisition of speaking ability. The students studying in urban colleges gain the advantage of attending spoken English tutorial classes in order to develop their speak ability. Such spoken English institutes sprout in towns and cities in large number. They impart teaching of spoken English by carrying on practice of grammar, usage of words and correct articulation with a view to developing the skills of speaking English. Their regular practices of exercise in these items of English cater to the need of students in respect of promoting their communicability in English.

The students of rural colleges on the other hand are deprived of such facilities of attending spoken English centers. As a result they cannot utter a single sentence correctly. They betray their inability and deficiency to communicate in English and consequently develop inferiority complex.

Another benefit reaped by the students of urban colleges is that most of them pass out of public schools or English medium schools with a fairly good standard in spoken English; whereas the students of rural colleges are mostly from regional medium schools with their deficiency in English. Their knowledge of English is comparatively poor and this poverty in English persists in their studies in rural colleges. These students are unfortunately deprived of exposure to English language practice. They continue to remain poor in writing, poor in comprehension and above all in oral communication.

Since teaching of grammar and vocabulary is never emphasized, students betray their poverty of grammatical knowledge without which one cannot acquire language. One, who is well up in English grammar, is supposed to have a wider vocabulary inasmuch as grammar teaches vocabulary by way of dealing with appropriate prepositions, synonyms and antonyms and substitution of one word for a phase or a long sentence. Thus lack of grammatical knowledge renders the students unable to speak English with the correct sentences and using right words.

The students of urban colleges are considerably exposed to spoken English as many intellectuals in the towns and cities frequently communicate in English. Educated parents and relatives often speak in English which students of urban areas listen to and emulate them. They also attend meetings in which speakers often address in English. This predominant exposure of students to spoken English exerts considerable impact on the mind of students. It also stimulates their interest in speaking and impresses on their mind certain language items such as usable words, befitting expressions and communicative sentences. Besides, they learn how to manipulate words in the appropriate context. Thus, the students in urban colleges find a congenial atmosphere of learning spoken English on account of the reasons mentioned above whereas the students of rural colleges find the rural life uncongenial, unfavourable and unproductive for acquisition of English language.

After expatiating on the disadvantages encountered by the students of rural colleges in regard to acquisition of communicability in English, a few suggestions are re-commended below as a panacea to these ever-existing problems. If the schemes chalked out here could be implemented successfully and effectively, the teachers and the students of rural colleges would overcome the impediments that stand on the way of teaching speaking ability.

First and foremost the bridge courses or remedial teachings of English should be introduced in rural colleges on top priority with the objective of remedying the deficiencies of students in English. Every day at least one remedial class should be taken for each year of students in order to teach them grammar, vocabulary and patterns of sentences. Besides, three spoken English classes should necessarily be taken to conduct conversation and interaction between the teacher and the students in which each student must be motivated and encouraged to speak a few sentences in English about his daily life, his hobby, his aim of life and his day-to-day experiences. While speaking if the student makes mistakes, the teacher must teach him effectively how to correct his sentences and expressions.

Another remedial class must be devoted to teaching of situational English to students. Situational English necessitates use of those sentences and words which are required for expression of one's activity in a particular situation, for example, a conversation between a fruit vendor and a buyer of it, between a T.T.E and a ticketless traveller in a train, between a doctor and a patient, and so on. The teacher has to create such situations innovatively and motivate students to converse with each other in relation to incidents taking place then and there. The teacher may teach the students such uses of English as are appropriate contextually. In like manner, the teacher may fabricate various day-to-day situations in order to teach situational English to students. The teacher has to insist the students on their practice of English in order to promote their speakability.

Another factor that is essential for teaching spoken English is organisation of seminars and symposia at regular intervals. Topics of general interest should be selected and notified to students a few days before so as to enable them to prepare and speak on the subject. Topics such as need of discipline in the academic institutions, merits and demerits of college election, terrorism in India, uses and abuses of TV, women education and language problems are to be given for discussion. Seminars and symposia are designed to provide positive motivation to students to participate in them. Their participation shall contribute to their improvement in speaking ability. Each of the students present there must be compelled to speak on the topic for two or three minutes. Credit should be given to those students who speak tolerably well but this should not dampen the spirit of other students who try but fail to speak well. Poor speakers must not be discredited or discouraged. On the contrary the teacher should conduct the seminar and symposia in such a way that even a poor speaker among the students shall be enthused to participate in the next seminars.

Apart from organisation of seminars and symposia, it is imperative upon rural colleges to introduce group discussions for each class per week. The entire class must be divided into certain groups consisting of four or five students and a commonplace topic of universal interest must be given for discussions frequent organisation of group discussions for each class shall provide positive reinforcement to students' speaking ability.

Besides, meeting should be organised for the students and by the students in order to motivate them to take part in its conduct. Students must be given guidance by the teacher how to welcome guests, introduce the invitees and offer a vote of thanks. Such practice and involvement on the part of students to preside over meetings must be given due emphasis from the viewpoint of promoting their speaking ability.

Over and above it is suggested to make the classroom teaching grammar based and oriented. All lessons such as prose poetry, one act play and drama must be taught grammatically. The relevance each item of grammar occurring in the lessons must be explained to students so as to strengthen their knowledge of it. The teacher in the course of curricular teaching must familiarise the students with different parts of speech, pattern of sentences and usage of grammatical items. While teaching poetry too the teacher has to explain the linguistic deviance and the unusual setting of words, which characterise a versification of poem and distinguish it from a prose piece.

Apart from this grammar oriented teaching, the teacher has to emphasise the teaching of vocabulary giving the synonyms and antonyms of the usable words. Contextual usage of words must be given due importance in order to acquaint the students how to use a word in a particular sense or situation Building of vocabulary is a part and parcel of language learning and speaking. Since words are essential to speaking and communicating one's views, thoughts and impressions, its teaching has to be accentuated in the perspective of improvement of students' skills of speaking. In the towns and cities the educated and elite public predominantly exposes students to learning of vocabulary as they listen frequently to usage of new words.

Another factor that facilitates better teaching of spoken English is the conduct of interview and personality test in the interest of development of students' speaking ability. The teacher motivates the students to face the interview as an interviewee and the teacher himself has to act as an interviewer.

The interviews conducted for students are intended to enable them to speak a few sentences readily, wittily and correctly.

If the measures suggested above are drastically given effect to rural colleges they will serve to revolutionise the methodology of teaching spoken English and contribute immensely to promotion of students' communicability in English. But implementation of these pedagogic devices has to face the problem of viability and feasibility from pragmatic viewpoint. Emphasis on coverage of courses, dearth of well trained teachers, and lack of adequate infrastructural facilities and administrative apathy of educational authorities are some of the deterrent factors that preclude significant advancement in this direction.

Nevertheless all these impediments have to be overcome for the sake of improvement in the teaching of spoken English in rural colleges. New strategies and skills of teaching of English have to be evolved, innovated and given effect on top priority. It is a blessing that the UGC has recently introduced remedial teaching in all colleges and provides finances for their sustenance. These remedial classes are designed to promote the existing standard of students in different curricular studies. These classes prove immensely beneficial and productive to students particularly of rural colleges in the acquisition of English language learning and speaking. The UGC should be prevailed upon to provide more finance to rural colleges for implementation of these recommendations intended for promotion of speaking ability of the students.

Besides, the teachers of English working in rural colleges must be directed to undergo training in the art of teaching spoken English. It must be binding upon them to do a course in PGCTE or PGDTE in the CIEFL or in any of its affiliated Institutes. Since these institutes impart training to teachers about the methodology of teaching spoken English, it is essential for the teachers of rural colleges to undergo a course in this line of studies and obtain a degree.

At the conclusion it is pertinent to advocate the organisation of refresher courses and orientation programmes in the teaching of spoken English for generation of a host of well-trained and competent teachers, who will be capable of producing good students of remarkable communicability in English. In the present context a revolutionary change in the method and skill of teaching English in rural colleges is warranted to achieve the desired objectives. The objective is obviously the promotion of communicability of students in English. In view of the incommunicability of the students of rural colleges, all these schemes suggested above have to be implemented uncompromisingly with a view to invigorating the methods of teaching spoken English. Any administrative slackness in materialising these objectives will further contribute inexorably to gradual impoverishment of students' standard in oral communication. Hence, it is incumbent on the UGC and the state governments to contemplate this academic issue on top priority from various angle of vision and contrive remedial measures for its solution.

21

200 Years of Indian English Literature: Shifting Paradigms of English in India

—Aju Mukhopadhyay

Introduction

Streams of invaders entered India from unrecorded time. Many of them left after plundering. The Mughals settled down gradually conquering almost the whole of India. They ruled for more than 200 years. Persian became the official language of India for some time. Later, Urdu, a mix of Hindi, Arabic and Persian, was born to become a fine literary language to take the place of Persian. Then came the British and ruled India for about 200 years. Their language, English, became the official language of India. In course of time it has become the international language, surpassing the claim of the French.

The introduction of English and its teaching among the younger generation in India was talked about for some time but it became effective only when such personalities as Raja Rammohan Roy, T.V. Macaulay, David Hare and Hyde East came forward with great interest to induce the government to take necessary steps to introduce it.

For dealing with the rulers, for getting modern education and for contacts with the outside world, the elites of India learnt English. With the development of the regional languages English too developed in post-colonial India. English is not the language of any particular community in any province of India but a language popular in the whole of India. Gaining popularity among the educated people, it has now acquired a firm position in the heart of Indians to become the literary link between Indian regions and a common link among the educated mass.

Indian English Literature

Coming up to this, we feel like defining what Indian English is and what is Indian English Literature. Raja Rao wrote in the foreword of his debut novel, *Kanthapura,* "English is not really an alien language to us. It is the language of our intellectual make-up like Sanskrit or Persian was before but not our emotional make-up. We are instinctively bilingual. We cannot write like the English. We should not. We cannot write only as Indians. We have grown to look at the larger world as part of us. Our method of expression therefore has to be as distinctive and colourful as the Irish or the American. Time alone will justify it."

Mulk Raj Anand wrote, "I generally translate or interpret my feelings or thoughts from Punjabi or Hindustani into the English language, thus translating the metaphor and imagery of my mothertongue into what is called Indo Anglo-Indian writing. . . ."

And Amaresh Dutta observed about such a language that the writers "almost forged a language with a new flavour and flexibility which went into the formation of an idiom capable of echoing the Indian voice." (Both as quoted in *A History of Indian Literature 1911-56* by Dr. Sisir Kumar Das. New Delhi; Sahitya Akademi, p.44)

This English language written by Indians may be termed as Indian English. At the beginning most of such writers were brought up in UK and wrote almost their English like the second generation writers of Indian origin, settled in England and America, have been writing in English regularly in their tone. Their orientation in the language was and is different; their language is akin to the nation in which their guardians settled. Yet when they write on India or Indian theme, even write on other themes, their mind remaining Indian, their subject in most cases and ideas remain Indian; their language is Indian English. Though some exceptions are there as it is reported that Hari Kunzru and some others have indicated that they belong to the nation they grew up from childhood.

Though Indian writers writing in English are scattered at many places in the globe; in and out of India, their mental makeup and thought process, at least up to a few generations to come, are likely to be Indian, at least of those who create literature on Indian subjects, partly or entirely. But they do not include writers of foreign origin settled in India and writing on Indian subjects. The poets and writers of Indian origin, living anywhere in the globe, may be called Indian English writers or poets.

The History of Growth of Indian English Literature

It has been held by the scholars that Cavelly Venkata Boriah's *Accounts of the Jains*, published in 1809, was the first evidence of Indian Writing in English. Raja Rammohan Roy was the first bilingual writer in India to use the English language in the nineteenth century. He translated *Katha, Kena, Isa, Mundaka* and other *Upanishads* in English. His campaign against Sati, polemics against Christian Missionaries, 'The Precepts of Jesus,' and his writing against Hindu Idolatry, writings towards social reforms, writings in Bangla, Sanskrit, Hindi and Persian, all were translated by him in English of which the readers were Indians as well as the British. Some of his writings were available as early as in 1916.

By the time the Raja left India for England in 1830, a group of students educated in the Hindu College (established in 1817), Calcutta, emerged in the scene to take up the cause of English. It started with Henry Louis Vivian Derozio (1809-1831), a Eurasian of Calcutta, who published his *Poems* in 1827 and a long poem, *Fakeer of Jungheera* in 1928. Kashi Prasad Ghose published his poems, titled, *The Shair and Other Poems*. Derozio's students, known as 'Young Bengal,' shook the Hindu Society of Calcutta. Of them the most famous was Michael Madhusudan Dutt, whose *The Captive Ladie and the Visions of the Past* with Rajnarain Dutt's *Osmyn: An Arabian Tale* was published with the publication of simultaneous works by some more of them.

At the early stage of Indian English Literature Toru Dutt, writing around 1876, recorded her fine literary works; poetry, translation and prose in English. Her translation work: from Bengali and French has been considered very fine, even as she wrote before her death at the age of 21 years. We must also add to this the debut novel of Bankim Chandra Chatterjee (1838-94), *Rajmohan's Wife*. Swami Vivekananda, the great preacher won the heart of young India. His poems and discursive prose dealing with religious, patriotic and theological issues were extensively read. There was almost no political leader who did not feel the impact of Vivekananda's religious, ideological assertions in a changing society. Then came Manmohan Ghose (1869-1924), Aurobindo Ghose (1872-1950), later known as Sri Aurobindo, and Sarojini Naidu (1879-1949). Of them Sri Aurobindo's works covered almost all aspects of life and literature; first and foremost he was a poet, he wrote volumes of poetry, then political essays, journalistic writings as editor of dailies and other periodicals, philosophy, essays on Indian culture, on human unity, translations from various Sanskrit, Vedic texts, from regional languages, writings on Indian epics and scriptures besides dramas. He wrote many dramas with source materials from Greek, Roman, Arabic and other worlds and from Indian epics and mythology. At the beginning he too wrote like his elder brother, almost as an English man as they were brought up there but later he changed his subjects and dictions to fit in Indian Writing in English of which he was the most prolific contributor so far. Manmohan produced *Primevara* a book of poems with three British poets and colleagues. His next long poem, *Love songs and Elegies* attracted the notice of many perceptive readers. But their impact on Indian readers was less. Sarojini Naidu became famous for her book of poems, *The Golden Threshold*.

Many great stalwarts of Indian politics found it convenient to reach larger number of audience including the foreign masters of the country through the medium of English. The maturity, vigour, precision and erudition of their works enriched Indian English literature. Even in this genre of political and discursive writings Sri Aurobindo was the pioneer through his dailies and periodicals: *Bande Mataram*, *Karmayogin* and others. We may name some remarkable works here, like Dadabhai Naoroji's *Poverty of India* and *Un-British rule in India*, Ranade's *Essays in Indian Economics*, Balgangadhar Tilak's *Orion*, Works of S. Subramania Iyer and V.S. Srinivasa Sastri, *Father India* by C. S. Ranga Iyer in reply to a notorious India bashing by one Catherine Mayo in her

Mother India just like Sri Aurobindo's voluminous *The Foundations of Indian Culture* in response to such a book by one William Archer and in support of *Is India Civilised*? by Sir John Woodroffe. In this group we add further such outstanding works as *A Nation in Making* by Surendranath Banerji, *The Story of my Deportation* by Lala Lajpat Rai, *Autobiography* by Jawaharlal Nehru, *Fragments of a Prisoner's Diary* by M.N. Roy, *Cast and Outcast* by Dhanagopal Mukherji, *The Indian Pilgrim* (translated) by Subhas Chandra Bose and *My Experiments with Truth* (translated) by Mohandas Karamchand Gandhi. Nirod C. Chaudhury appeared in the scene with his *Autobiography of an Unknown Indian*. And may we add *Autobiography of a Yogi* by Paramahansa Yogananda, read by millions in India and abroad? The names of B.R. Ambedkar and Radhakrishnan must also be added to this list. And there were more writers after them to take their positions in discursive writings. Tagore also came into the scene through the translation of his own poetry. He wrote directly in English too, both prose and short poems. His production was one of the largest in quantity.

Among the fiction writers Manjeri Isvaran (1910-66) was an expert short story writer, conscious of his art. His first collection of stories appeared in 1944 under the title, *Naked Shingles*. Other remarkable short story writers were the three novelists who pioneered in writing the Indian English fiction at the beginning; Mulk Raj Anand, R. K. Narayanan and Raja Rao. Raja Rao was an erudite scholar professor, who travelled throughout the globe. The subject of his works spread in several countries besides India. He has a moralistic, philosophic attitude with a one-sided devotion towards Advaita Vedanta philosophy of Sankaracharya. Raja Rao has the special capacity or weaving stories around legend and myths. His works have international flavour which is symbolic also. Anand had a leaning towards left politics. He sympathised with the poor and down trodden. He was a first rank member of the Progressive Writers Association. Both the writers were patriotic in their attitude. R. K. Narayanan has told the stories of middle class people in a very intimate and lovable way. His stories and novels enacted in an imaginary Malgudi land have made him remarkable as a writer. *Malgudi Tales* is one of the best of his works.

Raja Rao's *Kanthapura* and *The Serpent and the Rope,* Narayan's *Swami and Friends* and *Malgudi Tales* and Anand's *Untouchable* and *Coolie* are remarkable works of fiction to begin the world of fiction in the journey of Indian English literature at its early stage.

The number of titles by writers from the Indian diaspora makes a vivid impression in American market. The writers include V.S. Naipaul, Anita Desai, Bharti Mukherjee, Salman Rushdie, Bapsi Sidhwa, Jhumpa Lahiri, Chitra Banerjee Divakaruni, Anjana Appachana, Kiran Desai, Bharti Kirchner, Sujata Massey, Indira Ganesan, Shauna Singh Baldwin, Vikram Seth, Amitav Ghosh and others. Some such writers might have now settled in India. Shani Muthoo from Trinindad and Marina Budhos from Guyana too constitute the Indian diaspora. Some of the writers have been included in the list of writers in their respective country of settlement. The whole body of writers of Indian origin writing in English, including those who are residents in India and are writing in English may be grouped as Indian English writers. Most of such works are prose writings. Some of the prose writers, fiction, criticism and essay, lived or living in India are: Satyajit Ray, Amit Chowdhury, Meenakshi Mukherjee, Kiran Desai, Arundhati Roy, Upamanyu Chatterjee, Sashti Brata, Shobha De, Khushwant Singh, Ramen Basu, Manoj Das, Prema Nanda Kumar, Kunal Basu, Susan Visvanathan, Lata Mishra, K.V. Raghupathi, K.V. Dominic, P.C.K. Prem, Sachidananda Mohanti, T.S. Chandra Mouli, Jaydeep Sarangi, Amarendra Sharma, Binod Mishra and many others including me. Many are the editors of anthologies containing critical, discursive writings in recent years.

Indian Diasporic Literature

A few words about the Indian writers settled abroad: there are different types of exiles for writers; some are chosen some are compulsive. If a writer writing in his/her mother tongue other than English is settled elsewhere than his / her native place where his or her language has no roots, it becomes very difficult as it has been for Taslima Nasrin who could not stay even in Bengal, once out of Bangladesh. She is the victim of religious fundamentalism and political weakness of the rulers in both the countries. Even Sadat Hassan Manto felt himself a fish of Bombay out of water in Pakistan. Alexander Solzhenitsyn and Boris Pasternak were political exiles as Taslima is, in the right sense.

But in the modern global village the excitement is often by choice in search of new pasture though the progeny of the ones who were in exile voluntarily had no choice, like Jhumpa Lahiri and V.S. Naipaul.

Neel Mukherjee, fiction writer settled in London, chose to settle abroad. His view is, "Yes, it was a very deliberate move on my part . . . . The garden variety of nostalgia, which is nothing more than a spurious, confected sentimentality, has ruined the migrant novel" (Interview with *The Hindu*, dated 6.9.09). He is more attracted to miscegenation of cultures than harmony. This is something which regularly happens with the second generation migrants.

Nostalgia they will have but sometimes it is more than an emotion. To writers of Indian origin India is a subject; the theme they regularly utilise. For them who are settled abroad, writing as such has certain advantages over their counterparts living in India. Besides their stay in a foreign country their attitudinal expression also counts.

Tabish Khaire, in a write up in *The Hindu* (dated 6.9.09) opines, mentioning such writers as Salman Rushdie, V.S.Naipaul, Hari Kunzru and Zadic Smith, that "They are the mirror images that make the liberal West feel comfortable with itself, because it feels that in gazing on them (and their works) it is reading and championing the Other."

He further mentions, "But unfortunately even an Indian who writes about India in English is not likely to be made visible by agents, clubs and book chains in the West: she has to write about India in certain approved ways, ways that very often depend on a celebration of the 'multicultural' West either as actual presence or enabling possibility."

We may add that not only agents, clubs and book chains act in that way, our big media too act in the same way, preferring the multimedia, the writers from the diaspora or the very big publishers having international links. India bashing is an approved way, as we have seen in the Booker or Oscar ways of selection recently. Agents may take up such cases on special considerations.

"For years, in the wake of Rushdie, I had imagined magical realism to be the last refuge of the non-resident Indian . . . . But for me now, more than magical realism, it's the painstaking attempt at verisimilitude that more clearly betrays the anxiety about authenticity . . . . Quite apart from this whole slew of stay-at-home writers, home being in most cases somewhere outside India, are the ones who like Adiga, have taken the bus, or at least a hired taxi to the hinterland. They might have travelled on a boat and risked being eaten by a Royal Bengal Tiger or they have walked in the tight smelly alleys in the slums and if they are enterprising, meet a hired killer or two . . . . But reportage is only an inoculation against the charge of authenticity. It hides larger untruths," writes Amitava Kumar in an article titled, 'On Adiga's *The White Tiger* in *The Hindu* on 2 November, 2008.

It is said that *The White Tiger* has shown the world the 'Real India' and there lies its value. Fact is there are several layers of Real India like 'Real Europe' or 'Real America.' Suppose someone writes a truth about executing one of the most brave statesmen and freedom fighters of India in the country's capital on some charge by the foreigners, almost towards the end of the colonial rule in India, conjured by greater Indian statesmen, greater because they survived, whom it would help in the immediate future, and their spreading canard to hush up the real deed, would that be welcome idea in the present set up of the country? Even if that be a fiction, it would hurt the heart of the then statesmen's present progeny, known to represent 'Real India.' Indeed what we know may be far from what actually it was or is. So there will be many such findings of 'Real India' out of the unreal or not-so-real. The question remains, is 'Real India' a truth or falsehood or a mixture of the two?

Spread of Indian English Poetry in the Most Indigenous Way

Including some unreal stories, popular and selling high by publicity and award and such things, it is true that Indian English writing, specially poetry, has been fast expanding mainly through serious literary or little magazines without any help from the big press or media. This media has been called by Bernard M. Jackson, a senior poet of England, as the 'small Press.' He has written in an article titled, 'Within the Heartland of Contemporary British Poetry—The half-hidden World of Small Press Publication' published in *The Poetcrit*, Maranda, H.P., in their July 2009 issue, that "It is the small press which has firmly established itself at the vital hub of poetry activity in the U.K., at this present time, and there is every indication that here the central force of poetry is destined to remain." He has added that not only in U.K., in India too Indian English literature is flourishing through this path.

In his article he has discussed different phases of poetry movement in Britain and opined that by the sixties of the twentieth century "Standard poetry was on a noticeable decline . . . ."

Among other things he has written, "When we speak of English poetry, I suppose it would be only natural for those living abroad to summon up thoughts of William Wordsworth's frequently quoted verse, or perhaps one might address one's ideas to recall of some of William Shakespeare's better known sonnets. Perhaps, too, the names and poetry of John Keats, Percy Byshe Shelley, Alfred Lord Tennyson and Elizabeth Barrett Browning may equally spring to mind. However, what can nowadays be seen to be abundantly clear is the curious fact that we in the U.K. no longer have poets of that same high stature as those aforementioned giants of yesteryears' poetry world."

Indian English poets are mostly living in India. While some names of older and living poets are repeated by the media or the establishment, we do not hear of their newer products. We do not seem to have noticed some poets who suddenly appear on the pages of the big media. Large number of poets, old and young, are on the scene, regularly writing in poetry magazines or general literary magazines and in regularly flourishing ezines and are thriving without the support of any big media. As the number of such poets is quite big and scattered we may name some of them admitting that there are more of them writing in different corners of India and they might have recorded their global presence also. It may be said that all the ezines are open to all poets and writers of the world, depending on the policy of the magazines.

Of the poets Harindranath Chattopadhyay, Srinivasa Rangasamy, Kamala Das (Surayya), Krishna Srinivas, Niranjan Mohanty, A.K. Ramanujam, Nissim Ezekiel, Amiya Kanti Das, Nirodbaran and Dilip Chitre have died. Some of the others still writing or have retired are Amal Kiran (K.D.Sethna), Jayanta Mahapatra, P. Lal, Stephen Gill, Keki N.Daruwalla, H.R. Tulsi, Vikram Seth, R.K. Singh, N.P. Singh, N. Karthikeyan Osho, K.K. Menon, A.P.J. Abdul Kalam, I.K. Sharma, Nar Deo Sharma, Hazara Singh, Rita Malhotra, K.V. Dominic, Sajaat Hussain, Bhaskar Roy Burman, K.K. Srivastava, Rati Saxena, Mohammed Fakhruddin, Gulzar, S.L. Peeran, D.C. Chambial, Pronab K.Majumdar, A.K. Chaudhury, Syed Ameeruddin, Pritish Nandy, N.P.V. Laxmiprasad, Shaleen Kumar Singh, P.C.K. Prem, Haraprasad Sharma, Jashvinder Singh, Ram Sharma, K.V. Raghupathi, P. Raja, Ritanath Keshari, I.H. Rizvi, Swami Nem Pal, Abdul Bijapure, V.V.B. Rama Rao, Mahendra Bhatnagar (though mostly through his translated works), T.S. Chandra Mouli, Annie George and others. But this list is never conclusive which includes me too.

Position of English vis-à-vis Hindi

The present emerging trend of the languages spoken and learnt in India shows that Indians speak more English than any other language except Hindi. We further know that English speakers in India outnumber those in the whole of Western Europe except U.K. Indian English speakers are more than twice in number than the population of U.K.

"These facts emerge from recently released (census 2001) data on bilingualism and trilingualism in India," writes Subodh Mathur as forwarded by P.C. Mathur. According to it, the number of speakers of various major languages were: Hindi-551.4 million; English-125 million; Bengali 91.1 million; Telugu- 85 million; Marathi-84.2 million; Tamil-66.7 million; Urdu-59 million; Kannada-50.8 million; Gujarati-50.3 million; Oriya-36.6 million; Malayalam- 33.8 million; Punjabi-31.4 million and Assamese-18.9 million.

In 2006 English as a medium of instruction ranked fourth, behind Hindi, Bengali and Marathi but by 2007 it climbed to second place and grew even further in 2008, as reported in the latest edition of TOI-Crest. Regional language medium schools have witnessed steady erosion in their share over the years. Data collected by the National University for Education Planning and Administration (NUEPA) as a part of DISE, the monitoring system developed for the Sarva Shiksha Abhiyan programme, shows that the number of those opting for English medium from class one to seven has grown by 150 per cent between 2003 and 2008, while the number of students opting for Hindi grew by just 32 per cent.

The states with the highest number of students in English-medium schools have remained unchanged from 2004 till 2008, which are in order of position; Andhra Pradesh, Tamil Nadu, Maharashtra, Jammu & Kashmir, Karnataka, Kerala and Madhya Pradesh. In the two top states almost a fifth of all enrolled students are studying in English-medium schools. By 2008 many of the northern states too have joined the rush for English schooling. Haryana has recorded the highest growth. In Rajasthan students opting for English schooling increased more than three times; the growth between 2007 and 2008 alone was 130 per cent. Studies through English medium have been rapidly increasing in all important cities throughout India. This shows the prospect of the growing Indian English Literature.

Why Hindi has not grown as the only Link Language of India

Whereas the then leaders at the time of independence thought of one official language, an Indian language of course, for all Indians as the media of interstate communication and as the link between Indians and chose Hindi for the purpose as it had the largest number of speakers in India which is still a fact. But the idea has not caught fire in spite of all incentives and preferential treatments.

India is certainly one country politically, though that too is challenged, it is at the same time many; culturally, linguistically, in terms of growth of intellect, material wealth and in various other ways Indians are different. But one strange thing is that spiritually they were one, they are one. They are linked by spiritual affinity. The language of some people has not been accepted by the whole of the country as their own for every corner of India has its own language, the mother tongue, which they love. Nothing should be given preference at the cost of the mother tongue. It is of utmost importance that different languages in India develop to the extent their speakers are able to do it, given all opportunities. Hindi could be developed to be the link language, it is so to some extent, but the problem lies in preferential treatment as the native speakers of Hindi have an advantage over those who have learnt it as their second or third language. All Indians and their languages being equal no partial treatment could be accepted in favour of any. We need not elaborate this argument. It is understood. Indians have almost automatically chosen a neutral language as their link language for here no one has an edge over the other in this matter as it is a mother tongue of none. Dalits have welcomed this language most for they could be more known to all Indian people through this language. And English is different from Hindi; it is international and rich with literary treasures, easier to approach and to have access to it.

The Lost Possibility

There was another way of acceptability of a language to all Indians, obviously it was and still is, Sanskrit. The mother of most of the North Indian languages, its presence is inevitably felt in all the southern languages which are replete with Sanskrit words, open or hidden. It tells about the oneness of Indian linguistic culture. It might not be the language of commoners for all the regions had their own languages but Sanskrit was the language of the rituals all over India. Still it is so. It is respected by all. Sanskrit spread more through religious route than others. While the pure classical Sanskrit, rich with its literature and other wealth is little difficult to learn, it is our imperishable literary treasure, as the works of Kalidasa and many others. Our two grandiose epics, *Ramayana* and the *Mahabharata* speak in Sanskrit. But he simple Sanskrit is easier to spread which Indians would love if properly nurtured. This was the advice of the Mother of Sri Aurobindo Ashram, Pondicherry, who said that Sanskrit is the cultural language of India and it should be the true national language acceptable to all. But it has not been and with English rapidly growing we have to think introspectively.

The Desirable Attitude towards English

While all the regional languages along with Sanskrit should be encouraged to grow, English should not be treated as a foreign language. We have absorbed many foreign things and people in our national life. They have been Indianised as the English. We may say that English today is one of the Indian languages.

There is another reason for Indian writers adopting English as their medium of expression; it is the scope it offers. The readership of English is really vaster than any regional language and most of the regional literary establishments are perhaps monopolistic in nature, partial in dealing with their writers, offering narrow scopes to others than who are preferred. It seems that Indian English literature is broader in its application offering vaster opportunities. It is fact that English is going far to capture the heart of Indians.

Conclusion

In India Indian English Literature has been flourishing through the small press along with publications by big and multinational press with edge to represent themselves vigorously before the public. Where we stand exactly is difficult to say at the moment but true it is that English language and Indian English Literature has occupied an enviable position throughout the world. On one hand some talented writers of the Indian diaspora are getting prizes from their countries of settlement, are getting patronage by big media in our country and on the other hand Indians living in India and writing Indian English Literature are steadily growing in number and quality though not reasonably acknowledged or rewarded by the Governments and their agencies and establishments.

22

De-naturalisation of Socialistic Models and Roles of Women in Classroom Texts: A Gender Viewpoint Assessment in Shifting Paradigms

—Dr. T.R. Muralikrishnan

Introduction

Critics have shown that language is conventionally organised around male concerns, and that female thought cannot truly come into being because it is compelled to follow the lines imposed by men. The very strategies employed in language texts might be seen by some as being exclusive. Many have demonstrated the way in which the 'exclusiveness' of language is reflected in language materials themselves. Women in course materials, they argue, are either absent, disempowered or stereotyped in terms of their relationships and professional lives. The exclusiveness of language may also be seen to discriminate against people with disabilities, or those from ethnic groups, or some social classes. Because of this apparent, continued marginalisation of the so-called minority groups, the world picture presented within texts may easily be seen to be false or artificial, upholding a model of elitism which pertains to a different age from our own. The discourse of literary texts used to teach students and the exercises which are provided are worth to a scrutiny on these grounds. To teach from a feminist perspective, then, is to face the challenge of presenting an alternative and more accurate view of feminism than students typically bring to class. This reclamation of feminism is difficult for any teacher who does such work. The present paper proposes to discuss the issue from this perspective making use of the textbooks prescribed in the Government Schools in Kerala.

As it has been noted by Ansary and Babaii (2003), the study of language and gender began in 1975 by the three seminal publications in sociolinguistics, viz., Male/*Female Language* (M.R.Key), *Language and Women's Place* (R. Lakoff), and *Difference and Dominance* (Thorne & Henley). Later research studies by O'Barr & Atkins (1980), Cameron & Coates (1988), McLemore (1991), Macaulay & Brice (1994, 1997) focused on the role of language in locating and maintaining women in a disadvantageous position in society. Hartman and Jude (1978) examined the images of women and men in the TESOL textbooks in order to understand the stereotyped roles. They found evidence that ELT materials reflect sexist attitudes and values and this would "reinforce the second-place status of women and could, only a little effort, be avoided." Hellinger (1980) found that men participated in more than 93 per cent of the 131 passages studied in the three ELT texts used in Germany, while not even 30 per cent of the texts included women. Porreca (1984) conducted a content analysis of 15 widely used ESL books and she found that "there is evidence that sexism continues to flourish in ESL textbooks." Arnold-Gerrity (1978), who conducted a content analysis of primary reading textbooks, found that men were portrayed in four times as many paying occupations as women and that the females were most frequently portrayed in a housewife-mother capacity, occupied with household tasks and serving their children and husbands. Many such studies point out the fact that education materials provide students with values which covertly or overtly patriarchal. Of late the emerging commitment to non-sexist language is commendable but the old practices still linger in many texts. Hence is the need of this paper.

Method of Analysis

In any form of linguistic analysis, the concept of critical linguistics is vital. The understanding that language is central to the formation of subjectivity is crucial. Similarly, the assumption that certain groups in any society are privileged over the others and, the oppression that characterises contemporary societies is most forcefully reproduced when subordinates accept their social status as natural, necessary or inevitable. According to Terry Locke (2005), a rhetorical view of the text (that is the art of making language work), can indicate precisely what should be expected in a text.

- People construct texts to achieve a desired result with a particular audience.
- Textual form follows function.
- Texts assume a social complicity between maker and reader.
- The expectations of participants in such acts of complicity become formalised in the conventions of genre.
- These conventions relate to such language features as layout, structure, punctuation, syntax and diction.

Sara Mills (1995) has initiated the concept of feminist stylistics for reading texts, especially literary texts. It may well be noted that Virginia Woolf stated clearly about gendering of authorship. The language available to the woman is patriarchal and inherently sexist. But the woman author, having no other language at her command, forced to use this sexist language, a language that does not capture the woman's experience.

According to Sara Mills, the need is to have "two kinds of information to construct the possible readings of a text which might be arrived at. First we need to make a close textual analysis of the text, identifying certain features of form- literary conventions, syntax, lexis, and genre and so on: the cues of interpretation. Second we need to make some generalised predictions about groups of reader's background knowledge of language, of literary conventions and of their models of the world." In the academic text analysis such practices may not always be helpful but still there are some pointers which would provide relevant clues.

In 1996, the Japanese government promoted the concept of gender equality in its reform for Education. As per its declared norms, the attempt is to "correct a gender-fixed consciousness of sexual division of labour and to nurture a view of gender equality based on consciousness of human rights" and "plans to enrich education and learning that promote gender equality, in school and social education, by enriching training for teachers and persons concerned with education and developing teaching materials." Such progressive ideas need to be discussed in detail in our context where the status of women is undergoing a paradigm shift.

Gender sensitive information given in the learning material should be probed thoroughly. The texts selected for the present study belong to standards VIII, IX and X prescribed in the schools meant for the state syllabus. The study does not in any way question the competency and merit of the learning materials but it only to tries to see that from another angle possibly to highlight the contemporary requirement of certain healthy, inclusive practices necessary. The point of the study is to bring out certain assumptions when it comes to certain roles in social life. The need is to redefine and reconstruct the fundamental assumptions, which would help the girls and boys in the classroom, as they pass out from schools to seek higher responsibilities of life. The study looks at the role of women as projected in the texts. The young impressionable minds would naturalise certain notions, definitely preconceived, regarding social roles of women. The three significant areas are:

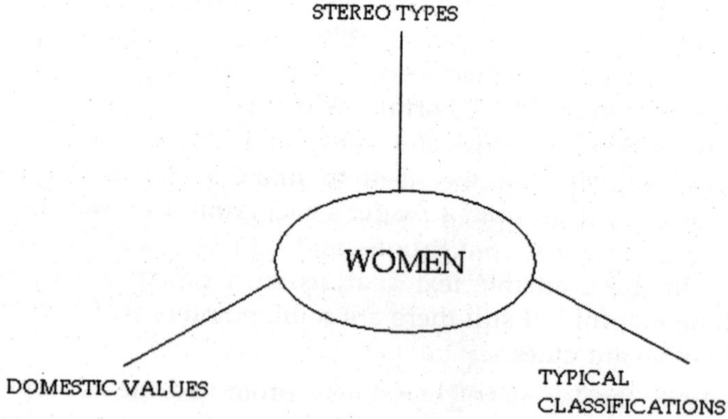

It may be noted that English language texts depend on social literature as well as creative writing for discussion. Varied themes such as history, art, science, culture, politics international issues, environment issues all are 'fit' material for texts. However textbooks do not promote gender equality much. Though Indian texts project women achievers such as Mother Teresa, Madam Curie, Indira Gandhi, Helen Keller, Rani Lakshmi Bai, the general representation remains far from satisfactory. Norms based on international understanding on women's issues enlist the following requirements:

- Women are protagonists.
- Women and men are not described according to stereo typical sexual division.
- Ways of living free of conventional ideas of femininity and masculinity are described positively.
- Topics encourage students to think about sexual discrimination and gender equality.
- Topics encourage students to reconsider various issues close to them from a gender perspective.
- Topics encourage students to think about women's human rights as a global issue.

Representation of Women as Stereotypes

The nature of human behaviour needs thorough scientific and psychological analysis before coming to rational conclusion. The texts which are put to scrutiny however posit certain problems. The women are attributed certain qualities which are in no way a reflection of the social reality but they are only characteristics promoted by films, advertisements, etc. In standard VIII text-book there is a communication exercise with a picture of two women talking standing side by side with a fence dividing them. The title is "A little gossip." An example of the talk goes like this:

Mrs Pillai: By the way...you haven't heard of Nancy recently, have you? She's marrying next month.

Mrs Menon: Really? She got her divorce only last month.

Mrs Pillai: Her first marriage lasted only two years, I think.

Mrs Menon: True. And her husband stayed with her only for three months.

Mrs Pillai: What a dreadful woman!

The talk presented here will reinforce the prevailing concept that when two women talk, the result or the nature of the talk is always a gossip. Feminists have argued that the male becomes the standard model for all things human. The woman is never seen as anything other than an object, a secondary figure to the primacy of the male. The values project men as rational and women as 'irrational' or emotional. The notion of 'subjectivity' is important here. While the man might be able to choose his subject position, woman's is pre-determined.

In the worksheet five of course book meant for standard IX, there is a question given for description. A picture of a young woman is given and the hints for description include lean, tall, fair, sunglasses, hair, dress, 20's, black eyes. The exercise can be seen as a first lesson for the school children in "male gaze." The traditional male oriented version of subjecting a woman to public exposure for "description" begins here. This stereo- typical attitude is blended into the textual material as "harmless." Patriarchal society attributes particular values to the woman's body and the woman assimilates these values. Feminists have objected to the objectification of woman's body such as beauty contests, where the body is a commodity for men's gaze.

In the standard X textbook there is a poem "Home they brought her warrior dead" by Tennyson. The questions given at the end include, 'Who succeeded where the attendants failed?' to which the students would certainly find the answer, a nurse of 90 years. But the question which goes unanswered is, why weeping in public an only alternative? Why should the textbook editor discuss the matter keeping in mind the possibility of woman as 'soft' 'tender' 'incapable of hard emotions'? Can't the wife live for herself? (Remember the last line "Sweet my child, I live for thee") The patriarchal values are reinforced through such subtle suggestions. Feminists argue that the values of motherhood are bestowed upon women by the society and these values are associated with the biological act of child-bearing. This becomes the central role for women to perform. The social values hence become attributed to biological acts.

Representation of Women as Domestic Help

The concept as such may not be novel but in a textbook for school students the continued portrayal of women as domestic help need to be analysed and questioned. One may not see men engaged in child caring or nursing. In the practice book meant for the standard IX, the task questions carry two pictures, one a man sitting pretty in the drawing room and another, a woman inside the kitchen. The question is, "Tom has invited a few of his friends to dinner. Tom and his wife have made all arrangements to entertain them. Now complete the sentences in the box using present perfect tense. The verbs given for the woman include, 'cook, arrange, keep, put.' Another question for using phrases (such as 'day by day,' 'day in day out') uses examples such as, "she cooked and cleaned ________for many years for them." "My father______ (read) the newspaper after returning from office and my mother ________ (cook) dinner for us" is a question on tense. Innumerable examples of such categorisation are found in course materials.

In the course book of standard X, the passage on reading goes like this:

"Last Friday, I took my wife and little daughter Sudha to see the Taj Mahal at Agra. We took the Taj Express. Sudha was very excited because she had never travelled by train before." The naiveté of Indian middle class woman is so blatantly asserted in the textbook. It may be worth mentioning what De Beauvoir stated. Her insight was that there is no 'essence' of a woman; a woman is constructed as such by man and society. "One is not born a woman but becomes one" (1984:267). Patriarchy makes use of sexual difference so as to maintain an inequality between men and women.

Representation of Women Cast in the Typical Social Model

The following examples help us to identify certain typical social situations in which the very nature of women becomes predictable. The society expects women and men to behave in pattern and the text is a representative sample to reinforce this thinking.

The course book of standard IX gives dialogue between a couple, Praveen and Priya. They were to meet at 4 o' clock in the restaurant. Praveen turns up late. Priya is angry. In the question, the tags are missing and the student needs to supply them.

Praveen: I'm little late, ______?

Priya: (Trying to hide her anger) No you aren't.

Praveen: You aren't angry with me, ______?

It is the woman who waits and it is her duty to 'hide' the feeling of frustration. In the same text, the students are given an option to choose jobs based on certain pictures interestingly the pictures follow the social norms in compliance with the prevailing patriarchal norms.

- Nurse- a woman
- Journalist- a man
- Beautician- a woman
- Pilot- a man
- Police officer- a man
- Driver- a man
- Teacher- a woman
- Military officer- a man

The society has bestowed certain preconceived norms and values for each profession and the textbooks we read only perpetuate these values. Feminists argue that gender is an ideology because it naturalises inequality between sexes by proposing that the biological differences are the determining factors rather than economic, social or educational ones. It also proposes and reinforces the difference in social performances regarding men's roles and women's roles as natural, pre-ordained and unalterable.

In the literary text for standard IX there is a poem meant to be appreciated titled, "The Beggar Maid." In the pre-reading part, the students are introduced to the poem with these words. "You have heard of great kings marrying beautiful princesses from famous families and celebrating the wedding on a grand scale. But have you ever heard of a king marrying a poor girl, that too, beggar? Here is poem in which a king meets a beautiful beggar maid and is carried away by her charm." The underlying notion of the male condescending to a poor girl is projected successfully which is already a reigning myth among the naïve middle class. Such values undermine the true identity of women.

Conclusion

Textbooks should not only reflect the times but prepare the learners for the future. Contemporary society calls for a better cooperation among men and women. In such a case textbooks should not project women as mere adjuncts. No doubt, text books function as a platform for the school students for furthering their linguistic skills. The language as such cannot be imbibed innocently. The material given for reading in the class room has some underlying socio-political values which have to be seriously looked into. It is important that authors should know how to ensure fair, accurate and equal treatment for men and women. The issue is not simply the use of pronouns and roles. There must be a serious analysis of present challenges taken up by women. In the learning material there must be a clear sexual division of labour, which includes gender in daily life, women's participation in society and nation building, human rights and violence, including domestic violence, and freedom from the shackles of femininity and masculinity.

Feminist pedagogy involves a commitment to gender equity in interacting with students. Not only must women students be acknowledged by validating their learning, but teachers must also be aware of the variety of ways in which they may, however unconsciously or unintentionally, discriminate against women in their classrooms. Women-oriented perspective will have to be given active consideration at the time for course content preparation. If not, the contemporary texts might continue to promote rigid patriarchal value systems without addressing women issues. The predictability of social roles and models of women in texts is a sure sign of academic double standards.

Works Cited

Ansari, H, E. Babaii. 'On the manifestation of Subliminal Sexism in Current Iranian Secondary School ELT Textbooks.' *Iranian Journal of Applied Linguistics* (IJAL) 6 (1): 40-56 March 2003.

Arnold-Gerrity, D. 'Sex stereotyping of women and girls in elementary textbooks and its implications for future work force participation.' Paper presented at the North Central Sociological Association. *Cincinnati*. May 1978.

De Beauvoir, Simone. (1984). *The Second Sex*. Trans. H.M.Parshley. Harmondsworth: Penguin.

Hartman, P. L., Jude E.L. 'Sexism and TESOL materials.' *TESOL Quarterly*. Vol. 12(4), 383-393.1978 .

Hellinger, M. 'For men must work, and women must weep: Sexism in English language textbooks used in German schools. In C. Kramerae (Ed.) *The Voices and Words of women and men*. Pergamon press: Elmsford, New York. 267-274.1980

Locke, Terry. (2005). *Critical Discourse Analysis*. London: Continuum.

Mills, Sara. (1995). *Feminist Stylistics*. London: Routledge.

Nayar, Pramod. K. (2010). *Contemporary Literary and Cultural Theory*. New Delhi: Pearson.

Porreca, K.L. 'Sexism in current ESL Textbooks.' *TESOL Quarterly*. Vol. 18(4), 704-724. 1984.

SCERT. (2006). *English Course book Standard IX*. Government of Kerala. Thiruvananthapuram.

______________ (2007). *English Practice book Standard IX*. Government of Kerala. Thiruvananthapuram.

______________ (2008). *English Course book Standard VIII*. Government of Kerala. Thiruvananthapuram.

______________ (2008). *English Course book Standard X* (Vol.I). Government of Kerala. Thiruvananthapuram.

23

Shifting Paradigms and Holistic Learning for Sustainable Development According to the Notion of Education for Sustainable Development (ESD)

—*Dr. Sarika Dubey*

Part I. Education for Sustainable Development means Self Learning

Since the notion of sustainable education has been introduced and emphasised it was understood that everyone already agreed to the concept of sustainability. This is especially true of the educational sector, which is a critical element for promoting sustainability and is a driving force for the change needed.

There is a paradox in our society that, while the mainstream economy and formal education is monetary oriented, the self sufficiency economy is also promoted following the King's concern about sustainable development and the people's well being. Unsurprisingly, we do have the promotion of greening the ground and saving the world, the environmental and energy saving, the social awareness for responsible and sustainable behaviour, the changing of consumption patterns, the improving resources management policy and practices and other humanised programmes. At the same time, our country has lost the national resources in proportion to trade her economic growth (GDP).

Considering the famous doctrine in Buddhist society, "Who create the cause deserve the consequences" should the past experiences be our lesson learned? Right from policy makers, economists, investors, producers, suppliers, marketing promoters to consumers, everyone at every stage of life, all over the country, are involved in this same situation. We are likely to share the same nightmare which are as follows: the global warming, the destruction of natural resources, the limitation of fertilised soil and fresh water, the shortage of food and agriculture production, the over consumption of luxury goods and instant productions and the overwhelming waste disposal. Who will be the first one to realise the real circumstances?

Looking at the above lesson from a self learning point of view helps to explain that the education for sustainable development (ESD) for Thai society is more than just about raising knowledge and promotion programmes. It should respond two-fold functions: to encourage social-engagement and as a change agent, in order to build partnerships of changing attitudes and responsibility for sustainable behaviour.

Part II. Holistic Education for promoting sustainability

The Education Reform Act (ERA) in 1999, to some extent, has been prepared for sustainability. It opened the opportunity for everyone to learn from different kinds of education programmes and curriculums such as home schools, non-formal education, and lifelong education, etc.

Unfortunately, the ERA practice did not interpret clearly the concept of personal development. Therefore, the ultimate goals of building a learning culture-based society, wisdom-based society and sustainable society were never reached. However, during the last decades, as a result of the Education Reform Act, alternative learning programmes and curriculums were launched in certain schools and institutions. The common goals were personal enlightenment, insight into self learning, interconnection and relationships between human communities and ecological communities.

Such a holistic education approach has easily led to learning to live sustainably and helped realise that everyone shares, as a part of mother earth, the partnership of responsibility. The crucial interventions which are required for promoting the holistic learning, as stated, to reach the ultimate goals, are the 3 components as followed:

The deep learning process aims to enlarge one's capability to learn (learning how to learn) in each proper stage of his/her life. Starting from basic self actualisation to self-directed learning, one can practice through different ethos such as Humanised Educare (Waldolf, Montessori, Reggio Emillia, Buddhist approach schools), brain-based learning, active learning, constructionism, dialogue, system thinking, contemplative education, mindfulness training. These learning processes directly influence the high proficiency learning outcome, providing that the learning partners (parents and teachers) are prompt to initiate those authentic learning atmosphere by themselves. Then the learner will be able to form their value systems and a vision of interrelationship of the whole oneness.

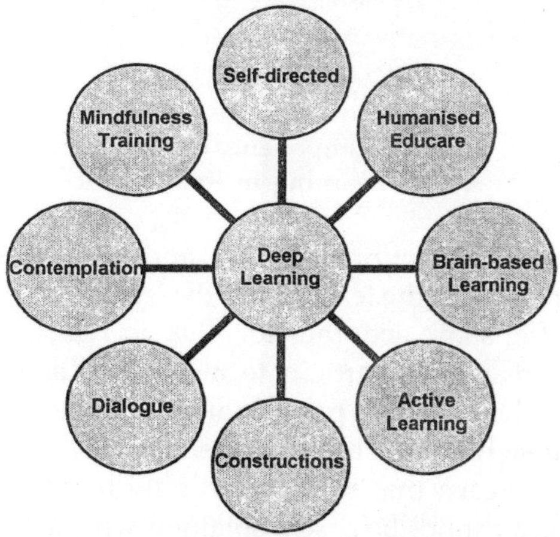

Figure 1. First Components of Holistic Learning Deep Learning Process

The Action-Learning in Real Sector: It aims directly to promote sustainable development parallel with social engagement. The real classrooms are usually waiting elsewhere outside the school. The learner should expose themselves to difference places and communities where the real living and earning activities happen. To deal with different cultures and ethnicities is also a prosperous experience. Various values, beliefs and visions are exchanged during these experiences. Many schools and institutions have already experimented this kind of special field study.

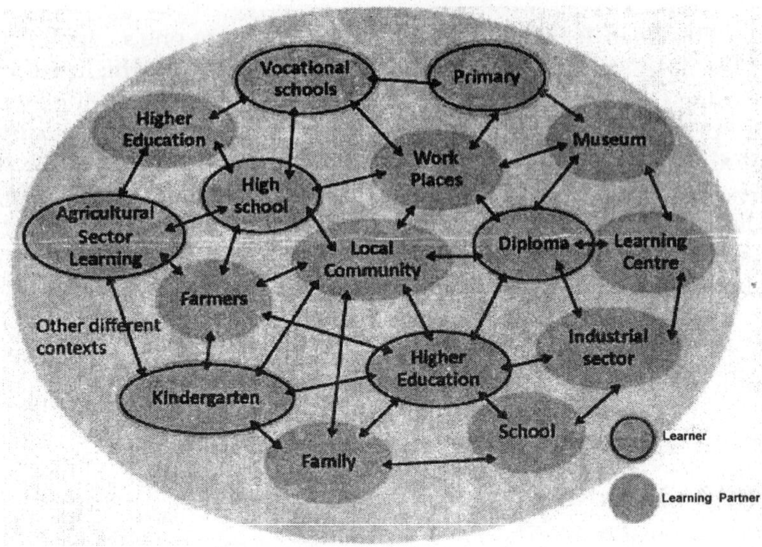

Figure 2. Second Components of Holistic Learning Action-Learning in Real Sector

The innovations of action learning and participation can be occurred by matching the learner and the learning partners to play their role in the same activities together in real time and place. In this, they can actually participate and equally share the existing situation, problem solving process and tacit knowledge. Finally they will realise how much effort one needs in order to do their jobs. They will learn that success can only be achieved by their own effort, and cannot be easily obtained with money like other commodities they are used to in the present world. Moreover, extra profits of knowledge and pride also come through this 'sweat your guts out' way. They will also learn the values of life through hard work, self-reliance and self sustainability.

The Interconnecting Communication-Based Learning aims to create a learning culture-based society. There are two important concepts behind this process:

- The dialogue in daily life practice, and
- The efficient public communication opened to real time/ live presentation.

Why is an interconnecting communication needed to be built in the education process? Actually, the present generation of mankind has to organise and deliver outside and the inside knowledge fluently. They are facing the difficulty of "literacy" in the sense of identifying, interpreting, and reflecting properly. Normally the root of constructions knowledge should originate from the inside rather than depending only on the outside instant information.

The (2 ways) interaction communication can be compared with the simultaneous information circuit of every cell in human body. Even though each cell is autonomous in its own function, but whenever unexpected situation is detected, the whole body cells automatically deliver and react to each other as soon as possible. If any single cell can stand alone, it doesn't deliver or react to other cells. It may become a free radical cell, which over consume other cells nearby, without knowing that the whole body will be destroyed, including itself.

From this example of cell's information circuit, one can imagine how to create the interconnecting circuit and how to use communication technology to serve efficiency in delivery and react system thoroughly. Getting to know each other all the time is the ideal learning process of mankind.

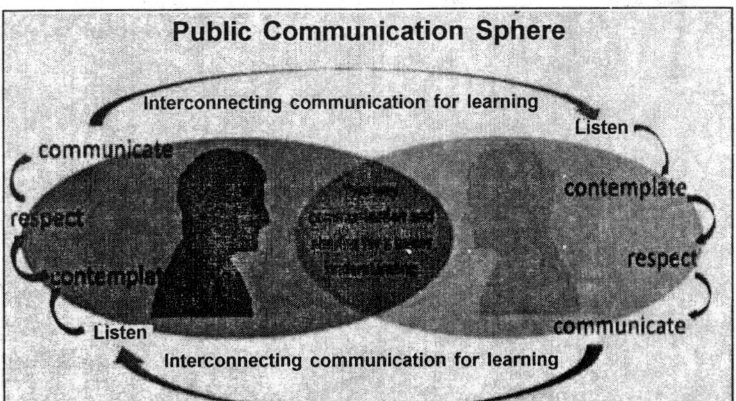

Figure 3. Third Components of Holistic Learning Interconnecting Communication-Based Learning:

In conclusion, the three components necessary for the holistic education has to be interrelated to one another in the same cycle. This input will promote a higher quality of learners and a learning-based society. Firstly, the systems thinking and deeper learning skills will support learners' self reliance and optimise their ability to learn, which encourages the formation of a wisdom-based society.

Secondly, the learning by doing skills and experiences through participation within the real sectors, will allow learners to truly engage with the complex connection of social issues, such as economic, ecological, social system, localisation, globalisation, technology, etc. The result will be the development of positive social attitudes towards a self-sustained economy society.

Thirdly, the interconnecting communication skills are the most efficient tools for being a lifelong learner, fitted with all kinds of context. Apart from self development, learners will be able to share and promote the social awareness issues along with civic participation. These abilities will contribute to the learning-culture society.

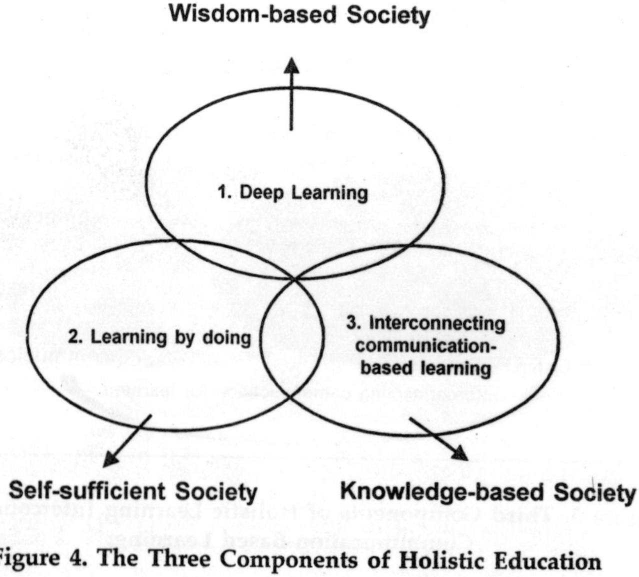

Figure 4. The Three Components of Holistic Education

Part III. The Implementation of Holistic Learning Approach to Promote ESD

What is important key factor of success in ESD under the concept of holistic learning? In general, teachers who are trained to be change agents will be firstly expected. It is also possible to design special teacher training programmes in order to achieve the well-round character of ESD teachers, as well as the design of whole ESD curriculum. But, carefully considering from the holistic point of view, those key factors are still the input from outside. They are separated from partnership building or the whole school participation, which are the real key factor of success and sustainability.

The implementation should start at the training of change agents through the building of partnerships, such as the model of learning cluster. In this model, whoever is ready to share and learn become change agents or learning partners of ESD. The whole process of implementing holistic learning into the education system to help promote ESD certainly requires strategic plan, and change agents.

One strategic plan suggested here has been developed from the sharing of experiences of a group of change agents who have been creating alternative schools and institutions during the last ten years. This group of change agents were networking and sharing their lesson-learned and tried to bring the development of human quality into social movements for the next decade. They proposed the model of Cluster of Learning Practices to represent holistic learning in practices as shown in the following diagram. The first agent to be changed should be the higher education institutes who will organise the research and development of each cluster.

The members of the cluster is composed of 2 partner groups, the learners and the learning partners. The main concept and input are the 3 components of holistic learning, as stated in part II. The process is the promotion of learning activities and training programmes, designed by both partners together.

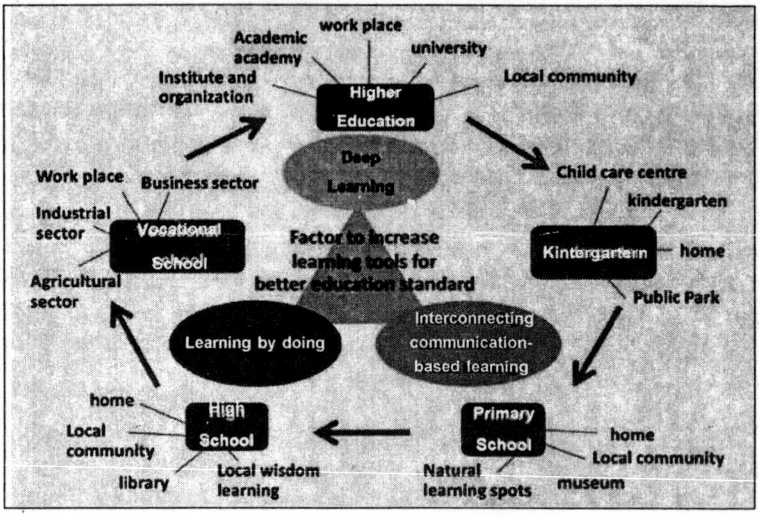

Figure 5. The cluster of learning practice (CLP model)

The cluster of learning practice (CLP model) should be functioned as an operating unit in term of research and development for ESD. The higher education institutes who have the experience in partnership building should operate the experiment together with their existing partners. The collaboration of partners can only be achieved when all parties are agreed on the 3 components of holistic learning. Any kind of training programmes, curriculum and pedagogy development should be designed in accordance with each pair partnership's requirement spontaneously. The sustainable ESD can only emerge when the CLP model has the right key factors, which are partnership building and the 3 components of holistic learning

REFERENCES

Institute of the Arts, Bangkok, Thailand.
Secretariat of Roong, Aroon School Foundation, at Singapore.

Bibliography

Abbott, G. & Wingard, P. (eds.) (1992) *Teaching of English as an International Language. A Practical Guide* Surrey: Nelson.

Ahulu, Samuel. (1997). General English. A Consideration of the Nature of English as an International medium. In *English Today,* vol. 13. no. 1: 17-24.

Akyel, A., & Yalcin, E. (1990). Literature in the EFL Class: A Study of Goal Achievement Incongruence. *ELT Journal, 44*(3). 174-180.

Allen, Virginia French. (1983). *Techniques in Teaching Vocabulary.* New York: Oxford University Press.

Allwright, D., & Bailey, K. B. (1991). *Focus on the Language Classroom.* Cambridge: Cambridge University Press.

Allwright, R.L. (1981). What do We Want Teaching Materials For? *ELT Journal, 36* (1). 5-18.

Alptekin, C. (1984). The Question of Culture: EFL Teaching in Non-English-Speaking Countries. *ELT Journal, 38*(1). 14-20.

_____________ , (1993). Target-language Culture in EFL Materials. *ELT Journal, 47*(2), 112-142. Al Seghayer K. (2001). 'The Effect of Multimedia Annotation Modes on L2 Vocabulary Acquisition: A Comparative Study.' *Language Learning and Technology* 5/1: 202232.

Anderson, P.S., & Lapp, D. (1988). *Language Skills in Elementary Education.* New York: MacMillan.

Annamalai, E. (2001). *Managing Multilingualism in India.* Sage Publications: New Delhi.

Arroyo C. (1992) 'What is the Effect of Extensive Use of Computers on the Teaching Achievement Scores of Seventh Grade Students?' (ERIC Document Reproduction Services No. ED 353544).

Arsham, H. (2005). *Impact of the Internet on Learning and Teaching.* Retrieved June 17, 2005 from http:// home.ubalt.edu/ntsbarsh/ interactive.htm.

Aston, G. (2000). Corpora and Language Teaching. In L. Burnard & T. McEnery (Eds.), *Rethinking Language Pedagogy from A Corpus Perspective: Papers from The Third International Conference on Teaching and Language Corpora* (pp. 7-17). Hamburg: Peter Lang.

Athlemoolan, L. (2006). 'The Role of Drama-in –Education in the English Second Language Classroom,' *The Journal of English Language Teaching* (India), Vol. 44/1.

Atkinson, T. & Davies, G. (2005). Computer Aided Assessment (CAA) and Language Learning, Module 4.1. *Information and Communications Technology for Language Teachers.*

Avery, P. & Ehrlich, S. (1992). *Teaching American English Pronunciation.* Oxford: Oxford University Press.

Bailey, Kathleen M., and Lance Savage. Eds. (1994). *New Ways in Teaching Speaking.* Alexandria, Virginia: Teachers of English to Speakers of Other Languages, Inc.

Baker, Ann, and Sharon Goldstein. (1990). *Pronunciation Pairs: Teacher's Manual.* Cambridge, England: Cambridge University Press.

Baker, Colin. (1988). *Key Issues in Bilingualism and Bilingual Education.* Clevedon: Multilingual Matters.

Bailey, Richard W. (1991). *Images of English. A Cultural History of the Language.* Cambridge: OUP.

Baldridge, Jason. (1996). *Reconciling Linguistic Diversity: The History and the Future of Language Policy in India,* http://www.ling.upenn.edu/jason2/papers/ natlang.htm [9 August 1998].

Bationo BD (1992) 'The Effects of Three Feedback forms on Learning Through a Computer Based Tutorial.' *CALICO 10/1:* 4552

Benson, P. (2001). *Teaching and Researching Autonomy in Language Learning.* Essex: Pearson Education Limited.

Barry, Peter. (2008). *Beginning Theory.* First Indian Edition. New Delhi: Viva Books Pvt. Ltd.

Bayer, Jennifer. (1990). *Language and Social Identity, Multilingualism in India.* Clevedon: Multilingual Matters Ltd: 101-111.

Benson Phil & Voller Peter. (eds.) (1997). *Autonomy and Independence in Language Learning.* London: Longman

Berg, C. (1990). Conversation Activities Based on Literary Readings. *The French Review, 63.*

Berge, Z. and Collins, M. (1995). *Computer-mediated Communication and The Online Classroom.* New Jersey: Hampton Press.

Bernstein, B. (1970). *A Socio-linguistic Approach to Socialisation.* In Gumperz and Hymes (eds.). 1972. *Directions in Sociolinguistics.* New York: Holt, Rinehart & Winston.

Bilaystok, (1990). *Communication Strategies.* Oxford: Basil Blackwell.

Biswas, A. and Agrawal , S .P. (1986). *Development of Education in India,* New Delhi: Vikas Publishing House.

Bonvillain, Nancy. (1993). *Language, Culture and Communication: The Meaning of Messages.* New Jersey: Prentice Hall.

Borg, S. (2007). Research Engagement in English Language Teaching. *Teaching and Teacher Education.* 23(5), 731-747.

Boulton, Marjorie. (2000). *The Anatomy of Language.* New Delhi: Kalyani Publisher.

Bowen, C. P. (1999). Technology Helps Students Learn Grammar. *Communication: Journalism Education Today.* 32(4), 17-18.

Bowen, J. Donald. (1979). Contextualising Pronunciation Practice in the ESOL Classroom. In *Teaching English as a Second or Foreign Language.* Marianne Celce-Murcia and Lois McIntosh. Eds. Rawley, MA: Newbury House Publishers, Inc.

_____________ Harold Madsen, and Ann Hilferty. (1985). *TESOL Techniques and Procedures.* Boston: Heinle & Heinle.

Bowen T. & Marks J. (1994). *Inside Teaching. Options for English Language Teachers.* Oxford: Heinemann.

Brandl K (1995). 'Strong and Weak Students' Preferences for Error Feedback Options and Responses.' *The Modern language Journal* 79/ 2: 194211

Braverman, Judi. (1994). Total Physical Response Vocabulary Practice. In *New Ways in Teaching Vocabulary.* Ed. Paul Nation. Alexandria, Virginia: Teachers of English to Speakers of Other Languages, Inc.

Breen, M. P. (2002). Syllabus Design. In R. Carter & D. Nunan (Eds.) *The Cambridge Guide to Teaching English to Speakers of Other Languages* (pp.151-159). Cambridge: Cambridge University Press.

Brett P (1995). 'Multimedia for Listening Comprehension: The Design of a Multi-media BasedResource for Developing Listening Skills.' *System* 23/1: 7785

_____________ (1997). 'A Comparative Study of the Effects of the Use of Multimedia on Listening Comprehension,' *System* 25/1: 3953.

_____________ (1998). 'An Intuitive, Theoretical and Empirical Perspective on The Effectiveness Question for Multimedia.,' http://perswww.wlv.ac.uk/~le1969/index.htm (last accessed, 14/ 4/04)

_____________ (2000). *The Design, Implementation and Evaluation of a Multimedia Application for Second Language Listening Comprehension.* http://perswww.wlv.ac.uk/~le1969/PhDthesis. html

_____________ & Motteram G. (Eds.) (2000). *A Special Interest in Computers.* Kent: IATEFL

Brown, H. D. (1994). *Teaching by Principles. An Interactive Approach to Language Pedagogy.* Prentice-Hall.

_____________ (1994). *Principles of Language Learning and Teaching* (3rd Ed.). Englewood Cliffs, NJ: Prentice Hall.

Brown, H. (1994). *Principles of Language Learning and Teaching*. New York: Pearson Education.

Brown, J. D. (1995). *The Elements of Language Curriculum: A Systematic Approach to Curriculum Development.* Boston: Heinle and Heinle.

Brown, Steven. (1993). Ten Things to Do Before Reading, in *New Ways in Teaching Reading*. Ed. Richard R. Day. Alexandria, Virginia: Teachers of English to Speakers of Other Languages, Inc.

Brumfit, C. J., & Johnson, K. (Eds.) (1979). *The Communicative Approach to Language Teaching.* Oxford: Oxford University Press.

_____________ (1980). *Problems and Principles in English Teaching.* Oxford: Pergamon.

_____________ (Ed) (1985). *Computers in English Language Teaching.* Oxford: Pergamon Press

Busbee, E. (2001a). The Computer and the Internet: Are They Really Destined to Play a Major Role in English Teaching? *English Teaching*. 56(1), 201-225.

Candido de Lima, D. (2001). English-as-a-foreign-language Teacher-training Programs: An Overview. *Linguagem & Ensino*. 4 (2), 143-153.

Carr, P. (1993). *Phonology*. London: Macmillan.

Carranza, M.A. (1982). "Attitudinal Research on Hispanic Language Varieties." In Ryan & Giles: 63-84.

Carrell, P., Devine, J. & Eskey, D. (Eds.) (1988). *Interactive Approaches to Second Language Reading.* Cambridge: Cambridge University Press.

_____________ (1998a). *'Introduction: Interactive approaches to Second Language Reading'* in Carrell, P., Devine J. & Eskey, D. (Eds.)

_____________ (1998b). 'Some Causes of Textboundedness and Schema Interference in ESL reading' in Carrell, P., Devine, J. & Eskey, D. (Eds.)

_____________ (1998c). 'Interactive Text Processing: Implications for ESL/Second Language Reading Classrooms' in Carrell, P., Devine, J. & Eskey, D. (Eds.)

_____________ & Eisterhold J (1988). 'Schema Theory and ESL Reading Pedagogy' in Carrell P, Devine J & Eskey D (Eds).

Carter, P. A., Holland, S. M., Mladic, S. L., Sarbiewski, G. M., & Sebastian, D. M. (1998). *Improving Student Writing Skills Using Wordless Picture Books.* Unpublished Master thesis. Saint Xavier University & IRI/ Skylight. ED 423 525.

Carter, R., & Long M. (1991). *Teaching Literature.* London: Longman.

Carter, R. (2007). Literature and Language Teaching 1986-2006: A Review. *International Journal of Applied Linguistics, 17,* 3-13.

Cartwright, L. (1977). The Teacher as Communicator. In M. Gill and W. J. Crocker (Eds.). *English in Teacher Education* (41-67). New England: University of New England.

Cassady, J. K. (1998). Wordless Books: No-risk Tools for Inclusive Middle-grade Classrooms. *Journal of Adolescent and Adult Literacy. 41,* 428-432.

Catford, J. C. (1977). *Fundamental Problems in Phonetics.* Edinburgh University Press.

Cazden, C. (2001). *Classroom Discourse: The Language of Teaching and Learning.* Portsmouth, NH: Heinemann.

Celce-Murcia, M., & Hawkins, B. (1985). Contrastive Analysis, Error Analysis, and Inter-language Analysis. In M. Celce-Murcia (Ed.). *Beyond Basics: Issues and Research in TESOL* (pp. 6-77). Rowley, MA: Newbury House.

____________ (1987). Teaching Pronunciation as Communication. In J. Morley (Ed.), *Current Perspectives on Pronunciation* (pp. 1-12). Washington, DC: TESOL

____________ (ed.) (1991). *Teaching English as a Second or Foreign Language.* Rowley, MA: Newbury House.

____________ Marianne, and Janet M. Goodwin. (1991). Teaching Pronunciation. In *Teaching English as a Second or Foreign Language.* Ed. Marianne Celce-Murcia. Boston: Heinle & Heinle.

____________ Brinton, D., & Goodwin, J. (1996). *Teaching Pronunciation: A Reference for Teachers of English to Speakers of Other Languages.* Cambridge: Cambridge University Press.

Chapelle, C. (1998). 'Multimedia Call: Lessons to Be Learned from Research on Instructed SLA,' *Language Learning and Technology.* Vol. 2. No. 1, 2234 http://polyglot.cal.msu.edu/llt/vol2num1/article1/index.html

____________ (2001). Computer Applications in Second Language Acquisition: Foundations for teaching, testing and research, Cambridge: OUP

Chatel, R. G. (2002). New Technology, New Literacy: Creating a Bridge for English Language Learners. *The New England Reading Association Journal. 38*(3). 45-49.

Chatterjee, K. K. (1976). *English Education in India: Issues and Opinions.* Macmillan: New Delhi.

Chaturvedi, A.K. (2006). *English Language Teaching in India, in Indian Book Chronicle.* ed. P. C. Mathur. Jaipur. October 2006.

Chaturvedi, M. G. (1974). *Language Teaching and Learning in India.* New Delhi: NCERT

Chen, C. Y., & Huang, H.Y. (2003). L2 Acquisition of Subject-Prominence by EFL Students in Taiwan. *English Teaching & Learning. 27*(4). 99-122.

Chen, H. C. (2000). Error Analysis of Some Features of English Article Usage. *Journal of Wu-Feng Applied Linguistics. 8.* 282-296.

Chen, H. J. (1999). 'Creating a virtual language lab: an EFL experience at National Taiwan Ocean University.' *ReCALL Online* 11/2: 2030 http://www.hull.ac.uk/cti/eurocall/recall/rvol11no2.pdf

Cheshire, Jenny. (1991). *English Around the World: Sociolinguistic Perspectives.* Cambridge: OUP.

_____________ (1991). Introduction: Sociolinguistics and English Around the World. In *Cheshire*: 1-12.

Chetty, Rajendra, Pier Paolo Piciucco (eds.), *Indians Abroad: The Diaspora Writes Back.* Johannesburg, STE Publishers. 2004

Chew, P. (2005). The Rise and Fall of Communicative Language Teaching. In Asian EFL Journal, May 2005, Conference Proceedings of The Future of English Education in Asia: 'Making Connections.' Pusan: *The Asian EFL Journal* Press.

Cho, K.S., & Krashen, S. (1994). Acquisition of Vocabulary from the Sweet Valley Kids Series. *Journal of Reading 37.* 662-667.

Chomsky, N. 1968. *Language and Mind.* New York: Harcourt Brace & World.

Chun, D. & J. Plass, (1996). 'Facilitating Reading Comprehension with Multimedia.' *System* 24/4: 503519

Chun, D. M. (2002). *Discourse Intonation in L2: From Theory to Practice.* Amsterdam: John Benjamins.

Clarke, M. (1988). *'The Short Circuit Hypothesis of ESL Reading or When Language Competence Interferes with Reading Performance'* in Carrell P., Devine J. & Eskey D. (eds.).

Clark, R.E. (1994). Media will Never Influence Learning. *Educational Technology Research and Development, 42*(2), 21-9.

Clément, R., Gardner, R. and Smythe, P.C. (1977), Motivational Variables in Second language Acquisition: A Study of Francophone Learning English. *Canadian Journal of Behavioural Science,* 9, 123-33.

Cobb, T. (1997). Cognitive Efficiency: Towards a Revised Theory of Media. *Educational Technology Research and Development. 45*(4). 21-35.

Collentine, J. (2000). Insights into the Construction of Grammatical Knowledge Provided by User-Behavior Tracking Technologies. *Language Learning & Technology.* 3(2). 44-57.

Collerson, J. (1977). Language in Teacher Education. In M. Gill and W. J. Crocker (Eds.), *English in Teacher Education* (98-134). New England: University of New England.

Cook, V. (1996). *Second Language Learning and Teaching*. London: Edward Arnold.

Cotterall, S. (1999). *Key Variables in Language Learning: What do Learners Believe about Them? System*. 27. 493-513.

_____________ (2000). Promoting Learner Autonomy Through Curriculum: Principles for Designing Language Courses. *ELT Journal 54* (2), 109-117.

Crawford, J. (1990). How Authentic is the Language in Our Classrooms? *Prospect*. *6*(1). 47-54.

Cronnell, Bruce. (1979). Spelling English as a Second Language. In *Teaching English as a Second or Foreign Language*. Eds. Marianne Celce-Murcia and Lois McIntosh. Rowley, MA: Newbury House Publishers, Inc.

Crystal, David. (1987). *The Cambridge Encyclopedia of Language*. Cambridge, England: Cambridge University Press.

_____________ (1988). *The English Language*. London: Penguin Books. Ltd.

_____________ (1995). *The Cambridge Encyclopedia of the English Language*. Cambridge: OUP.

Cullen, R. (2001). The Use of Lesson Transcripts for Developing Teachers' Classroom Language. *System, 29* (1), 27-43.

Cunningsworth, A. (1984). *Evaluating and Selecting EFL Teaching Materials*. London: Heinemann Educational Books.

_____________ (1995). *Choosing Your Course Book*. Oxford: Macmillan Heinemann.

Dubin F, Eskey D. & Grabe, W. (eds.), (1986). *Teaching Second Language Reading for Academic Purposes*, Reading Massachusetts: Addison Wesley

Dalton, C. & Seidlhofer, B. (1994). *Pronunciation*. Oxford: Oxford University Press.

Dalton, D. (1997). Some Techniques for Teaching Pronunciation. *The Internet TESOL Journal*. 3 (1). January.

D'Angelo, K. (1979). Wordless Picture Books: Also for the Writer. *Journal of Language Arts*. *56* (7), 813-814.Degler, L. S. (1979). Putting Words into Wordless Picture Book. *The Reading Teacher*. 32 (4). 399-402.

Dang, A. (2004). Reasons for Poor Teaching Quality. *Improving English Teaching*, Hanoi: Vietnam National University.

Das Gupta, J. (1970). *Language Conflict and National Development: Group Politics and Language Policy in India*. University of California

Davies, M. & Crowther, D. (1996). 'The Benefits of Using Multimedia in Higher Education: Myths and Realities.' Active Learning 3. http://www.ilt.ac.uk/public/cti/ActiveLearning/issue3/crowther/index.html

Day, R. & Conklin, G. (1992), March). *The Knowledge Base in ESL/EFL Teacher Education.* Paper Presented at the 1992 TESOL Conference. Vancouver. Canada.

______________ (1993). Models and the Knowledge Base of Second Language Teacher Education. *University of Hawai'i Working Papers in ESL. 11* (2). 1-13.

______________ (1993). Ed. *New Ways in Teaching Reading.* Alexandria, Virginia: Teachers of English to Speakers of Other Languages, Inc.

Demir, B. (2004). *An Investigation into the Effects of Motivational Factors and of Primary School Students on Learning English as a Foreign Language.* Unpublished *Attitudes* M.A. thesis. Çanakkale: Çanakkale Onsekiz Mart University.

Dewey, G. (1971). *English Spelling: Roadblock to Reading.* New York: Columbia University Press.

Dickinson, L. (1978). Autonomy, Self-Directed Learning and Individualisation. In *Individualisation and Autonomy in Language Learning* (pp.7-28). London: Modern English Publications and the British Council.

______________ (1987). *Self-Instruction in Language Learning.* Cambridge: Cambridge University Press.

______________ (1988). Learner Training. In A. Brookes & P. Grundy (Eds.) *Individualisation and Autonomy in Language Learning* (pp. 45-53). London: Modern English Publications and the British Council.

______________ (1992). *Learner Autonomy 2: Learner Training for Language Learning.* Dublin: Authentik.

______________ (1993). Talking Shop: Aspects of Autonomous Learning. *ELT Journal 47* (4), 330-336.

______________ (1995). Autonomy and Motivation: A Literature Review. *System, 23*(2), 165-174.

Dickinson, L. & Carver, D. J. (1980). Learning How to Learn: Steps Towards Self-Direction in Foreign Language Learning in Schools. *English Language Teaching Journal. 35,* 1-7.

______________ & Wenden, A. (1995). Autonomy, Self-Direction and Self-Access in Language Teaching and Learning. Special issue of *System.* 23 (2).

Dittmar, Norbert. 1976. *Socio-linguistics.* London: Edward Arnold Publishers.

Doff, Adrian.1988. *Teach English-A Training Course for Teachers.* Cambridge, England: Cambridge University Press.

Donaldson, R. P., & Kotter, M. (1999). Language learning in Cyber Space: Teleporting the Classroom into the Target Culture.*CALICO Journal. 16* (4). 531-557.

Donato, R., & Brooks F. B. (2004). Literary Discussions and Advanced Speaking Functions: Researching the (dis) connection. *Foreign Language Annals. 37* (2).

Dörnyei, Z. (2001). *Teaching and Researching Motivation.* Essex: Longman.

______________ (2001). *Motivational Strategies in the Language Classroom.* Cambridge: Cambridge University Press.

Dursun, E. (2007). *An Investigation into Reasons of Gender Differences in Foreign Language Learning Process at University Level Prep Classes.* Unpublished M.A. Thesis. Çanakkale: Çanakkale Onsekiz Mart University.

Edge, J. (1994). Toward Communication in and about Second Language Teacher Education. *TESOL Quarterly. 28* (2). 395-400.

Educational Testing Service. (1996). *TOEFL Test of Written English Guide.* Princeton. NJ: ETS.

Edwards, John R. (1982). "Language Attitudes and Their Implications." In Ryan & Giles: 20-33.

Egbert, J. (May 2002). A Project for Everyone: English Language Learners and Technology in Content-area Classrooms. *Learning and Leading with Technology. 29*(8). 36-41.

Ellis, Greg. (1996). How Culturally Appropriate is the Communicative Approach? *ELT Journal. 50* (3). 213-18.

______________ & Sinclair, B. (1989). *Learning to Learn English: A Course in Learner Training.* Cambridge: Cambridge University Press.

Ellis, R. (1986). Activities and Procedures for Teacher Training. *ELT Journal. 40* (2). 91-99.

______________ (1990). Activities and Procedures in Teacher Education. In J. Richards and D. Nunan (Eds.). *Second Language Teacher Education.* Cambridge: Cambridge University Press.

______________ (1991). *Understanding Second Language Acquisition.* Oxford: OUP.

______________ (1994). *The Study of Second Language Acquisition.* Oxford: Oxford University Press.

______________ (1997). *The Study of Second Language Acquisition,* Oxford: Oxford University Press.

______________ (1997). *SLA Research and Language Teaching.* Oxford: Oxford University Press.

______________ (2003). *Task Based Language Learning and Teaching.* Oxford: Oxford University Press.

______________ (2005). Principles of Instructed Language Learning. *Asian EFL Journal,* 7(3).

______________ & Barkhuizen, G. (2005). *Analysing Learner Language.* New York: Oxford University Press.

EnGauge. North Central Regional Educational Laboratory. Retrieved May 31, 2002 from http://www.ncrel.org/engauge/skills/21skills.htm

Ersöz, A. (2004). Key to Effective Teaching: Intrinsic Motivation. In G.Durmuþoðlu-Köse (Ed.) *Proceedings of the 5th International Inged-Anadolu ELT Conference* (pp.51-54). Eskiºehir, Turkey.

Esch, E. M. (1997). Learner Training for Autonomous Language Learning. In P. Benson& P. Voller (Eds.) *Autonomy and Independence in Language Learning* (pp.164-175). London: Longman.

Eskey, D. (1973). 'A Model Program for Teaching Advanced Reading to Students of English as a Second Language.' *Language Learning* 23/2: 169184

______________ (1988). *'Holding in the Bottom: An Interactive Approach to The Language Problems of Second Language Readers'* in Carrell P, Devine J. & Eskey D. (Eds.)

______________ & Grabe, W. (1988). 'Interactive Models for Second Language Reading: Perspectives on Instruction' in Carrell P, Devine J. & Eskey D. (Eds.)

Fasold, Ralph. (1984). *The Socio-linguistics of Society.* Oxford: Basil Blackwell.

Finch, A.E. (1998). Designing and Using a Learner Journal for False Beginners: Self- Assessment and Organisation of Learning. *Self-Access Language Learning Newsletter,* Retrieved June 25, 2006 from http://lc.ust.hk/HASALD.

Fishman, J.A. (1972). "The Relationship Between Micro-and Macro-socio-linguistics in the Study of Who Speaks What Language to Whom and When." In Pride, J. B. & Holmes, Janet (eds). *Socio-linguistics.* Harmondsworth: Penguin Books Ltd: 15-32.

Freeman, D. (1989). Teacher Training, Development and Decision Making: A Model of Teaching and Related Strategies for Teacher Education. *TESOL Quarterly.* 23 (1). 27-45.

______________ & Richards, J. (eds). (1996). *Teacher Learning in Language Teaching.* Cambridge: Cambridge University Press.

______________ (2002). Second Language Teacher Education. In R. Carter & D. Nunan (Eds.), *The Cambridge Guide to Teaching English to Speakers of Other Languages* (pp. 72-79). Cambridge: Cambridge University Press.

Fry, Edward Bernard. (1963). *Teaching Faster Reading: A Manual.* Cambridge, MA: The University Press.

Gardner, R.C. (1980), On the Validity of Affective Variables in Second Language Acquisition: Conceptual, Contextual and Statistical Considerations, *Language Learning.*

_____________ (1985). *Social Psychology and Second Language Learning. The Role of Attitudes and Motivation.* London: Edward Arnold Ltd.

_____________ (1988). The Socio-Educational Model of Second Language Learning: Assumptions, Findings, and Issues. *Language Learning.* 38. 101-126.

_____________ ; (1996), Motivation and Second Language Acquisition: Perspectives. *Journal of the CAAL.* 18 (2): 19-42.

Gardner, R.C., Lalonde, R.N. and Moorcroft, R. (1985), The Role of Attitudes and Motivation in Second Language Learning: Co-relational and Experimental Considerations. *Language Learning: A Journal of Applied Linguistics.* 35/2: 207-227.

_____________ and Lambert, E. (1972), *Attitudes and Motivation in Second Language Learning.* Rowley. MA: Newbury House.

_____________ and Macintyre, P.D. (1993), A Student's Contributions to Second Language Learning: Part II: Affective Variables. *Language Teaching.* 26/1:1-11.

_____________ and Smythe, P.C. (1981), On the Development of the Attitude/Motivation Test Battery. *Canadian Modern Language Review.* 37. 510-525

_____________ Smythe, P., Clement, L. & Glicksman L. (1976). Second Language Learning: A Social Psychological Perspective. *Canadian Modern Language Review.* 32. 198-213.

Garinger, D. (2001). Textbook Evaluation. *TEFL Web Journal. 1.*

_____________ (2002). *Textbook Selection for the ESL Classroom.*

Ghosn, I. (2002). Four Good Reasons to Use Literature in Primary School ELT. *ELT Journal. 56* (2). 172-179.

Gibbons, P. (2006). *Bridging Discourses in the ESL Classroom: Students, Teachers and Researchers.* London; New York: Continuum.

Gimson, A.C. (1989). *An Introduction to the Pronunciation of English.* London: Edward Arnold.

Gleason, H. A. (1955). *An Introduction to Descriptive Linguistics.* New York: Holt, Rinehart & Winston.

Goodman, K. (1967). 'Reading: A Psycho-linguistic Guessing Game.' *Journal of the Reading Specialist* 6: 126135

Goodwin-Jones, B. (2004). Emerging Technologies, Language in Action: From Web quests to Virtual Realities. *Language Learning & Technology. 8* (3). 9-14.

Gonzalez-Bueno, M., & Perez, L.C. (2000). Electronic Mail in Foreign Language Writing: A Study of Grammatical and Lexical Accuracy, and Quantity of Language. *Foreign Language Annals. 33* (2). 189-198.

Gorlach, M. (1991). *Studies in Varieties of English Around the World.* 1984-1988. Amsterdam/Philadephia: John Benjamin's Publishing Company.

______________ (1995). *More Englishes: New Studies in Varieties of English 1988-1994.* Amsterdam: John Benjamin's.

Gower, R., Phillips, D. & Walters, S. (1995). *Teaching Practice Handbook.* Oxford: Heinemann.

Graddol, David. "Thoughts from Kolkata on English in India." *English Today* 100, Vol. 25, No. 4 (December 2009). United Kingdom: Cambridge University Press, 21.

Granger, S. (1994). The Learner Corpus: A Revolution in Applied Linguistics. *English Today. 10* (3), 25-29.

Graves, D. H. (1983). *Writing: Teachers and Children at Work.* New Hampshire: Heinemann Educational Books.

Green, J. L. (1983). Exploring Classroom Discourse: Linguistic Perspectives on Teaching-Learning Processes. *Educational Psychologist. 18,* 180-99.

______________ & Wallat, C. (1981). Mapping instructional conversations: A socio-linguistic Ethnography. In J. L. Green, & C. Wallat (Eds.), *Ethnography and Language in Educational Settings.* Norwood: Ablex.

Green, S. (ed.), (2000). *New Perspectives on Teaching and Learning Modern Languages. Clevedon: Multilingual Matters.* Review by D. Ayoun.

Gruba, G. (2004). Computer Assisted Language Learning (CALL). In A. Davies & C. Elder (eds.), *Handbook of Applied Linguistics.* Oxford: Blackwell.

Gutierrez, K. D. (1994). How Talk, Context, and Script Shape Contexts for Learning: A Cross-Case Comparison of Journal Sharing. *Linguistics and Education. 5,* 335-65.

Gupta, Anthea Fraser, (1996). "Reading A : English and Empire: Teaching English in Nineteenth Century India." In Mercer, Neil & Swann, Joan. *Learning English: Development and Diversity.* London: Routledge: 188-194.

Haddad, Wadi D., & Jurich, Sonia. (2002). ICT For Education: Potential and Potency, in Haddad,W. & Drexler, A. (eds), *Technologies for Education: Potentials, Parameters, and Prospects.* Washington DC: Academy for Educational Development and Paris: UNESCO.

Halliday, M. A. K. 1970. *Language Structure and Language Function.* In John Lyon (ed.), *New Horizons in Linguistics.* New York: Penguin Books. 140-165.

______________ ; (1973). *Explorations in the Functions of Language.* London: Edward Arnold.

Hall, R.A. (Jr.), (1969). *Introductory Linguistics.* Delhi: Motilal Banarasidas.

Halsall, Paul. "Thomas Babington Macaulay On Indian Education." 17 Oct. 2007 <http:// www.fordham.edu/halsall/mod/1833macaulay-india.html>

Hamers, Josiane F. & Blanc, Michel H. A. (1989). *Bilinguality and Bilingualism.* Cambridge: OUP.

Hammond, R. M. (1995). Foreign Accent and Phonetic Interference: The Application of Linguistic Research to the Teaching of Second Language Pronunciation. In P. Eckman (Ed.), *Second Language Acquisition: Theory and Pedagogy.* New Jersey: Lawrence Erlbaum Associates.

Hampel, R., & Baber, E. (2003). Using Internet-Based Audio-Graphic and Video Conferencing for Language Learning. In U. Felix (Ed.), *Language learning on-line: Towards best practice.* Lisse. The Netherlands: Swets & Zeitlinger.

______________ & Hauck, M. (2004). Towards an Effective Use of Audio Conferencing in Distance Language Courses. *Language Learning & Technology. 8* (1), 66-82.

Handscombe, J. (1994). Putting it All Together. In F. Genesee (Ed.), *Educating Second Language Children: The Whole Child, The Whole Curriculum, The Whole Community.* New York: Cambridge University Press.

Harris, D. P. (1986). *Testing English as a Second Language.* New York: McGraw Hill.

Harklau, L. (2005). Ethnography and Ethnographic Research on Second Language Teaching and Learning. In E. Hinkel (Ed.), *Handbook of Research in Second Language Learning and Teaching.* Mahwah. NJ: Lawrence Erlbaum.

Harmer, J. (1991). *The Practice of English Language Teaching* (rev. Ed.). Longman.

______________ (2000). *How to Teach English.* Beijing: Foreign Language Teaching and Research Press & Pearson Education Limited.

Harsch, Kenny. (1994). Vocabulary Enrichment Through Word Association. In *New Ways in Teaching Vocabulary.* Ed. Paul Nation. Alexandria, Virginia: Teachers of English to Speakers of Other Languages, Inc. 128-129.

Harwood, N. (2005). What do We Want EAP Teaching Materials for? *Journal of English for Academic Purposes.* 4 (2), 149-161.

Hatch, E. & Wagner-Gough, J. (1976). Explaining Sequence and Variation in SLA. *Language Learning. Special Issue. 4,* 39-47.

Heaton, J.B. (1990). *Writing English Language Tests* (3rd ed.). New York: Longman.

Hedge, T. (1993). Key Concepts in ELT. *ELT Journal 47* (2), 92.

______________ (2000). *Teaching and Learning in the Language Classroom.* Oxford: Oxford University Press.

Heldenbrand, B. (2003). Drama Techniques in English Language Learning. *Korea TESOL Journal. 6* (1), 27-37.

Henry, L. (2003). *Creative Writing Through Wordless Picture Books.* Newark, DE: International Reading Association. (ERIC Document: Reproduction Service No. ED 477 997).

Hertel, T.J. (2003). Using an E-mail Exchange to Promote Cultural Learning. *Foreign Language Annals. 36* (3), 386-396.

Higgins, A. & Postle, G. (1993). Changing Paradigms: From Correspondence Schools to open Learning. *Towards 2000: Schooling Through Distance Education,* SPERA Proceedings of the First National DE Conference, Toowoomba: Australia.

Hillman, J. (1995). *Discovering Children's Literature.* Englewood Cliffs, NJ: Prentice Hall.

Hoch, F. S. (1985). Computer Literacy and the Foreign Language Teacher. *CALICO Journal. 3* (1), 17-18, 32.

Holmes, Janet. (1992). *An Introduction to Socio-linguistics.* London: Longman Group UK Ltd.

Hopkins, L. B. (1979). Look! No Words. *Teacher. 23* (4), 28-31.

Hoven, D. (1999), 'A Model for Listening and Viewing Comprehension in Multimedia Environments,' *Language Learning and Technology.* 3/1: 88103.

Hsieh, L. T. (2001). Business English: How and What to Teach. *The Bulletin of National Ping Tung Institute of Commerce. 3,* 59-70.

Huang, S. J. & Liu, H.F. (2000). Communicative Language Teaching in a Multimedia Language Lab. *The Internet TESL Journal, 6* (2). Retrieved May 23, 2005. from http://iteslj.org/Articles/Lee-CALLbarriers.html

Hughes, A. (2003). *Testing for Language Teachers* (2nd ed.). Cambridge: Cambridge University Press.

Huntoon, Diane. (1994). Verb Pass for Fluency Development. In *New Ways in Teaching Speaking.* Alexandria, Virginia: Teachers of English to Speakers of Other Languages, Inc.

Hutchby, I. (2001). *Conversation and technology: From the telephone to the Internet.*Malden. MA: Blackwell.

Hyman, L. (1975). *Phonology: Theory and Practice.* New York: Holt.

Hymes, D. (ed.), (1964). *Language in Culture and Society.* New York: Harper and Row.

India (1996). *A Reference Annual.* 1997. New Delhi: Ministry of Information and Broadcasting. Government of India. Publications Division.

Indian Constitution. (1998). Available at: http://www.uni_wuerzburg.de/law/,00034_.html [9 August 1998].

Indian Culture. (1998). Available at: http://www.anand.to/india/culture.html [9 August 1998].

Isbell, K. (1999). Intercultural Awareness Through Drama. *English Teaching Forum Online, 37*(1). Retrieved December 13, 2006 from http://exchanges.state.gov/forum /vols/vol37/no1/p10.htm

Jain, R.K. (1985). *Essentials of English Teaching.* Agra: Vinod Pustak Mandir.

Jalongo, M.R. (ed.), (2002). Using Wordless Picture Book to Support Emergent Literacy. *Early Childhood Education Journal. 29* (3), 167-177.

Jan, L.C. (2000). An Experimental Computer and Internet Based English Writing Course in CCIT. *Journal of C.C.I.T. 19,* 229-261.

______________ (2002). Interactive Online Discussion in an Internet Assisted English Writing Course. *Journal of C.C.I.T. 31* (1), 39-58.

Jayshree Mohanraj, *Spoken Conversational English.* CIEFL. Hyderabad.

Jenkins, J. (2003). *World Englishes: A Resource Book for Students.* London: Routledge.

Jespersen, O. (1922). *Language: Its Nature, Development and Origin.* New York: W. W. Norton & Company Inc.

Jordan, R.R. (1997). *English for Academic Purposes: A Guide and Resource Book for Teachers.* Cambridge: Cambridge University Press.

Kachru, Braj B. (1982). "English in South Asia." In Bailey & Görlach. *World Englishes.* 353-383.

______________ (1983). *The Indianisation of English. The English Language in India.* Oxford: OUP.

______________ (1986a). *The Alchemy of English. The Spread, Functions and Models of Non-Native Englishes.* Oxford: Pergamon Press Ltd.

______________ (1986b). *"English Education in India: A Socio-linguistic Profile of Indian English."* Nagoya Gakuin Daikagu Gaikokugo Kyoiku Kiyo, No. 15:11-30.

______________ (1986). *The Alchemy of English: The Spread, Function and Models of Non-native Englishes.* New York: Pergamon Press Inc., p.12.

______________ (1986c). "The Power and Politics of English." In *World Englishes,* Vol. 5, No. 2/3: 121-140.

______________ (1987). "The Spread of English and Sacred Linguistic Cows." In Gurt. *Language Spread and Language Policy Issues,*

Implications and Case Studies. Washington DC: Georgetown University Press: 207-228.

_____________ (1994). "English in South Asia." In Robert Burchfield (ed.). *The Cambridge History of the English Language.* Vol. V: *English in Britain and Overseas. Origins and Development.* Cambridge: OUP: 497-626.

_____________ (1996). "Opening Borders with World Englishes: Theory in the Classroom." In: On *JALT 96: Crossing Borders. The Proceedings of the 23rd Annual JALT International Conference on Language Teaching/Learning.* Hiroshima. Japan: 10-20.

_____________ 1997. "World Englishes and English-using communities." In Annual Review of Applied Linguistics 17: 66-87.

Kannan, J. & Macknish C. (2000). Issues Affecting On-line ESL Learning: A Singapore Case Study. *The Internet TESL Journal, 6* (11).

Kandiah, Triru. (1991). "Variation in Society—The Background and Its Impact." In *Cheshire*: 271-287.

Kao, C.C. (1999). An Investigation into Lexical, Grammatical, and Semantic Errors in English Compositions of College Students in Taiwan. *Fu Hsing Kang Journal. 67,* 1-32.

Kavitha, V. *Attitudinal Factor in Second Language Acquisition An Illustrative Example from a Class in University.* Language in India, Volume 9: 5 May 2009, http://www.languageinindia.com/may2009/kavithaattitudinal.html, 12 March 2010.

Kavanagh, F.J. & Mattingly, G. (eds.), (1972). *Language by Ear and by Eye,* Cambridge, MA: MIT Press

Kelly, G. (2000). *How to Teach Pronunciation.* Essex: Longman

Kenworthy, J. (1987). *Teaching English Pronunciation.* London: Longman.

Kern, R. & Warschauer, M. (2000). Introduction: Theory and Practice of Networked-based Language Teaching. In M. Warschauer & R. Kern (Eds.), *Network-based Language Teaching: Concepts and Practice.* New York: Cambridge University Press.

Kim, M. (2004). Literature Discussions in Adult L2 Learning. *Language and Education. 18* (2), 145-166.

Kitade, K. (2000). L2 Learners' Discourse and SLA Theories in CMC: Collaborative Interaction in Internet Chat. *Computer Assisted Language Learning. 13* (2), 143-166.

Kitao, S. Kathleen, (1993). Teaching Transitions. In *New Ways in Teaching Reading.* Ed. Richard R. Day. Alexandria, Virginia: Teachers of English to Speakers of Other Languages, Inc.

Kodchedkar, S. (2002). *Readings in English Language Teaching in India.* Chennai: Orient Longman.

Kohonen, V. (1987). *Towards Experiential Learning of Elementary English 1. A Theoretical Outline of an English and Finnish Teaching Experiment in Elementary Learning*. Tampere: University of Tampere.

_____________ (1989). *Experiential Language Learning Towards Second Language Learning as Learner Education*. Bilingual Research Group Working Papers. Santa Cruz, CA.: University of California.

_____________ (1992a). Experiential Language Learning: Second Language Learning as Cooperative Learner Education. In D. Nunan (Ed.), (1992a) *Collaborative language learning and teaching* (pp. 37-56). Cambridge: Cambridge University Press.

_____________ (1996). Learning Contents and Processes in Context: Towards Coherence in Eduational Outcomes Through Teacher Development. In L. Lösfman, L. Kurki-Suonio, S. Pellinen & J. Lehtonen (Eds.). *Effectiveness of teacher education: New challenges and approaches to evaluation* (pp. 63-84). Tampere: Reports from the Department of Teacher Education in Tampere University.

_____________ (1999). Authentic Assessment in Affective Foreign Language Education. In J. Arnold (Ed.) *Affect in Language Learning*. Cambridge: Cambridge University Press.

Kramsch, C. (1985). Literary Texts in the Classroom: A Discourse Perspective. *The Modern Language Journal. 69*(4), 356-366.

_____________ & Andersen, R.W. (1999, January). Teaching Text and Context Through Multimedia. *Language Learning & Technology, 2* (2), 31-42. Retrieved June 7, 2004, from http://llt.msu.edu/vol2num2/article1/

Krashen, S.D. (1988). *Second Language Acquisition and Second Language Learning*. London: Prentice Hall.

Kreutzer, M., & Neunzig, W. (1997). Computer Assisted Learning, Teacher Training and An Evaluation of a Seminar for Language Teachers. *CALICO Journal. 14* (2-4), 65-79.

Ladefoged, P. (1982). *A Course in Phonetics*. New York: Harcourt Brace.

Lambert, W.E. (1963b), Psychological Approaches to the Study of Language Part II: On the Second Language Learning and Bilingualism. *Modern Language Journal*. 14, 114-121.

_____________ (1974). *Culture and Language as Factors in Learning and Education*. In F. F. Aboud & R. D. Meade (Eds.), *Cultural Factors in Learning and Education*. Bellingham: Western Washington State University.

Lao, C.Y., & Krashen, S. (2000). The Impact of Popular Literature Study on Literacy Development in EFL: More Evidence for the Power of Reading. *System 28*. 261- 270.

Lazar, G. (1993). *Literature and Language Teaching: A Guide for Teachers and Trainers*. Cambridge, England: Cambridge University Press.

_____________ (1993). *Literature and Language Teaching*. Cambridge: Cambridge University Press.

_____________ (1994). Using literature at lower levels. *ELT Journal, 48*(2), 115-124.

Lee, I. (1998). Supporting Greater Learner Autonomy in Language Learning. *ELT Journal. 52*(4), 282-291.

Lee, K. (2000). English Teachers' Barriers to the Use of Computer-Assisted Language Learning. *The Internet TESL Journal. 6* (12).

Lee, S. (2000). Teaching Writing Using a Bulletin Board on the Internet: A Preliminary Study. *English Teaching. 55* (3), 171-191.

_____________ & Krashen, S. (2002). Predictors of Success in Writing English as a Foreign Language: Reading, Revision Behavior, Apprehension, and Writing. *College Student Journal. 36*, 532-543.

Lee, W.R. (1994). *Language Teaching Games*. Oxford: Oxford University Press.

Lennon, P. (1989). Introspection and Intentionality in Advanced SLA. *Language Learning. 39*, 375-395.

Leech, G. (1998). Preface. In S. Granger (Eds.), *Learner English on Computer*. London and New York: Addison Wesley Longman.

Lemke, J. L. (1990). *Talking Science: Language, Learning, and Values*. Norwood, NJ: Ablex.

Levy, M. (1997). *Computer-Assisted Language Learning: Context and Conceptualisation*. London: Clarendon Press.

_____________ & Hill, J. (1992) *Practical Techniques for Language Teaching*. Hove: Language Teaching Publications.

Liaw, M. L. (2001). Exploring Literary Responses in an EFL Classroom. *Foreign Language Annals. 34*, 35-45.

Li, G. (2000a). *A New English Course*. Book Five. Shanghai: Shanghai Foreign Language Education Press.

_____________ (2000b). *A New English Course*. Book Six. Shanghai: Shanghai Foreign Language Education Press.

Lightbown, P. (1985). Great Expectations: Second Language Acquisition Research and Classroom Teaching. *Applied Linguistics. 6* (2), 173-189.

Lightbown, P.M. & Spada, N. (1993). *How Languages are Learned*. Oxford: Oxford University Press.

Lindauer, S. K. (1988). Wordless Books: An Approach to Visual Literacy. *Children's Literature in Education. 19* (3), 136-142.

Lin,Yen-Chi A. (2004). *An Assessment of the International Students' Attitudes Toward Technology-Based Learning: English as a Second Language (ESL) Implication*. Mississippi State University. DAI. A 65/02, 478.

Liou, H. C., & Yeh, H. Y. (2000). *A Study of Using Web Articles to Support College English Students' Ideas in Writing*. Paper presented in Learning Societies in the New Millennium: Creativity, Caring & Commitments. International Conference on Computers in Education/International Conference on Computer-Assisted Instruction, Taipei, Taiwan.

Littlewood, W. (1990). *Communicative Language Teaching*. Cambridge: Cambridge University Press.

_____________ (2000). Do Asian Students Really Want to Listen and Obey? *ELT Journal*. *54* (1), 31-35.

Llosa, L. (2007). Validating a Standards-based Classroom Assessment of English Proficiency: A Multi-trait-Multi-method approach. *Language Testing*. *24* (4), 489–515.

Long, M. (1985) Input and Second Language Acquisition Theory. *Input in SLA Acquisition, 377-93.*

Logan, S. & Moore, N. (2004). Implementing Learner Training from a Teacher's Perspective. In H. Reinders (et al) (Eds.), *Supporting Independent Learning in the 21st Century: Proceedings of the Independent Learning Association Conference*, the University of Melbourne, Australia.

Loveday, Leo. (1982). *The Socio-linguistics of Learning and Using a Non-Native Language*. Oxford: Pergamon Press Ltd.

Lukmani, Y.M. (1972). Motivation to Learn and Language Proficiency. *Language Learning*. 22, 261-273.

Lynch, B. & T. Hudson, (1988). EST Reading. In M. Celce-Murcia (Ed.), *Teaching English As A Second or Foreign Language*. Boston: Heinle & Heinle.

MacCarthy, P. (1978). *The Teaching of Pronunciation*. Cambridge: Cambridge University Press.

MacDonald, M., Badger, R., & White, G. (2001). Changing Values: What Use are Theories of Language Learning and Teaching? *Teaching and Teacher Education*. *17* (8), 949-963.

McKay, S. (1982). Literature in the ESL Classroom. *TESOL Quarterly*. *16* (4), 529-36.

Mantero, M. (2001). *The Reasons We Speak: A Socio-cultural Discourse Analysis of Text-based Talk in a University Level Foreign Language Classroom*. The Florida State University.

Maddox, H. (1998). *How to Study*. New Delhi: Rupa Paperbacks.

Mahapatra, B.P. (1990). "A Demographic Appraisal of Multi-lingualism in India." In Pattanayak: 1-14.

Majumdar. S. (Ed.), (2005). Regional Guideline for Teacher Development for Pedagogy Technology Integration. Thailand: UNESCO.

MacCarthy, P. (1978). *The Teaching of Pronunciation.* Cambridge: Cambridge University Press.

Matas, C.P. & Birch, G. (2000). Web-based Second Language Grammar Development: Researching the Options. *CALL-EJ Online, 1* (3).

McCarthy, C.P. (1998). Learner Training for Learner Autonomy on Summer Language Courses. *The Internet TESL Journal 3* (7).

McCrum, Robert, Cran, Willian, McNeil, Robert. (1988). *The Story of English.* London: Faber& Faber Ltd. & BBC Books.

McEnery, T. & Others (1995). A Statistical Analysis of Corpus Based Computer vs. Traditional Human Teaching Methods of Part of Speech Analysis. *Computer-Assisted Language Learning. 8* (2-3), 259-74.

McGrath, I. (1995). *Feeding, Leading, Showing, and Throwing: Process Choices in Teacher Training and Trainer Training, in Learning to Train: Perspectives on the Development of Language Teacher Trainers.* Prentice Hall Europe, in association with the British Council.

McGregor, L., Tate M.and Robinson, K. (1977). *Learning through Drama: Report of the School Council Drama Teaching Project* (10-16).

McNamara, J. (1973). Nurseries, Streets and Classrooms: Some Comparisons and Deductions. *Modern Language Journal. 57,* 250-255.

Meganathan, Rama. *English Language Education in Rural Schools of India: The Situation, the Policy and the Curriculum.30 .10. 2009.* http://www.teachingenglish.org.

Mehan, H. (1979). *Learning Lessons: Social Organisation in the Classroom.* Cambridge, MA: Harvard University Press.

Mehrotra, R.R. English in *India*: The Current Scene *ELT Journal.* 1977 XXXI (2): 163-170. London: OUP. 1977.

Methods of Teaching English (PGCTE). CIEFL. Hyderabad.

Meunier, L. E. (1994). Computer-assisted Language Instruction and Co-operative learning. *Applied Language Learning 5* (2), 31-56.

Milton, J. & Garbi, A. (2000). VIRLAN: Collaborative Foreign Language Learning on the Internet for Primary Age Children: Problems and a Solution. *Educational Technology & Society. 3* (3).

Mo, L. (1999). On the Participants of English Listening Course and Their Functions. *Journal of PLA University of Foreign Languages. 109*(4), 75-78.

Morley, J. (1987). *Current Perspectives on Pronunciation.* Washington. DC: YESOL.

_____________ (1991). The Pronunciation Component in Teaching English to Speakers of Other Languages. *TESOL Quarterly. 25* (1), 51-74.

_____________ (1991). Listening Comprehension in Second/Foreign Language Instruction. In *Teaching English as a Second or Foreign Language*. Ed. Marianne Celce-Murcia. Boston: Heinle & Heinle.

Mullins, P. (1992). *Successful English Language Learning Strategies of Students Enrolled in the Faculty of Arts, Chulalonkorn University, Bangkok Thailand*. United States International University. San Diego, CA.

Mynard, J. (1999). *Motivation for Learning English Among First Year Female University Students in Abu Dhabi*. Exeter: The University of Exeter.

Nation, Paul. (1994). (Ed.), *New Ways in Teaching Vocabulary*. Alexan- dria, Virginia: Teachers of English to Speakers of Other Languages, Inc.

NCERT. (2005). *National Curriculum Framework*. New Delhi: NCERT.

Nunan, D. (1989) *Designing Tasks for the Communicative Classroom*. Cambridge: Cambridge University Press.

_____________ ;(2002). Learner Strategy Training in the Classroom: An Action Research Study. In J.C. Richards & W. A. Renandya (Eds.), *Methodology in Language Teaching*. Cambridge: Cambridge University Press.

_____________ and Lindsay Miller. (Eds). 1995. *New Ways in Teaching Listening*. Alexandria, Virginia: Teachers of English to Speakers of Other Languages, Inc.

Nunn, R. (2005). Competence and Teaching English as an International Language. *Asian EFL Journal*. 7 (3). Retrieved Mar. 5, 2007 from http://www.asian-efljournal.com/September_05_ rn.php

Nutta, Joyce (1998). Is Computer-based Grammar Instruction as Effective as Teacher-Directed Grammar Instruction for Teaching L2 Structures? *CALICO Journal. 16* (1), 49-62.

Nystrand, M. (1997). *Opening Dialogue: Understanding the Dynamics of Language and Learning in the English Classroom*. New York: Teachers College Press (with A. Gamoran, R. Kachur, & C. Prendergast).

O'Brien, T. (1981). The E-R-O-T-I Model: A Stimulating Guide for Teacher Training. *In British Council ELT Documents. 110*, 54 - 61.

Oberprieler, G. (1999). Outcome-based Learning and The Role of CALL in South Africa. In R. Debski & M. Levy (Eds.), *WorldCALL: Global Perspectives on Computer-assisted Language Learning*. Swets & Zeitlinger.

O'Grady, William, Michael Dabrovolsky, and Mark Aronoff. (1993). *Contemporary Linguistics: An Introduction*. New York: St. Martin's Press.

Oxford, R.L. (2006). Task-based Language Teaching and Learning: An Overview. *Asian EFL Journal. 8* (3).

Ozad, B. (1999). *Process in Teacher Training*. Retrieved from http:// sfl.emu.edu.tr/tu /oldconferences/ 19992000/papers.htm

Palmer, H.E. (1917). *The Scientific Study and Teaching of Languages.* London: Harrap.

Parkinson, B., & Thomas H.R. (2000). *Teaching Literature in a Second Language.* Edinburgh: Edinburgh University Press.

Patrikis, P.C. (1997). The Evolution of Computer Technology in Foreign Language Teaching and Learning. In R. Debski, J. Gassin & M. Smith (Eds.), *Language Learning Through Social Computing* (p.176). ALAA& The Horwood Language Centre.

Pennington, M.C. (1990). A Professional Development Focus for the Language Teaching Practicum. In J. Richards and D. Nunan, (Eds), *Second Language Teacher Education* (pp. 132 - 151). Cambridge: Cambridge University Press.

Parrott, M. (1993). *Tasks for Language Teachers.* Cambridge: Cambridge University Press.

Philips, M. (1987). Potential Paradigms and Possible Problems for CALL. *System. 15*(3), 275-287.

Pray, L. (2005). How well do Commonly Used Language Instruments Measure English Oral-Language Proficiency? *Bilingual Research Journal. 29* (2), 387-409.

Pathak, R.S. (1999). *Teaching English in India.* New Delhi: Creative Books.

Pattanayak, D.P. (1990). *Multilingualism in India* (Ed.). Clevedon: Multilingual Matters Ltd.

_______________ (2005). *India: A Multilingual Perspective.* A Report. New Delhi: NCERT.

Pennycook, Alastair. (1994). *The Cultural Politics of English as an International Language.* Harlow: Longman Group Ltd.

Plaister, Ted. (1994). My Friends Call Me Ted. In *New Ways in Teaching Speaking.* Alexandria, Virginia: Teachers of English to Speakers of Other Languages, Inc.

Plaister, Ted. (1994). Using a Box of Raisins to Promote Speech. In *New Ways in Teaching Speaking.* Alexandria, Virginia: Teachers of English to Speakers of Other Languages, Inc

Platt, J., Weber, H., Ho, M.L. (1984). *The New Englishes.* London: Routledge & Kegan Paul.

Poplack, Shana. (2001). 'Code Switching: Linguistic' in *International Encyclopedia of the Social & Behavioral Sciences,* Elsevier Science Ltd.

Prator, Jr., Clifford H. and Betty Wallace Robinett. (1972). *Manual of American English Pronunciation.* Third Edition. New York: Holt, Rinehart and Winston, Inc.

Price, Karen. (1987). The Use of Technology: Varying the Medium of Language Teaching. In Wilga M. Rivers (ed.), *Interactive Language Teaching.* (pp.155- 169). Melbourne, CUP.

Raimes, Ann. (1983). *Techniques in Teaching Writing*. New York: Oxford University Press.

Ramanathan, H. (2008). Testing of English in India: A Developing Concept. *Language Testing*. *25* (1), 111-126.

Rayner, K. & Pollatsek, A. (1989). *The Psychology of Reading:* New Jersey: Prentice Hall.

Reese, C. (1996). Story Development Using Wordless Picture Books. *The Reading Teacher*. *50*, 172-173.

Richard, A.P. (1987). *Making it Happen. Interaction in the Second Language Classroom: From Theory to Practice*. Harlow: Longman.

Richard C. Jack (2006), "Intro: New Interchange. English for International Communication." Cambridge: OUP.

Richards, J.C. and Rodgers, T.S. 2002. *Approaches and Methods in Language Teaching*. Delhi, Cambridge University Press.

_____________ & Nunan, D. (eds.). (1990). *Second Language Teacher Education*. Cambridge: Cambridge University Press.

R.N. Ghosh, *Indian Bi-lingualism and the Teaching of English*. CIEFL, Hyderabad.

Roach, P. (2000). *English Phonetics and Phonology*. Cambridge: Cambridge University Press.

Robinett, B.W. (1978). *Teaching English to Speakers of other Languages: Substance and Technique*. Minneapolis: University of Minnesota Press.

Robinson, P. (2001). *Cognition and Second Language Instruction*. Cambridge: Oxford University Press.

_____________ (2002). The Pervading Influence of Neo-Confucianism on the Korean Education System. *Asian EFL Journal*. *4* (2).

_____________ (2003). Teaching English Pronunciation Skills to the Asian Learner. A Cultural Complexity or Subsumed Piece of Cake? *Asian EFL Journal*. June.

Romaine, Suzanne. (1995). *Bilingualism* (2nd ed.). Oxford: Blackwell Publishers.

Rost, M. (1990). *Listening in Language Learning*. London: Longman.

_____________ (2001). Listening. In R. Carter & D. Nunan (Eds.), *The Cambridge Guide to Teaching English to Speakers of other Languages* (pp. 7-13). Cambridge: Cambridge University Press.

Ryan, Ellen Bouchard & Giles, Howard. (1982). *Attitudes Towards Language Variation*. London: Edward Arnold. 1982

Saghal, Anju. (1991). "Patterns of Language Use in a Bi-lingual Setting in India." In Cheshire: 299-307.

Salem, N. M. (2006). *The Role of Motivation, Gender and Language Learning Strategies in EFL Proficiency*. Lebanon: American University of Beirut.

Salmien, J. (1998). *Using Wordless Books in Your ESL Class.* Paper presented at the Annual Meeting of the Teachers of English to Speakers of Other Language. P. 17-21.

Sankoff, D. (1998). 'A Formal Production-based Explanation of the Facts of Code Switching.' *Bi-lingualism: Language and Cognition.* I (1): 39-50.

Sanyal, S.C. (1987). *English Language in India & Indo-Anglian Prose Style.* London: TEFL.

Sapir, E. (1919). *Selected Writings in Language, Culture and Personality.* Berkeley and Los Angeles: University of California Press.

______________ (1921). *Language: An Introduction to the Study of Speech.* New York: Harcourt, Brace &World.

Saussure, Ferdinand de. (1983). *Course in General Linguistics.* Eds. Charles Bally and Albert Sechehaye. Trans. Roy Harris. La Salle, Illinois: Open Court.

Schacter, John. *The Impact of Educational Technology on Student Achievement. What the Most Current Research has to say.*

Schegloff, E., Jefferson, G., & Sacks, H. (1977). The Preference for Self-correction in the Organisation of Repair in Conversation. *Language. 53* (2), 361-382.

______________ (1979). The Relevance of Repair to Syntax-for-conversation. In T. Givon (Ed.), *Syntax and Semantics. Volume 12. Discourse and Syntax.* (pp. 261-286). New York, Academic Press.

Schinitzer, E. (1995). English as an International Language: Implications for the Inter-culturalists and Language Educators. *International Journal of Intercultural Relations. 19*(2), 227-236.

Schnackenberg, H.L. (1997). *Learning English Electronically: Formative Evaluation in ESL Software.* ERIC Document Reproduction Service No. ED403877.

Scovel, T. (1969) Foreign Accent: Language Acquisition and Cerebral. Dominance. *Language Learning. 19,* 245-254.

Schemidt, R.W. (1996). *Developing Basic Conversational Ability in a Second Language.*

Scott, Baldauf. (November 23, 2004). "A Hindi-English Jumble, Spoken by 350 Million." *Christian Science Monitor.* http://www.csmonitor.com/2004/1123/p01s03-wosc.html.

Scrimshaw, P. (ed), (1993), *Language, Classrooms and Computers* Routledge: London

Scrivener, J. (1994). *Learning Teaching: A Guidebook for English Language Teachers.* Oxford: Heinemann.

Sebastian, Richard J. (1982). "An Integrative Perspective for the Study of Attitudes towards Language Variation." In Ryan & Giles: 1-19.

Seelye, H. (1984). *Teaching Culture: Strategies for Inter-cultural Communication*. Revised edition. Lincolnwood, IL: National Textbook Company.

Shanahan, D. (1997). Articulating the Relationship between Language, Literature, and Culture: Toward a New Agenda for Foreign Language Teaching and Research. *The Modern Language Journal. 81*, 164-74.

Sharkova, Krassimira D. (1996). *A Reflective Model of Language Teacher Education: An Integration of Theoretical with Competency based Training in an Awareness Raising Context*. Paper presented at the 1996 IALS Symposium for Language Teacher Educators.

Sharma, Pete. (2009). *Controversies in Using Technology in Language Teaching*. Retrieved January 18, 2010 from http://www.teachingenglish.org.uk/think/articles/controversiesusingtechnologylanguageteaching 18-1-10.

Sheerin, S. (1997). An Exploration of the Relationship between Self-access and Independent Learning. In P. Benson & P. Voller (Eds.), *Autonomy and Independence in Language Learning* (pp. 54-65). London: Longman.

Sheorey L Ravi (2006), "Learning and Teaching English in India." New Delhi: Sage Publications India Pvt. Ltd.

Siemens, George. & Tittenberger, Peter. (2009) *Handbook of Emerging Technologies for Learning*. Retrieved January 18, 2010 from http://umanitoba.ca/learning_technologies /cetl/ HETL.pdf

Singleton, D. (1989). *Language Acquisition: The Age Factor*. London: Multilingual Matters. Skiba, Richard. (1997). 'Code Switching as a Countenance of Language Interference,' *TESL Journal. Vol. III, No. 10, October 1997*, http://iteslj.org/, accessed on 15 Jan 2010.

Skidmore, D. (2000). From Pedagogical Dialogue to Dialogical Pedagogy. *Language and Education. 14* (4), 283-296.

Slimani, A. (1989). The Role of Topicalisation in Classroom Language Learning. *System. 17*, 223–234.

Smith, H. (2001). Smart Board Evaluation: Final Report. Retrieved from http://www.kented.org.uk/ngfl/ict/IWB/whiteboards/report.html#11

Sook, K.H. (2003). The Types of Speaking Assessment Tasks used by Korean Junior Secondary School English Teachers. *Asian EFL Journal*. Retrieved 23 March 2008 from www.asian-efl-journal/dec_03_sub.gl.htm

Somaratne, W. (1957). *Aids and Tests in the Teaching of English*. Oxford: Oxford University Press.

Spolsky, R. (1978). *Educational Linguistics: An Introduction*. Rowley. Mass: Newbury House.

Srivastava, A.K. (1990). "Multilingualism and School Education in India: special features, problems and prospects." In Pattanayak: 37-53.

Stockwell, G., & Harrington, M. (2003). The Incidental Development of L2 Proficiency in NS-NNS Email Interaction. *CALICO Journal. 20* (2), pp. 337-360.

Strevens, P. (1974). Some Basic Principles of Teacher Training. *ELT Journal,* 29 (1), 19-27.

_______________ (1977). *New Orientations in the Teaching of English.* Oxford: Oxford University Press.

Swain, M. (1985). *Communicative Competence: Some Roles of Comprehensible input and Comprehensive output in its Development.* Massachusetts: Gass and Madden.

Swan, M. & Smith, B. (eds.). (1987). *Learner English: A Teacher's Guide to Interference and other Problems.* Cambridge: Cambridge University Press.

Sweet, H. (1899). *The Practical Study of Languages: A Guide for Teachers and Learners.* London: JM Dent.

Sweet, Henry. (1964). *The Practical Study of Languages.* London: OUP.

Tarone, E. (1987). Some Influences on the Syllable Structure of Interlanguage Phonology. In S. Weinberger (Ed.), *Interlanguage Phonology: The Acquisition of a Second Language Sound System.* Cambridge, Newbury House Publishers.

Taylor, R.P. (ed.), (1980). *The Computer in the School: Tutor, Tool, and Tutee.* New York: Teachers College Press.

TE Editor. *Podcasting for ELT (2005) retrieved January 18, 2010 from* http:/ /www. teachingenglish.org.uk/think/articles/podcasting-elt.

The Beginnings of English Literary Study in British India. *Oxford Literary Review,* IX. London: OUP, 1987.

The Hindu on Indiaserver, Science and Technology Briefs. (1997, 3 February). Pagers on Indian Tongues Launched. Available at: ttp:/ /www.indiaserver.com/thehindu/1997/ 03/ test/03/thb10.htm [9 August 1998].

The New Encyclopedia Britannica (Macropaedia). (1974). 15th ed., Vol. 9. Chicago: Helen Hemingway Benton.

Thirumalai, M. S. (1977). *Language, Thought, and Disorder.* Mysore: Central Institute of Indian Languages.

Thompson, T., & Gaddes, M. (2005). The Importance of Teaching Pronunciation to Adult Learners. *Asian EFL Journal.* 1.

Thornbury, Scott. (2009). *On Interactive Whiteboards (again!)* Retrieved January 18, 2010 fromhttp://www.teachingenglish.org.uk/blogs/ scott-thornbury/interactive-whiteboards -again.

Tickoo, M.L. 2003. *Teaching and Learning English.* New Delhi, Orient Longman Pvt. Limited.

Tarone, E. & Yule, G. (1989). *Focus on the Language Learner*. Oxford: Oxford University Press.

Troudi, S. (1994). *The Nature of Speaking Opportunities in English as a Second Language Class*. The Florida State University

Trudgil, P. (1974). *Socio-linguistics: An Introduction*. Harmondsworth: Penguin Books.

Tseng, D.S.D. (1980). Error Analysis, Contrastive Analysis, and The Acquisition of English Communicative Competence. *Journal of the Taiwan Provincial College of Education*. 4, 69-105.

Tully, Mark. (1997). "English: and Advantage to India?" In *ELT Journal*. vol. 51 No. 2:157 164.

Twaddell, W. Freeman. (1973). Vocabulary Expansion in the ESOL Classroom. *TESOL Quarterly*. 7:1, 61-78.

Tyrwhitt-Drake, H. (1999). Responding to Grammar Questions on the Internet. *ELT Journal*. *53* (4), 281-88.

Underhill, N. (1987). *Testing Spoken Language: A Handbook of Oral Testing Techniques*. Cambridge: Cambridge University Press.

Ur, P. (1996). *A Course in Language Teaching: Practice and Theory*. Cambridge: Cambridge University Press.

Vale, David, & Anne Fountain. (1995). *Teaching Children English*. Cambridge, England: Cambridge University Press.

Verma, M.K. (1998). (Ed.) *Socio-linguistics, Language and Society*. New Delhi: Sage Publications.

Victori, M. & Lockhart, W. (1995). Enhancing Meta-cognition in Self-directed Language Learning. *System*. 23 (2), 223-234.

Viswanathan, Gouri. (1989). *Masks of Conquest: Literary Study and British Rule in India*. New York: Columbia University Press.

Vygotsky, L. S. (1962). *Thought and Language*. Cambridge, MA: The M.I.T. Press.

Wallace, J.M. (1991). *Training Language Teachers*. Cambridge University Press: Cambridge.

Wallace, M. (1991). *Training Foreign Language Teachers: A Reflective Approach*. Cambridge: Cambridge University Press.

Walsh, S. (2006). *Investigating Classroom Discourse*. London and New York: Routledge.

Wan, S.E.L. (2004). Second Language Socialisation in a Bilingual Chat room: Global and Local Considerations. *Language Learning & Technology*. *8* (3), 44-65.

Wang, Y.P. (2004). Distance Language Learning: Interactivity and Fourth Generation Internet-Based Video-conferencing. *CALICO Journal*. *21*(2), 373-395.

Warschauer, M., & Healey, D. (1998). Computers and Language Learning: An Overview. *Language Teaching*. *31*, 57-71.

______________ & Meskill, C. (2000). Technology and Second Language Learning. In J. Rosenthal (Ed.), *Handbook of Undergraduate Second Language Education* (pp. 303-318). Mahwah, New Jersey: Lawrence Erlbaum

Warschauer, M. (2001). Online Communication. In R. Carter & D. Nunan (Eds.), *The Cambridg Guide to Teaching English to Speakers of other Languages* (pp.207-212). Cambridge: Cambridge University Press.

Wei, C.L. (2002). DFLL Learners' Perceptions of Internet Assisted English Writing Instruction: A Case Study. *Journal of Humanities, College of Liberal Arts*. NCHU, 32, 483-503.

Wells, G. (1999a). *Dialogic Inquiry: Toward Socio-cultural Practice and Theory of Education*. Cambridge, UK: Cambridge University Press.

______________ (1999b). Language and Education: Re-conceptualising Education as Dialogue. *Annual Review of Applied Linguistics, 19*, 135-155.

______________ (2005). *Toward Dialogue in the Classroom*. Unpublished manuscript, Retrieved May 17, 2005, from http://education.ucsc.edu/faculty/gwells/Files/PapersFolder/-ClassroomDialogue.html

Wenden, A. (1987). Incorporating Learner Training in the Classroom. In A. Wenden and J. Rubin (Eds.), *Learner Strategies in Language Learning* (pp. 159-168). New York: Prentice Hall International.

Wenden, A.L. (1998a). Learner Training in Foreign/Second Language Learning: A Curricular Perspective for the 21st Century. *ED 416 67.*

______________ (1998b). Meta-cognitive Knowledge and Language Learning. *Applied Linguistics. 19* (4), 515-537.Z

West, Michael. (1953). *Learning to Read a Foreign Language*. Longman: London.

Whalen, L. (1974). Wordless Picture Books: Every Picture Tells a Story, doesn't it? *Emerging Librarian. 21* (5), 14-17.

Williams, M. & Burden, R.L. (1997). *Psychology for Language Teachers.* Cambridge: Cambridge University Press.

Whitman, R., & Jackson, K. (1972). The Unpredictability of Contrastive Analysis. *Language Learning. 22*, 29-41.

Widdowson, H.G. (1968). "The Teaching of English Through Science." J. Dakin et al., OUP, London

______________ (1978). *Teaching Language as Communication.* Oxford: Oxford University Press.

______________ (1979). Explorations in Applied Linguistic. OUP, London.

______________ (1983). *Learning Purpose and Language Use*. Oxford: Oxford University Press.

_____________ (1984). *Stylistics and the Teaching of Literature.* Essex: Longman.

_____________ (1984). Teaching Language as and For Communication. In H. Widdowson (Ed.), *Explorations in Applied Linguistics* 2 (pp. 229-246). Oxford: Oxford University Press.

Willis, J. (1981). *Teaching English through English.* London: Longman.

_____________ (1996) *A Framework for Task-Based Learning.* Harlow, Essex: Longman.

Wong, R. (1987). *Teaching Pronunciation: Focus on English Rhythm and Intonation.* Englewood Cliffs, NJ: Prentice Hall Regents.

Woodward, T. (1991.) *Models and Metaphors in Language Teacher Training: Loop Input and Other Strategies.* Cambridge: Cambridge University Press.

Woodward W. Suzanne, (1997), "Fun with Grammar: Communicative Activities for the Azar Grammar series." Prentice Hall: Regents.

Wright, C. (ed). (2000). *Issues in Education and Technology: Policy Guidelines and Strategies.* London: Commonwealth Secretariat.

Wright, T. & Bolitho, R. (1993). Language Awareness: A Missing Link in Language Teacher Education. *ELT Journal. 47*(4), 292-304.

Yadav, S. (2007). *Language, Literature and Education.* New Delhi: Academic Excellence.

Yang, N. (1998). Exploring a New Role for Teachers: Promoting Learner Autonomy. *System. 26,* 127-135.

Yang, P. J. (1998). Networked Multimedia and Foreign Language Education. *CALICO Journal. 15* (1-3), 75-88.

Yan, X., Zhou, Z., & Dai, P. (2007). Principled Eclecticism in College English Teaching in China. *Professional Teaching Articles of Asian EFL Journal. 17* (Article 1).

Yeh, A. (2003). Telling True Stories: Blending Multimedia in a Task-based Activity. *The Internet TESL Journal. 9*(8).

Yuksel, D., & Yu. (2008). Inside the Classroom: Student and Teacher Questions in a Foreign Language Literature Class. *TESL Reporter, 41*(1), 12-32.

Zhenhui, R. (2001). Matching Teaching Styles with Learning Styles in East Asian Contexts. *The Internet TESL Journal. 3* (7). Retrieved from http://iteslj.org/Techniques/Zhenhui-Teaching Styles. html

Research-oriented Journals: Applied Linguistic Journals

APAC of News (membership to APAC: Associació de Professors d'Anglès de Catalunya) It's for Teachers (Philology UB library) (available in Barcelona's bookstores) Also on line at http://its-online.com

ELT Journal: An International Journal for Teachers of English to Speakers of Others Languages; Oxford University Press in association with the British Council and with IATEFL (Educational UB Library).

English Journal National Council of Teachers of English, (Educational Library) (TM) TESOL Matters (Educational UB Library).

Practical English Teaching: A Magazine for Teachers of English as Foreign Language London: Mary Glasgow Publications.

Primera Clase. *The Heinemann English Teaching Magazine*. Macmillan Heinemann. English Language Teaching.

(TQ) TESOL Quarterly : Teachers of English to Speakers of Other Languages Quarterly (Educational UB Library).

Some Online EFL/ESL and CALL Resources

Asian EFL Journal: http://www.asian-efl-journal.com/index.html

Boggle's *World (ESL teacher resources, job boards and worksheets)*: http://bogglesworld.com

English-to-go: http://www.english-to-go.com/

English-4U (English Lesson Plan): http://www.english-4u.com/

ESL Teachers Board: http://www.eslteachersboard.com/cgi-bin/articles/index.pl?read=917

Randall's *ESL Cyber Listening Lab*: http://www.esl-lab.com/

Teaching English as a Foreign or Second Language: http://www.kyoto-su.ac.jp/information /tesl-ej/index.html

The Internet TESL Journal: http://iteslj.org/

Index